General Principles of European Community Law

EUROPEAN MONOGRAPHS

Editor-in-Chief Prof. Dr. K.J.M Mortelmans

1. Lammy Betten (ed.), *The Future of European Social Policy* (second and revised edition, 1991).
2. J.M.E. Loman, K.J.M. Mortelmans, H.H.G. Post, J.S. Watson, *Culture and Community Law: Before and after Maastricht* (1992).
3. Prof. Dr. J.A.E. Vervaele, *Fraud Against the Community: The Need for European Fraud Legislation* (1992).
4. P. Raworth, *The Legislative Process in the European Community* (1993).
5. J. Stuyck, *Financial and Monetary Integration in the European Economic Community* (1993).
6. J.H.V Stuyck, A.J. Vossestein (eds.), *State Entrepreneurship, National Monopolies and European Community Law* (1993).
7. J. Stuyck, A. Looijestijn-Clearie (eds.), *The European Economic Area EC-EFTA* (1994).
8. R.B. Bouterse, *Competition and Integration–What Goals Count?* (1994).
9. R. Barents, *The Agricultural Law of the EC* (1994).
10. Nicholas Emiliou, *The Principle of Proportionality in European Law: A Comparative Study* (1996).
11. Eivind Smith, *National Parliaments as Cornerstones of European Integration* (1996).
12. Jan H. Jans, *European Environmental Law* (1996).
13. Siofra O'Leary, *The Evolving Concept of Community Citizenship*: From the Free Movement of Persons to Union Citizenship (1996).
14. Laurence Gormley (ed), *Current and Future Perspectives on EC Competition Law* (1997).
15. Simone White, *Protection of the Financial Interests of the European Communities: The Fight against Fraud and Corruption* (1998).
16. Morten P. Broberg, *The European Commission's Jurisdiction to Scrutinise Mergers* (1998).
17. Doris Hildebrand, *The Role of Economic Analysis in the EC Competition Rules* (1998).
18. Christof R.A. Swaak, *European Community Law and the Automobile Industry* (1999).
19. Dorthe Dahlgaard Dingel, *Public Procurement: A Harmonization of the National Judicial Review of the Application of European Community Law* (1999).
20. J.A.E. Vervaele (ed.), *Compliance and Enforcement of European Community Law* (1999).
21. Martin Trybus, *European Defence Procurement Law: International and National Procurement Systems as Models for a Liberalised Defence Procurement Market in Europe* (1999).
22. Helen Staples, *The Legal Status of Third Country Nationals Resident in the European Union* (1999).
23. Damien Geradin (ed.), *The Liberalization of State Monopolies in the European Union and Beyond* (2000).
24. Katja Heede, *European Ombudsman: Redress and Control at Union level* (2000).
25. Ulf Bernitz, Joakim Nergelius (eds.), *General Principles of European Community Law* (2000).

KLUWER LAW INTERNATIONAL

EUROPEAN MONOGRAPHS

General Principles of European Community Law

Reports from a Conference in Malmö, 27–28 August 1999

Organised by the Swedish Network for European Legal Studies and the Faculty of Law, University of Lund

Edited by

Ulf Bernitz
Joakim Nergelius

Wolters Kluwer
Law & Business

AUSTIN BOSTON CHICAGO NEW YORK THE NETHERLANDS

Published by Kluwer Law International
P.O. Box 85889
2508 CN The Hague, The Netherlands
sales@kli.wkap.nl
http://www.kluwerlaw.com

Sold and distributed in the USA and Canada by
Kluwer Law International
675 Massachusetts Avenue
Cambridge, MA 02139, USA

Sold and distributed in all other countries by
Kluwer Law International
Distribution Centre
P0. Box 322
3300 AH Dordrecht, The Netherlands

A C.I.P. Catalogue record for this book is available from the Library of Congress

Cover design: Bert Arts

Printed on acid-free paper

ISBN: 90-411-1402-5

Kluwer Law International incorporates the publishing programmes of Graham & Trotman Ltd, Kluwer Law and Taxation Publishers and Martinus Nijhoff Publishers.

Table of contents

Preface

This book on the General Principles of European Community Law deals with an area of European law of enormous and ever growing importance which, so far, does not seem to have attracted all the attention it deserves. Due to their complex nature, the general principles offer a more or less unlimited field for theoretical legal studies. At the same time, the general principles play a very important role in legal practice, not the least when used as instruments for the protection of individuals and firms against too far reaching measures taken by the European institutions or Member States.

It is a difficult task already to try to define what is a general principle as opposed to a normal legal rule. Some of the principles are unwritten and very broad, others have a more clear shape and have found an expression in Treaty articles of a general character. The general principles applied in Community law are derived from many different sources. On the whole, it seems possible to recognise three main categories of general principles within the Community legal system, viz. principles of international law applied within Community law, principles specifically developed to fit the needs and purposes of Community law and principles common to the laws of the Member States (or at least a number of them) which have been accepted by the European courts as principles of Community law.

In order to enhance the understanding of these general principles a European study conference was organised in the city of Malmö, Sweden, 27–28 August 1999 by the Swedish Network for European Legal Studies in cooperation with the Faculty of Law at the University of Lund. The conference attracted a large number of eminent legal scholars in the field as well as judges of the European courts and national appellate and supreme courts and other experts. The Swedish Network for European Legal Studies is a network set up with funds allocated to it by the Swedish Parliament, intended to promote closer cooperation between researchers within the field of European Law.

The object of the Network is to establish a forum that will allow researchers to meet, discuss and open up new paths of investigation within the field of European Law, not only within their respective Faculties but also at a national and European level. The Network arranges conferences, symposia and seminars and also actively supports the publishing of research material. More information about the Network can be found at: http://www.juridicum.su.se/nef

The fundamental purpose of the conference has been to analyse the general principles and their scope in the EU legal order with special emphasis on their role in the creation of a "*jus commune europaeum*". Consequently, a major theme of the conference has been to analyse the impact of the general principles of Community law at the national level and to study how these principles have been "transformed" into the national legal systems of the EU Member States. Another important aspect has been to assess to what extent the general principles function as tools for a "soft harmonisation" of the law applicable at the national level. Also, it has been an aim to study the creative process behind the shaping and further development of the general principles and their application. Important issues observed include the judicial activism of the EC Court, the use of the comparative methodology in order to develop the principles and the gap filling function of the general principles within the Community legal system.

This book is based on a selection of the papers presented at the conference. However, the papers have been rewritten and edited extensively in order to form the base for the analysis presented here. Two persons in particular have been responsible for the intellectual efforts in preparing the conference papers and for the successful completion of this volume, Dr Joachim Nergelius, associate professor of constitutional law at the University of Lund and Mr. Xavier Groussot, researcher in European law, especially the general principles of law, at the same university. I wish to thank them most sincerely for their eminent work on this project.

Ulf Bernitz
Professor of European Law at Stockholm University
Chairman of the Swedish Network for European Legal Studies.

1. General Aspects

1.1 The Origins and Development of the General Principles of Community Law

*Matthias Herdegen**

1.1.1 Introduction: General Principles and the Rule of Law

Ever since its inception the European Union has conceived itself as a "a community based on the rule of law".[1] Characteristically, the European Court of Justice was amongst the first to express this aspiration.[2] It is only fairly recently that explicit references to the rule of law as one of the constitutional foundations of the Union are to be found in the constituent treaties of the European Union, initially hidden in a preambular paragraph[3] and, since the entering into force of the *Amsterdam* Treaty, also in a more prominent position in the operative part of the Treaty on European Union.[4]

References to the rule of law in this context are not concerned with the formal notion of parliamentary sovereignty, which lies at the heart of the English concept of the rule of law. Rather, the invocation of the rule of law in the Community context is akin to the German notion of *Rechtsstaat* which imposes procedural and substantive limitations upon the exercise of power by all three branches of government.[5]

However, the constituent treaties of the European Communities contain only rudimentary substantive standards against excessive encroachment of Community power upon the individual. In particular, the European Union does not yet possess a written Bill of Rights, which is today considered an essential element of a *Rechtsstaat*. Important principles associated with the rule of law such as legal certainty, legitimate

---

* The author thanks *Dr. Thilo Rensmann LL.M.* for his valuable assistance.

1. Case 294/83, *Les Verts v. Parliament*, [1986] ECR 1339, at 1365, para. 23; Opinion 1/91, *European Economic Area*, [1991] ECR, I-6079, at 6102, para. 21.
2. See note 1.
3. See, however, the former Art. J.1 para. 2 TEU (now: Art. 11 para. 1 Treaty on European Union [hereinafter: TEU]).
4. Art. 6 para. 1 TEU: "The Union is founded on the principles of liberty, democracy, respect for human rights and fundamental freedoms, and the rule of law, principles which are common to the Member States."
5. As to the divergent notions of the "rule of law", "l'état de droit" and "Rechtsstaat" in England, France and Germany see *C. Grewe/ H. Ruiz Fabri*, Droits Constitutionnels européens (1995), p. 22 et seq.; *R. Grote*, Rule of Law, Rechtsstaat and "Etat de droit", in: Ch. Starck (ed), Constitutionalism, Universalism and Democracy – A Comparative Analysis, p. 269 et seq.

Ulf Bernitz and Joakim Nergelius (eds.), General Principles of European Community Law, 3–23

expectations and, until fairly recently proportionality[6] and transparency[7] are also not expressly laid down in the Treaties.

Despite these *lacunae* in the text of the founding treaties, the European Union may nevertheless today be considered a "community based on the rule of law". This is largely due to the jurisprudence of the European Court of Justice, which has gradually developed a body of general principles of law, encompassing all essential features of a *Rechtsstaat*, including the protection of fundamental human rights.

Accordingly, the rule of law in the European Union, although now entrenched in Art. 6 para. 1 of the TEU, is still mainly built on general principles of law. At the same time reliance by the Court of Justice on general principles of law touches upon a fundamental problem posed by the rule of law: the limits of the law-making capacity of the judiciary.

In the light of this problem the treatment of the "origins and development of general principles" should not be understood as a mere exercise in historiography. Although this paper will try to identify the main stages of development of the jurisprudence of the ECJ on general principles the emphasis will be on the conditioning factors and the methodological approach which lend legitimacy to the body of general principles of law created by the Court.

1.1.2 Origins

1.1.2.1 The Early Case-Law on General Principles

Relatively early in its jurisprudence the European Court of Justice was faced with the problem that the Community legal order did not contain any coherent body of general rules of administrative law. In the *Algera* case, when confronted with the issue of whether certain decisions of the Assembly of the ECSC could be revoked, it seemed a matter of course for the Court[8] to resolve the problem of *lacunae* in the ECSC Treaty by reference to the national legal systems of the Member States:[9]

> "The possibility of withdrawing such measures is a problem of administrative law, which is familiar in the case-law and learned writing of all countries of the Community, but for the solution of which the Treaty does not contain any rules. Unless the Court is to deny justice it is therefore obliged to solve the problem by reference to the rules acknowledged by the legislation, the learned writing and the case-law of the member countries."

---

6. See Art. 5 EC-Treaty [hereinafter: ECT] and Protocol to the Amsterdam Treaty on the Application of the Principles of Subsidiarity and Proportionality.
7. See now Art. 1 para. 2 TEU. *Cf.* also the transparency-related amendments by the Amsterdam Treaty in Arts. 207, 248, 255 and 285 ECT. On these amendments see *P. Craig/G. de Burca*, EU Law (2nd ed. 1998), p. 370. *Cf.* also Case T-14/98, *Heide Hautala v. Council*, judgment of 19 July 1999, nyr.
8. At the time it sat as the Court of Justice of the European Coal and Steel Community.
9. Joined Cases 7/56 & 3-7/57, *Algera & Others v. Assembly*, [1957/58] ECR 39, at 55.

The dogmatic justification for resorting to general principles of law is hence to avoid a *déni de justice* (which is in itself a general principle of law).[10] This argument was clearly inspired by Art. 4 of the Code Napoléon to which Advocate General *Lagrange* had made explicit reference in an earlier case decided by the Court.[11] A closer analysis must, however, focus on presumptive powers under the relevant treaty: The Member States, having entrusted the Court with adjudicating certain categories of cases, must be deemed to have endowed the judges with a sufficient body of law to enable them to guarantee effective judicial protection. It is a rather academic issue whether this dynamic concept of the ECJ's functions is covered by the doctrine of "implied powers".[12]

The limits of this argument may be illustrated by the more modern example of Member State liability for breaches of community law: the creation of general principles of Community law to enhance effective judicial protection may easily encroach upon the sovereign powers of the Member States. It seems rather doubtful whether the Member States can really be considered to have empowered the Court to rely on general principles of Community law in order to extend the reach of Community law far into what was originally thought to be encompassed by the Member States' "procedural autonomy".[13]

Lacunae in Community law can be filled by two sources: either international law or national law (as filtered through a comparative analysis). The previously quoted passage from the *Algera* case reveals that the Court's recourse to national law was mainly led by practical considerations: The problems of administrative law which the Court had to address were well-known in national law. International law at the time[14] did not contain any applicable rules. The judges and the Advocates General were familiar with their respective national laws (rather than with public international law) and it could be expected that decisions based on a legal approach which was accepted in all legal orders of the Community would not meet with any resistance from the ranks of the Member States.[15]

---

10. Note that Art. 40 ECSC Treaty – unlike Art. 288 (ex 215) para. 2 EC Treaty (and Art. 188 para. 2 Euratom Treaty) – does not contain any reference to "general principles of law". As to the reasons for the different wording of these provisions see *S. Jacoby*, Allgemeine Rechtsgrundsätze (1997), p. 225 et seq.
11. Case 8/55, *Féderation Charbonnière de Belgique v. High Authority of the European Coal and Steel Community*, [1954 to 1956] ECR 245, at 277 et seq.
12. As to the doctrine of "implied powers " see International Court of Justice, *Reparation for Injuries Suffered in the Services of the United Nations*, ICJ Reports 1949, 174, at 182; *Certain Expenses of the United Nations*, ICJ Reports 1962, 151, at 168.
13. *Cf. M. Herdegen/T. Rensmann*, Die neuen Konturen der gemeinschaftlichen Staatshaftung, Zeitschrift für das gesamte Handelsrecht und Wirtschaftsrecht 161 (1997), p. 522, at 532 et seq.
14. As to an emerging international administrative law see *e.g. C.F. Amerasinghe*, Principles of Institutional Law of International Organizations (1996), p. 452 et seq.
15. See quotation in note 9: "... to solve the problem by reference to rules *acknowledged* by the legislation, the learned writing and the case-law of the member countries...".

At first sight it seems surprising that the European Court of Justice did not refer to Art. 38 para. 1 *lit.* c of the Statute of the International Court of Justice which includes "general principles of law recognised by civilised nations" amongst the sources of international law. This would have been a much more straightforward explanation than the somewhat cryptic invocation of *déni de justice*. Whereas the recourse to general principles of national law shows a certain deference to the sovereignty of the Member States, the reluctance to justify their use by reference to the Statute of the International Court of Justice is evidence of the self-confidence of being a Court within an autonomous legal order rather than an ordinary international Court. Advocate General *Lagrange* pointed out that comparisons with the International Court of Justice were faced with the objection[16]

> "that our Court [i.e. the Court of Justice of the European Coal and Steel Community as it then was] is not an international court but the court of a Community created by six States on a model which is more closely related to a federal than to an international organisation and that although the Treaty which the Court has the task of applying was concluded in the form of an international treaty and although it unquestionably is one, it is nevertheless, from a material point of view, the charter of the Community, since the rules of law which derive from it constitute *the internal law of that Community*."

As regards the sources of Community law the Advocate General concludes that[17]

> "there is obviously nothing to prevent them being sought, where appropriate, in international law, but normally and in most cases they will be found rather in the internal law of the various Member States."

The Court's approach to general principles of law was therefore probably inspired rather by the *Conseil d'Etat's* recourse to *principes géneraux* in French administrative law[18] than the Statute of the International Court of Justice. General principles are thus not used as a source of *international law* but as an autonomous source of *Community law*.

1.1.2.2 Fundamental Rights

The pioneering cases in which the European Court of Justice pronounced fundamental rights as being enshrined in general principles of Community law need hardly be recalled: The praetorian development of the Community's Bill of Rights began in the late 1960s and early 1970s with *Stauder*,[19] *Internationale*

16. *Féderation Charbonnière de Belgique* (note 11), at 277 [Emphasis in the original].
17. Ibid.
18. See *A. Bleckmann*, Europarecht (6th ed. 1997), § 580.
19. Case 29/69, *Stauder v. City of Ulm*, [1969] ECR 419.

Handelsgesellschaft[20] and *Nold*.[21] By today the Court has succeeded in vesting fundamental rights with rather clear contours. This may be illustrated by the protection of an applicant for a position within the public services of the Communities against unwarranted medical scrutiny.[22]

A view currently still quite popular in Germany credits the Federal Constitutional Court with having provided the decisive impulse for the strengthening of fundamental rights at Community level.[23] In 1974, the controversial "*Solange I*"-decision subjected the implementation of Community acts in Germany to review by the German Constitutional Court in the light of the fundamental rights of the Basic Law.[24] The German Constitutional Court reserved such constitutional control to itself so long as the Community system remained devoid of a Bill of Rights and a truly democratic legislative process. The German claim of having laid the ground for the adequate protection of fundamental rights at Community level (especially by the ECJ) is, however, challenged by prominent players on the European scene.[25] Whatever the contribution of the German Constitutional Court may have been, it seems safe to assume that the development of fundamental rights has drawn considerable benefit from the interplay between the two courts.[26]

1.1.2.3 Beyond Fundamental Rights

Beyond the area of fundamental rights, general principles of Community law are of essential importance to the continuing evolution of an autonomous body of general administrative law. Since the *Algera* case[27] the Court has identified such fundamental principles as proportionality,[28] legal certainty[29] and the protection of legitimate expectations[30] which provide the foundation of today's European Administrative Law.[31]

---

20. Case 11/70, *Internationale Handelsgesellschaft v. Einfuhr- und Vorratsstelle für Getreide und Futtermittel*, [1970] ECR 1125.
21. Case 4/73, *Nold v. Commission,* [1974] ECR 491.
22. Case C-404/92 P, *X. v. Commission*, [1994] ECR I-4737, at paras. 17 et seq.
23. *H. Steinberger*, Entwicklungslinien in der neueren Rechtsprechung des Bundesverfassungsgerichts zu völkerrechtlichen Fragen, ZaöRV 48 (1988), 1, at 9 et seq.
24. BVerfGE 37, 271; English translation in [1974] 2 CMLR 540.
25. *U. Everling*, Weiterentwicklung des Grundrechtsschutzes durch den Europäischen Gerichtshof, in: W. Weidenfeld (ed.), Der Schutz der Grundrechte in der Europäischen Gemeinschaft, (1992), p. 73, at 74 ("Der Gerichtshof entscheidet nicht mit dem Blick auf nationale Gerichte, sondern aus Verantwortung für die ihm anvertraute Aufgabe. ").
26. See *infra sub* 1.1.3.1.
27. See *supra* note 9.
28. See *e.g.* Case 25/70, *Köster*, [1970] ECR 1161, at 1175, para. 8.
29. See *e.g.* Case 13/61, *Bosch & van Rijn,* [1962] ECR 45, at 52.
30. *Algera* (note 9), at 55.
31. See in particular *J. Schwarze*, Europäisches Verwaltungsrecht (2 Volumes, 1988); English translation: European Administrative Law (1992).

This development has culminated in the ECJ's rulings on the liability of Member States for violations of Community law.[32] In this context, the Court's case law raises serious doubts about its methodological foundations. In *Francovich* the Court had relied mainly on the fundamental principle of "effective and uniform application of Community law" to justify the creation of Member State liability as a rule of community law.[33] It was only after the Member States submitted in *Brasserie* du *Pêcheur* that the ECJ had exceeded its powers by pronouncing a general right to reparation for individuals[34] that the Court thought it appropriate to base its decision in addition on a "general principle familiar to the legal systems of the Member States."[35] It appears difficult, however, particularly with regard to liability for legislative acts, to rest a broad principle of Member State liability on a convincing comparative analysis of national laws.[36] On the other hand, the traditional reluctance of national courts to admit liability for wrongful legislative acts has for quite some time been severely criticised for its insensitivity to fundamental rights issues and for its inherent failure to synchronise administrative law with constitutional dynamics.[37] With its bold judgements on liability, the ECJ has made an important contribution towards weeding out anachronistic features still prevailing in many administrative laws.

1.1.2.4 General Principles in the Treaties

General principles of law are undisputed today as a source of Community law. They have found express recognition as a source of law in the provisions of the EC-Treaty governing non-contractual Community liability (Art. 288 para. 2 ECT)[38] and more recently with regard to fundamental rights in Art. 6 para. 2 TEU which is now fully justiciable by the Court.[39]

---

32. See in particular Case C-6/90 & C-9/90, *Francovich,*[1991] ECR I-5357; Joined Cases C-46 & 48/93, *Brasserie du Pêcheur v. Germany; Regina v. Secretary for Transport, ex parte Factortame Ltd*, [1996] ECR I-1029.
33. *Francovich* (note 32), at 5413–14, paras. 31 et seq.
34. *Brasserie du Pêcheur* (note 32), at 1143, para. 24.
35. *Brasserie du Pêcheur* (note 32), at 1144, para. 29.
36. See Advocate General *Léger*, Case 5/94, *Hedley Lomas*, [1996] ECR I-2553, at 2579: "...as far as state liability for legislative action is concerned, there are no general principles which are truly common to the Member States. "
37. See *M. Herdegen*, Die Haftung der Europäischen Wirtschaftsgemeinschaft für fehlerhafte Rechtsetzungsakte (1983), at 55 et seq.
38. See also the corresponding Art. 188 para. 2 Euroatom-Treaty.
39. See Art. 46 *lit. d* TEU.

1.1.3 The Development of Fundamental Rights and their Protection

1.1.3.1 Clashes over Authority: The ECJ and the German Constitutional Court

The fundamental rights jurisprudence of the European Court of Justice emerged in the context of a battle with the German Federal Constitutional Court for supremacy over Community law. It is probably no coincidence that the main challenge to the supremacy of Community law originated in Germany. In the late fifties Germans gradually became accustomed to the principle that each and every governmental act could be reviewed by the Federal Constitutional Court with respect to its compatibility with the fundamental rights enshrined in the German Constitution.[40] From a German perspective, therefore, the idea that sovereign powers transferred to the Community level lay completely outside the reach of the German bill of rights seemed hard to fathom.

Initially however, the European Court of Justice appeared oblivious to the seriousness of this challenge to the supremacy of Community law. In *Stork* the complaint of a German coal wholesaler that a decision of the High Authority violated fundamental rights as laid down in the Basic Law was brushed aside by the Court with the remark that "the High Authority is not empowered to examine a ground of complaint that, when it adopted its decision, it infringed principles of German constitutional law." [41] It was not until ten years later that the Court in *Stauder* (a case which ironically brought to fame the name of a German citizen who fought for the right not to reveal his identity) took up the challenge and proclaimed that "fundamental rights [were] enshrined in the general principles of Community law and [hence] protected by the Court."[42]

However, the U-turn in the Court's jurisprudence came too late to avert a head-on collision with the German Federal Constitutional Court. Although in the *Internationale Handelsgesellschaft* case the Court – almost pleadingly – emphasised the existential importance for the Community of upholding the supremacy of Community law,[43] it had missed the opportunity to prove that the protection of fundamental rights could effectively "be ensured within the framework of the structure and objectives of the Community."[44] It was not so much the fact that in the case at hand the Court held that the German applicant's fundamental rights were not disproportionately affected by the impugned Community regulation but rather the failure to

40. See the two seminal decisions BVerfGE 6, 32 (*Elfes*) and 7, 198 (*Lüth*) rendered by the Federal Constitutional Court in 1957 and 1958 respectively.
41. Case 1/58, *Stork v. High Authority*, [1959] ECR 17, at 26, para. 4.
42. *Stauder* (note 19), at 425, para. 7.
43. *Internationale Handelsgesellschaft* (note 20), at 1134, para. 3: "In fact, the law stemming from the Treaty, an independent source of law, cannot because of its very nature be overridden by rules of national law, however framed without being deprived of its character as Community law and without the legal basis of the Community itself being called into question. "
44. Ibid., at 1134, para. 4.

have provided sufficient underpinnings by an established case law which led the Federal Constitutional Court to challenge the supremacy of Community law with respect to the German Bill of Rights in its famous *Solange I* judgment.[45]

It took another twelve years to remedy the situation. In its *Solange II* ruling the Federal Constitutional Court reviewed the case law of the European Court of Justice on fundamental rights since 1974 and gave it its "seal of approval", *de facto* reinstating the supremacy of Community law despite the admonition that its jurisdiction would be resuscitated should fundamental rights protection in the Community fall substantially below the German standard.[46]

However, the European Court of Justice's battle for supremacy in the field of fundamental rights protection does not yet seem to be over. In the wake of the *Matthews* judgment of the European Court of Human Rights,[47] claims to supremacy suddenly appear to be discernible from Strasbourg.[48] And in Germany the Community's quota system for bananas is challenged before the Federal Constitutional Court as violating the "indispensable" core of fundamental rights protected by the Basic law despite the ECJ's 1994 judgment[49] reaffirming conformity with the Community's fundamental rights standard.[50]

1.1.3.2 Deficient Judicial Control?

Until now, the ECJ has not developed a coherent system of scrutiny for Community acts encroaching upon individual rights protected by general principles. As a rule, the Court has confined itself to mere references to the fundamental rights concerned on the one hand and conflicting interests on the other, coupled with

---

45. BVerfGE 37, 271; English translation in [1974] 2 CMLR 540.
46. BVerfGE 73, 339, at 387; English translation in [1987] 3 CMLR 225, at 265:
"In view of these developments, it must be held that, *so long as* the European Communities, and in particular the case law of the European Court, generally ensure an effective protection of fundamental rights as against the sovereign powers of the Communities which is to be regarded as substantially similar to the protection of fundamental rights required unconditionally by the Constitution, and in so far as they generally safeguard the essential content of fundamental rights, the Federal Constitutional Court will no longer exercise jurisdiction to decide on the applicability of secondary Community legislation cited as the legal basis for any acts of German courts or authorities within the sovereign jurisdiction of the Federal Republic of Germany, and it will no longer review such legislation by the standard of the fundamental rights contained in the Constitution. "
See also *Maastricht* judgment, BVerfGE 89, 155, at 174 et seq.; English translation in [1994] 1 CMLR 57, at 78 et seq. and Art. 23 para. 1 Basic Law.
47. *Denise Matthews v. United Kingdom*, Judgment of 18 Feb., 1999, reprinted in Europäische Zeitschrift für Wirtschaftsrecht [EuZW] 1999, p. 308.
48. See *infra sub* 1.1.3.3.1.
49. Case C-280/93, *Germany v. Council*, [1994] ECR I- 4973.
50. *Cf.* the decision by the Frankfurt Administrative Court referring the case to the Federal Constitutional Court for a preliminary ruling, EuZW 1997, p. 182.

rather crude considerations of the plausibility of excessive burdens having been placed upon the individual.[51] These flaws in the Court's fundamental rights jurisprudence generate the potential for conflicts with national constitutional courts.[52]

The defects of the ECJ's scrutiny are highlighted by the ECJ's judgment in the *Bananas* case[53]. When a former judge of the European Court of Justice – who is known rather for his courtesy than for his belligerence – publicly expresses his "perplexity"[54] and "astonishment"[55] at a judgment rendered by the Court, when he accuses the reasoning of his former colleagues of "inadequacy"[56] and when he questions whether the Court takes fundamental rights seriously,[57] it is clear that something has gone seriously wrong. Indeed the handling of the fundamental rights issues in the *Bananas* case is widely considered to prove the deficiency of fundamental rights review by the European Court of Justice.[58] What went wrong in the Bananas case?

The general methodological framework of the Court's fundamental rights analysis is similar to the approach of the Federal Constitutional Court in Germany or the European Court of Human Rights in Strasbourg:

> "[Fundamental rights] are not absolute but must be viewed in relation to their social function. Consequently, the exercise of [those rights] may be restricted ... provided that those restrictions in fact correspond to objectives of general interest pursued by the Community and do not constitute a disproportionate and intolerable interference, impairing the very substance of the rights guaranteed."[59]

However, in applying the balancing test required by the concept of proportionality the Court's judgment in the *Bananas* case proves to be seriously flawed and displays a problematic bias against the individual.[60] In the field of the Common Agricultural Policy the Court accords a far-reaching margin of discretion to the Community organs, which reduces the standard of review to flagrantly disproportionate

51. See *e.g.* Case 44/79, *Hauer*, [1979] ECR 3727, at 3725 et seq.
52. *M. Herdegen*, Europarecht (2nd ed., 1999), at 160.
53. See *supra* note 49.
54. *U. Everling*, Will Europe Slip on Bananas? The Bananas Judgment of the Court of Justice and National Courts, CML Rev. 33 (1996), p. 401, at 413.
55. Ibid., at 413 et seq.
56. Ibid., at 417 note 33.
57. Ibid., at 419.
58. See *J. C. Cascante/G.G. Sander*, Der Streit um die EG-Bananenmarktordnung (1999), p. 54 et seq.; *P. Selmer*, Die Gewährleistung des unabdingbaren Grundrechtsstandards durch den EuGH (1998), each with further references.
59. *Germany v. Council* (note 49), at 5065, para. 78.
60. As to the following see in particular *Everling* (note 54), at 410 et seq.; *M. Nettesheim*, Grundrechtliche Prüfdichte durch den EuGH, EuZW 1995, p. 106 et seq.

measures.[61] In addition, the Court fails to identify clearly the intensity of the individual interest affected, which is a precondition for a meaningful balancing test.

On the other hand, the consequences of the *Bananas* judgment should not be overdramatised.[62] The Court subsequently tried to mitigate the consequences of its judgment by applying the hardship clause (contained in the applicable regulation) in favour of the individuals concerned.[63] Consequently, the Federal Constitutional Court, before which the *Bananas* case is currently pending,[64] will presumably stop short of precipitating a constitutional crisis in the European Union by declaring that the "level of protection of basic rights is [not] essentially comparable to that afforded by [the] Basic law."[65]

However, the *Bananas* judgment has certainly left a dark stain on the record of the Court's fundamental rights jurisprudence. It poses the question whether in view of the different constitutional traditions of the Member States general principles of law are an adequate instrument for devising a subtle fundamental rights methodology. A comparison with other constitutional courts demonstrates that the praetorian development of a conceptual framework for fundamental rights protection will take some time. In this process, the European Court of Justice can count on the spirit of "cooperation" which the German Federal Constitutional Court conjured up in its *Maastricht* judgment in a slightly patronising manner.[66] It may be expected that the Federal Constitutional Court's *Bananas* judgment will give some guidance for the future development of the European Court of Justice's methodology and hence open another chapter in the "judicial dialogue" between the two courts. On the other hand it seems safe to assume that the ECJ will receive grandseigneurial offers of cooperation extended by national courts without exuberant enthusiasm.

1.1.3.3 The "Special Significance" of the European Convention on Human Rights

It is only after France followed the other Member States in joining the European Convention on Human Rights in 1974 that the Court could openly refer to the

61. *Germany v. Council* (note 49), at 5065 para. 78 and Advocate General *Gulmann*, ibid., at 5006 et seq., paras. 82-99. See also the clearer expression in Case C-306/93, *SW Winzersekt/Land Rheinland-Pfalz,* [1994] ECR I-5555, at 5581, para. 21: "... in matters concerning the common agricultural policy the Community legislature has a broad discretion which corresponds to the political responsibilities given to it by Articles 40 and 43 of the Treaty and ... the Court has, on several occasions, held that the lawfulness of a measure adopted in that sphere can be affected only if the measure is manifestly inappropriate, having regard to the objective which the competent institution is seeking to pursue. "
62. See *I. Pernice*, in: R. Dreier (ed.), Grundgesetz-Kommentar, Vol. 2 (1998), Art. 23, at para. 79.
63. Case C- 68/95, *T. Port v. Bundesanstalt für Landwirtschaft und Ernährung*, [1996] ECR, I-6065, at 6099-6101, para. 34 et seq.
64. See *supra* note 50.
65. *Cf.* Art. 23 para. 1 of the Basic Law.
66. See *Maastricht* judgment (note 46), BVerfGE 89, 175; [1994] 1 CMLR 79.

Convention in its effort to ascertain whether and to what extent certain rights had entered the body of general principles of Community law.[67] Since then the Convention has become an important point of reference in the Court's effort to establish the constitutional values common to all Member States.[68] Although the Court has reaffirmed the "special significance" of the Convention, it has never considered the Community to be formally bound by it.[69] In fact, in Opinion 2/94, the Court held that the Community lacked competence to accede to the Convention.[70] The special significance of the Convention has found its positive legal expression in Article 6 para. 2, which – since the amendments effectuated by the Amsterdam Treaty – also constitutes the formal basis of the Court's fundamental rights mandate.[71]

1.1.3.3.1 The *Matthews Case*: The European Court of Human Rights as a "Surrogate Constitutional Court"

The particular importance of the European Convention on Human Rights goes far beyond it being a convenient restatement of the consensus amongst the Member States on human rights matters. The *Matthews* judgment[72] recently rendered by the European Court of Human Rights serves as a reminder that the Member States of the European Union *in principle* remain responsible for ensuring that acts of the European Union do not violate the rights guaranteed in the Convention and that the Strasbourg Court has concomitant jurisdiction. The *Matthews* judgment concerned the exclusion of the British citizens in Gibraltar from elections to the European Parliament by the 1976 "Act Concerning the Election of the Representatives of the European Parliament by Direct Universal Suffrage". The Strasbourg Court held that the exclusion of Gibraltan citizens from the ballot box constituted a violation of the right to vote as laid down in Art. 3 of the First Protocol and that the violation was attributable to the United Kingdom. As to the question of imputability of Community acts to the Member States, the European Court of Human Rights observed in the *Matthews* case[73]

---

67. See the first cryptic reference in *Nold* (note 21), at 507, para. 13: "Similarly, international treaties for the protection of human rights on which the Member States have collaborated or of which they are signatories, can supply guidelines which should be followed within the framework of Community law." Specific references may first be found in Case 36/75, *Rutili v. Minister for the Interior*, [1975] ECR 1219, at 1232, para. 32.
68. See *e.g.* Case 222/84, *Johnston*, [1986] ECR 1651; Cases 46/87 and 227/88, *Hoechst AG v. Commission*, [1989] ECR 2859.
69. *Johnston* (note 68), at 1682, para. 18; *Hoechst AG* (note 68), at 2923, para. 13; Opinion 2/94 on Accession by the Community to the ECHR, [1996] ECR I-1759, at 1789, para. 33.
70. Opinion 2/94 (note 69), at 1787–89, para. 23 et seq.
71. See Art. 46 *lit.* d TEU.
72. See *supra* note 47.
73. See *supra* note 47, at 309, para. 32.

> "that acts of the EC as such cannot be challenged before the Court because the EC is not a Contracting Party. The Convention does not exclude the transfer of competences to international organisations provided that Convention rights continue to be 'secured'. Member States' responsibility therefore continues even after such a transfer."

A closer look at the further reasoning reveals that the *Matthews* decision is perhaps not quite the bombshell suggested by some initial comments.[74] It seems rather to be in line with the views previously expressed by the European Commission on Human Rights in a decision which had declared as inadmissible an application against the execution of an ECJ judgment on the basis that the system of fundamental rights review developed in the case law of the European Court of Justice offered sufficient legal protection to the applicants.[75] *Matthews*, however, concerned an Act of primary law, which although adopted within the Community framework had the status of a treaty and could thus not be challenged before the European Court of Justice.[76] It is only due to this gap in the Community system of judicial protection that the Member States could be considered to have failed to discharge their responsibility under Art. 1 of the Convention to "secure" the effective protection of Convention rights and that the Strasbourg Court could step in as a "surrogate Constitutional Court".

In conclusion, *Matthews* appears to provide a sense of *déjà vu* with respect to the German Federal Constitutional Court's *Solange II* decision: Strasbourg will not intervene, so long as fundamental rights are efficiently protected at the Community level.

1.1.3.3.2 The Need to Harmonise Human Rights Jurisprudence in Luxembourg and Strasbourg

As a consequence, the European Court of Justice will need to pay particular attention to the case law of its learned friends in Strasbourg in order for conspicuous discrepancies to be avoided.[77] On the other hand it should not be expected that Convention rights will always be identically interpreted in Strasbourg and Luxembourg, just as national courts at times construe Convention rights differently. However, it ought to be borne in mind that – in contrast to national courts – opinions of the European Court of Justice which are at odds with the Strasbourg Court's construction of certain Convention Rights may only be referred to the European Court of Human Rights under exceptional circumstances.[78] Both European Courts should therefore take

74. See *e.g. Ch. Lenz*, Case note, EuZW 1999, p. 311 ("Paukenschlag "); for a more cautious evaluation *cf. H.G. Schermers,* Case note, CML Rev. 36 (1999), p. 673 et seq.
75. Application No. 13258/87, *Melchers v. Germany,* DR 64, 138.
76. *Matthews* (note 47), at 309, para. 33.
77. See Advocate General *Darmon* in Case C-49/88, *Al-Jubail Fertilizer Co et al. v. Council,* [1991] ECR I-3187, at 3230-1, para. 111.
78. See *supra* text at note 72 et seq.

adequate care to avoid unnecessary discrepancies in interpreting Convention Rights lest the moral authority of the "European Bill of Rights" be undermined.

So far the European Court of Justice seems to have attempted to pay due regard to the Strasbourg case law. Divergent opinions appear mainly to be due to the European Court of Human Rights subsequent dissension from the ECJ's construction of certain Convention rights. A case in point is the *Hoechst* decision in which the European Court of Justice held, in keeping with the older and ambiguous case law of the European Commission of Human Rights,[79] that Art. 8 of the Convention does not extend to business premises.[80] It was only a few years later that the European Court of Human Rights came to the opposite conclusion in *Niemitz v. Germany.*[81] In its recent fundamental rights jurisprudence the European Court of Justice regularly refers to the case law of the European Court of Human Rights.[82]

1.1.4 THE ECJ'S MANDATE TO ENGAGE IN LAW-MAKING

The Court bases the legitimacy of the recourse to general principles of law on its judicial mandate under Article 220 ECT.[83] In the *Brasserie du Pêcheur* case the Court – in the light of the severe criticism generated by its *Francovich* decision[84] – felt the need to justify the praetorian recognition of the principle of Member State liability for breaches of Community law:[85]

> "Since the Treaty contains no provision expressly and specifically governing the consequences of breaches of Community law by Member States, it is for the Court in pursuance of its task conferred on it by Art. 164 [now Art. 220] of the Treaty of ensuring that in the interpretation and application of the Treaty the law is observed,

79. *Cf. M. Herdegen*, in: R. Dolzer (ed.), Bonner Kommentar, Art. 13, at para. 13 with further references.
80. See *supra* note 68, at 2924, para. 18. The Court, in fact, pays a special tribute to the Strasbourg Court by expressly stating that "... it should be noted that there is no case-law of the European Court of Human Rights on that subject."
81. Series A, No. 251, para. 31. See also *Funke v. France*, Series A, No. 256 A, in which the European Court of Human Rights "overruled" the ECJ's *previously* held view that Art. 6 of the Convention did not encompass the right not to give evidence against oneself, *cf.* Case 374/87, *Orkem v. Commission*, [1989] ECR 3283, at 3350, para. 30. See, however, Case C-60/92, *Otto B.V.*, [1993] ECR, I-5683, at 5711, para. 11.
82. See *e.g.* Case C-368/95, *Vereinigte Familia Press,* [1997], I-3689, at 3717, paras. 25–6; Case C-199/92 P, *Hüls v. Commission*, judgment of 8 July 1999, para. 150, nyr.; Case C-185/95 P, *Baustahlgewebe v. Commission*, [1998] ECR, I-8417, at 8499, para. 29; Case C-249/96, *Grant*, [1998] ECR , I-621, at 648, para. 34; Case T-213/95 & T-18/96, *SCK & FNK v. Commission*, [1997] ECR, II-1739, at 1765, para. 57.
83. As to specific references to general principles of law in Art. 288 para. 2 ECT and Art. 6 para 2 TEU see *supra sub* 1.1.2.4.
84. See *supra* note 32.
85. *Brasserie du Pêcheur* (note 32), at 1144, para. 27.

to rule on such a question in accordance with generally accepted methods of interpretation, in particular by reference to the fundamental principles of the Community legal system and, where necessary, general principles common to the legal systems of the Member States."

The European Court of Justice thus considers general principles common to the legal systems of the Member States to be part of the "law", the observance of which it ensures.[86] Article 220 ECT, indeed, seems to suggest that the duty to observe "the law" goes beyond what is laid down in the Treaties. Viewed in conjunction with the specific references to general principles in Article 288 para. 2 ECT and Article 6 para. 2 TEU it is justifiable today to argue that the body of "law", the observance of which is to be ensured by the Court, encompasses the fundamental values embodied in the national constitutional traditions of the Member States, or in the words of *Pierre Pescatore*:[87]

> "[le] fonds commun d'idées d'ordre, de justice et de raison qui sont à la base de la civilisation juridique à laquelle appartiennent les Etats membres."

It remains unclear in the previously quoted statement from the *Brasserie du Pêcheur* decision whether the Court deems general principles of law to be merely "a generally accepted method of interpretation" or an independent source of law.[88] General principles of law may in fact serve both functions. In the context of international treaties the "ordinary meaning" of the text[89] is considered to be the meaning which is assigned to certain terms in the national laws of those States party to the treaty.[90] Since the very beginning of the Court's jurisprudence, comparative law analysis has been employed in this sense in order to shed light on the exact meaning of certain provisions in the constituent treaties of the Communities.[91]

---

86. See also *Nold* (note 21), at 507, para. 13: "... fundamental rights form an integral part of the general principles of law, *the observance of which it ensures.*" [Emphasis added].
87. *P. Pescatore*, Rôle et chance du droit et des juges dans la construction de l'Europe, in: Die europäische Rechtsprechung nach zwanzig Jahren Gemeinschaftsleben (FIDE VI, 1976), p. 9, at 123.
88. See quotation *supra* note 85: "... in accordance with *generally accepted methods of interpretation*, in particular by reference to the fundamental principles of the Community legal system *and*, where necessary, general principles common to the legal systems of the Member States. "
89. *Cf.* Art. 31 para. 1 of the Vienna Convention on the Law of Treaties.
90. See *Schwarze* (note 31), Vol. I, at 74-93; Vol. II, at 1380. *Cf.* also with regard to the European Convention on Human Rights *L. Wildhaber/ St. Breitenmoser*, in: Golsong *et al.* (eds)., Internationaler Kommentar zur Europäischen Menschenrechtskonvention (Looseleaf), Art. 8, para. 23 with further references.
91. The earliest example is the comparative law analysis by Advocate General *Lagrange* of the concept of "misuse of power " within the meaning of Art. 33 para. 2 ECSC-Treaty, see Case 3/54, *ASSIDER v. High Authority of the European Coal and Steel Community*, [1954 to 1956] ECR 63, at 74 et seq.

In the case of Member State liability, as in the other cases discussed so far, general principles common to the laws of the Member States are, however, used to fill (perceived) *lacunae* in the treaty. Here, general principles serve as a proper source of law, since the Treaties remain tacit on the point of law in question. It may, however, be questioned whether in such cases general principles of law may be regarded as the true source of law or whether they only serve as a veil which barely cloaks – as one observer put it – "the nakedness of judicial law-making".[92] This takes us back to the old English controversy about the nature of Common Law. As with English Common Law the *ius commune europaeum,* of which the general principles common to the legal systems of the Member States are said to be an emanation, is not a pre-existing body of principles, which merely needs to be "discovered" by the Community judge. To develop a concrete rule from at times divergent legal traditions will always entail a fair amount of law-making. The decisive question is therefore not so much whether the judges or a *ius commune europaeum* can be considered the true source of the wisdom of the Court's attempts to fill the gaps in the Community legal system. Rather, the legitimacy of the European Court of Justice's jurisprudence depends on a transparent methodological approach in developing and applying general principles of law and a judicial process, which takes into account the interests of all parties concerned.

1.1.5 METHODOLOGY

1.1.5.1 A Selective Approach

A perusal of the case law of the European Court of Justice reveals comparatively few clear statements on the methodological approach followed in developing and applying general principles of law. This is partly due to the relatively brief and at times cryptic style adopted by the Court in drafting its judgments. But even taking into account the more detailed opinions of the Advocate Generals, fairly little guidance as to the proper method of "discovering" general principles may be gleaned. This nurtures the suspicion that we are confronted with a process of judicial law-making guided mostly by common sense rather than a hermeneutical process informed by a generally accepted methodology.

However, some methodological guiding-posts may be identified: a closer look at Article 288 para. 2 ECT and Article 6 para. 2 TEU reveals that general principles result from a double process of abstraction. The normative point of reference for the development of general principles of law is not the specific national legal provisions but rather the underlying ideas or principles.[93] Accordingly, in the field of fundamental rights the Treaty on European Union does not refer to the national Constitutions but rather to the "constitutional traditions" of the Member States.[94]

92. *T.C. Hartley,* The Foundations of European Community Law (4th ed. 1998), p. 130.
93. Art. 288 ECT does not refer to specific legal provisions but "general principles" which need to be common to the laws of the Member States.
94. See Art. 6 para. 2 TEU.

After having identified the principles upon which the individual national legal provisions are based, some sort of common denominator needs to be found. Even if a highest common denominator can be discerned this is likely to be on such a level of abstraction that it would not provide a rule operable in an individual case. At the very latest, at this juncture it becomes apparent that in most cases comparative analysis is not sufficient to solve individual cases, but that it can provide at most the normative framework within which a concrete rule may be developed.[95] Distilling concrete operable rules from general principles of law is hence primarily a process of value judgement and choice.[96] That this was even true for a Community of six found a clear expression in the opinion of Advocate General *Lagrange* in the *Hoogovens* case in which he analyses the early jurisprudence of the Court on the process of developing general principles of law:[97]

> "... the case law of the court, in so far as it invokes national laws (as it does to a large extent) to define the rules of law relating to the application of the Treaty, is not content to draw on more or less arithmetical 'common denominators' between the different national solutions, but chooses from each of the Member States those solutions which, having regard to the objects of the Treaty, appear to be the best or, if one may use the expression, the most progressive."

Similarily, in its fundamental rights jurisprudence, the Court considers the "constitutional traditions" of the Member States as a mere "source of inspiration" in the process of ensuring the protection of fundamental rights "within the framework of the structure and objectives of the Community."[98]

It is maybe no coincidence that Advocate General *Lagrange* in the *Hoogovens* case found the most appropriate solution in the French *droit administratif.* National legal approaches may not therefore simply be transplanted into the Community legal order. The Court must rather choose or devise the "best" solution in the light of the structure and objectives of Community law. Advocate General *Roemer* characterised this process as "wertende Rechtsvergleichung".[99] In this teleological process different considerations will apply depending on the context in which *lacunae* have to be filled.

---

95. As to this "negative function" of general principles see Advocate General *Roemer*, Case 25/62, *Plaumann v. Commission*, [1963] ECR 95, at 117: "I am therefore of the opinion that the Court is relatively free under the second paragraph of Article 215 in the dogmatic assessment of individual problems but that in the results of its investigation into the law concerning the legal liability of the Community it must remain within a framework common to the laws of the Member States."
96. See with regard to fundamental rights *Hartley* (note 92), at 136: "... it all depends on the policy of the European Court." *Cf.* in the context of Art. 215 para. 2 ECT *Herdegen* (note 37) at 38 et seq.
97. Case 14/61, *Hoogovens v. High Authority*, [1962] ECR 253, at 283 et seq.
98. *Internationale Handelsgesellschaft* (note 20), at 1134, para. 4; *Nold* (note 21), at 507, para. 13.
99. Case 5/71, *Schöppenstedt*, [1971] ECR 975, at 989.

Whereas the Court's fundamental rights jurisprudence may, to some extent, be guided by the maxim in *dubio pro libertate*, weighing the interests of the Community and the individual in the context of non-contractual liability will sometimes stop short of maximising the interests of the individual.[100]

1.1.5.2 Sources of Inspiration

It is a most intriguing question whether other instruments, apart from constitutional traditions of Member States and the European Convention of Human Rights, can serve as a source of inspiration for general principles of Community law. Certain OSCE principles – such as those enshrined in the Charter of Paris[101] referred to in Article 11 para. 1 TEU – might be relied upon, for example, in order to concretise the principles of liberty, democracy and the rule of law laid down in Article 6 para. 1 TEU.

General principles might also be drawn from a survey of protocols and joint declarations of the *Maastricht* and *Amsterdam* intergovernmental conferences. Thus the "Protocol on the System of Public Broadcasting in the Member States" annexed to the Treaty of Amsterdam and other instruments could inspire a general principle leading to an interpretation of the EC competition rules in favour of the maintenance of certain basic services as a constitutional value of the European Community.[102] Of course, reliance on such instruments meant for specific sectors cannot erode competition principles enshrined in the EC Treaty itself.

1.1.5.3 Judicial Dialogue between the ECJ and National Courts

The lack of normative predetermination inherent in the Court's reliance on general principles of law does not, however, necessarily render the Court *legibus solutus* or lead to a *gouvernement des juges*. It is in particular the "judicial dialogue" between the European Court of Justice and national courts as well as the discourse with other national and Community institutions which lends legitimacy to judicial law-making within the Community legal order.

In fact in many cases the Court appears deliberately to initiate such a discoursive process in order to secure the acceptance and legitimacy of its pronouncements on

100. *P. Gilsdorf/P. Oliver* in: H. v.d. Groeben/H, Thiesing/C.-D. Ehlermann, Kommentar zum EU-/EG-Vertrag, Vol. 5 (5th ed. 1997), Art. 215, at para. 12.
101. Reprinted in ILM 30 (1990), p. 190.
102. *Cf.* for the view that access to universal services constitutes a basic value of the European Community: Art. 16 ECT and *European Commission*, Services of General Interest in Europe, OJ 1996 C 181/3, para. 1 (n. 1). On the interplay between EC competition law and "basic services" see *M. Herdegen,* Constitutional Rights and the Diminishing State, in: Starck (note 5), p. 183, at 185 et seq.

general principles of law.[103] Again the Court's case law on Member State liability for breaches of Community law may serve as a pertinent example: although the Court in *Francovich* was only asked to adjudicate the specific question of liability relating to the failure to implement a provision of a directive (which was not directly applicable), the Court pronounced a sweeping principle of Member State liability for each and every breach of Community law.[104] Since the European Court of Justice is dependent on the impulse of preliminary references by national courts to develop its jurisprudence, it quite often deliberately posits general legal principles going far beyond the case at issue. This is intended to provoke further references providing the Court with the opportunity to refine its jurisprudence. At the same time the Court will take notice of any reaction from other Community organs, Member States and public opinion. Justified criticism may be countered by introducing conditions limiting the application of the legal principle at issue. This is precisely what happened in the wake of the *Francovich* decision. The *Francovich dictum* triggered a series of preliminary references from Germany and the United Kingdom. The European Court of Justice took the opportunity to reaffirm and broaden the dogmatic underpinnings of the principle of Member State liability[105] while at the same time heading off concerns expressed. The Court drastically restricted the ambit of Member State liability[106] by introducing the limiting condition of the violation of Community law having to be "sufficiently serious".[107] It seems that the initial indignation caused by *Francovich* has ebbed away. Today the legitimacy of the praetorian development of Member State liability from general principles of national and Community law no longer appears to be seriously questioned. In fact, the faithful implementation by national courts of the principle of Member State liability may be considered a (quasi-) "ratification" of the Court's jurisprudence.[108]

At first sight the Court's fundamental rights jurisprudence appears to fall in line with the discoursive development of general principles exemplified by the evolving concept of Member State liability, as it too is the result of an intensive dialogue

103. As to the following see in particular *U. Everling*, Der Ausschluß der Rückwirkung bei der Feststellung der Ungültigkeit von Verordnungen durch den Gerichtshof der EG, in: J. F. Baur *et al.* (eds.), Festschrift für Bodo Börner (1992), p. 57, at 73 et seq.; *Herdegen/Rensmann* (note 13), at 524 et seq. (with further references).

104. *Francovich* (note 32), at 5415, para. 37.

105. *Brasserie du Pêcheur* (note 32), at 1144, paras. 27–30. See also Case C-392/93, *British Telecommunications,* [1996] ECR I-1631; Case C-5/94, *Hedley Lomas*, [1996] ECR I-2553; Case C-178, 179, 188, 189 & 190/94, *Dillenkofer*, [1996] ECR I-4845; Case C-283 & 291/94, *Denkavit,* [1996] ECR I-5063.

106. *Cf. Herdegen/Rensmann* (note 13), at 545 et seq. The former Advocate General *W. van Gerven* even goes so far as to pose the question "whether the principle of liability, as applied by *Brasserie*, has not been rendered devoid of practical significance outside the *Francovich* situation." (id., Bridging the Unbridgeable: Community and National Tort Law After Francovich and Brasserie, ICLQ 45 [1996], p. 507, at 527).

107. *Brasserie du Pêcheur* (note 32), at 1149-50, paras. 51, 55.

108. *Herdegen/Rensmann* (note 13), at 533.

between the European Court of Justice and national courts. However, in the case of fundamental rights the decisive impulse for their entrenchment as general principles of law in the Community legal order did not come from the Court itself but from national, namely German courts.[109] Once in place the legitimacy of the European Court of Justice's recognition of fundamental human rights as general principles, common to the constitutional traditions of the Member States was never questioned as such. Criticism today is merely aimed at the Court's standard of review, which is deemed by some to be too lenient with regard to Community measures. Some might even consider the terms judicial "dialogue" or "discourse" inappropriate euphemisms in this context bearing in mind the at times harsh rhetoric surrounding what the German Constitutional Court describes as its "relationship of cooperation"[110] with the European Court of Justice.

1.1.6 PERSPECTIVES

1.1.6.1 The Evolution of a Common Constitutional Law beyond Fundamental Rights?

It is one of the great achievements of the European Court of Justice to have contributed to the gradual evolution of a Common European Administrative Law.[111] First glimpses of a budding Common Constitutional Law may also be discerned.[112] Many elements of the rule of law (in its broad sense of the German notion of *Rechtsstaat)* have become principles common to all Member States through the jurisprudence of the European Court of Justice.[113] For example the principle of proportionality – the roots of which may be traced back to Prussian Law – made its way via the jurisprudence of the European Court of Justice into the legal system of the United Kingdom.[114] In concretising other fundamental principles of constitutional law in the Community context comparative analysis will, however, be of more limited value due to the fundamental structural differences remaining between the European Union and its Member States.

This holds particularly true for the different expressions of the federal principle. However, the development of certain broader concepts such as "the duty of close cooperation" between the Member States and the Community with regard to mixed

109. See *supra sub* 1.1.3.1.
110. See *supra* note 66.
111. See *e.g. Schwarze* (note 31), *passim*; *T. von Danwitz*, Verwaltungsrechtliches System und Europäische Integration (1996), p. 194 et seq.
112. See *e.g. R. Bieber/P. Widmer*, The European Constitutional Area (1995); *P.-C. Müller-Graff/E. Riedel*, Gemeinsames Verfassungsrecht in der Europäischen Union (1998).
113. See the survey in *J. Schwarze (ed.)*, Das Verwaltungsrecht unter europäischem Einfluß (1996).
114. *G. de Burca,* The Influence of European Legal Concepts on UK Law: Proportionality and *Wednesbury* Unreasonableness, European Public Law 3 (1997), p. 561.; *J. A. Usher*, General Principles of EC Law (1998), at 151 et seq.

agreements[115] might draw on parallels with models of loyal co-operation within federally structured Member States.

The development of unwritten standards of democracy calls for a high degree of caution, since democratic participation must primarily follow the structure of the treaties.[116] However, the regime for political parties[117] and participation of European citizens in the political process might be influenced by general democratic principles, as cautiously indicated in the *Piermont* judgment of the European Court of Human Rights.[118]

1.1.6.2 The Proper Province of General Principles

The invocation of general principles enhancing social justice, in particular social and economic rights, calls for a caveat. The proper domain of general principles of law lies in steering the exercise of Community powers and the fulfilment of the Member States' obligations as they flow from the Treaties. General principles provide no leverage for distorting the constitutional balance between the Communities and its Member States by extending Community powers beyond the terms of the Treaties. Neither the ECJ nor the academic community have a mandate to change the constitutional balance through the development of general principles of law. Thus, the strict commitment to price stability and budgetary discipline enshrined in the EC Treaty[119] cannot be diluted by reference to vague general principles of social justice. Such changes are reserved to a revision of the founding treaties by the constituent powers of the Communities, *i.e.* the Member States. General Principles are no tool for constitutional poetry.

1.1.6.3 Codification and Integration

The importance of general principles common to the legal systems of the Member States as a source of law may gradually decrease in the continuing process of European integration. On the one hand principles which the European Court of Justice originally developed by a comparative analysis of the Member States' national laws are by now so entrenched in the case law of the European Court that they have in reality become fundamental principles *of Community law*. Their national pedigree has long been forgotten.

---

115. See Opinion 1/94 (*Re WTO Agreement*), [1994] ECR I-5276, at 5389 & 5395.
116. On the principle of democracy in the Community context see Case C-65/93, *Parliament v. Council*, [1995] ECR I-643, at 668, para. 21; Case T-135/96, *UEAPME v. Council*, [1998] ECR II-2335, at 2371, para. 88.
117. See Art. 191 ECT.
118. Series A, No. 314 (1995).
119. Arts. 4 para. 3, 104 para. 1, 105 para. 1 (1) ECT. See also *M. Herdegen*, Price Stability and Budgetary Restraints in the Economic and Monetary Union: The Law as Guardian of Economic Wisdom, CML Rev. 35 (1998), p. 9 et seq.

On the other hand there is an increasing tendency to codify principles which the Court previously applied as general principles of law. A pertinent example is the principle of proportionality, which may now be found in Art. 5 ECT and in the "Protocol on the application of the principles of subsidiarity and proportionality". At the Cologne Summit an initiative to codify fundamental rights in the European Union was set in motion.[120] Many protagonists in the current discussion would welcome a solemnly declared European Bill of Rights as a catalyst for the formation of a European *demos*. Quite apart from these high-flying expectations such a Bill of Rights would have a tangible impact: it would provide the impetus for more coherent standards of judicial scrutiny, thus enhancing the legitimacy of the judicial architecture of fundamental rights.

120. See Presidency Conclusions, Cologne European Council, 3/4 June 1999, paras. 44–46 and Annex IV ("European Council Decision on drawing up a Charter of Fundamental Rights of the European Union").

1.2 General Principles of Law in European and National Systems of Law: A Comparative View

*T. Koopmans**

1.2.1 Introduction

General principles of law are, in a certain sense, commuters. Frequently, they travel from national legal systems to European Community law, as principles common to the legal systems of the Member States. Subsequently, after having been baptized as general principles of Community law, they travel back to national systems as part of the influence of Community law on national law. On their way back, however, they are not always recognised as having originated in the national legal system; they have, metaphorically speaking, a new attire.

The "principles common to the legal systems of the Member States" are mentioned in the provision of the EC-treaty which concerns extra-contractual liability of the Community.[1] For this subject, these common principles are to serve as a source of law. In practice, the Court of Justice of the European Communities (which I shall call ECJ) also relied on such principles in other areas of the law, as it did in the early years of the European integration process, under the Treaty establishing the European Coal and Steel Community. The leading judgment concerned a staff case, which raised a well-known problem of administrative law not covered by the provisions of the Treaty. The ECJ considered that it had to solve the problem since it was not allowed to deny justice to a petitioner, and that it could only do so by examining the legal systems of the Member States (then only six) and by trying to find its inspiration in the principles adopted in these systems.[2] More than forty years later, it is generally accepted that principles common to the legal systems of the Member States constitute one of the major sources of European Community law.[3]

This reception of elements of national legal systems into Community law does not imply that these elements will necessarily have the same shape. On the one hand, there may be differences between the national systems even though the solutions to be adopted are very similar: differences in terminology, in scope, in legal effect. On the other hand, the ECJ will mould the principles so as to fit them in the system of

* Goodhart Professor of Legal Science, 1999-2000, University of Cambridge; former judge of the Court of Justice of the European Communities.

1. Art. 288 (ex 215), para. 2, EC-treaty.
2. Cases 7/56 and 3-7/57, Algera [1957-58] ECR 55.
3. See T. C. Hartley, The Foundations of European Community Law (4th ed., Oxford 1998), p. 130–132.

Ulf Bernitz and Joakim Nergelius (eds.), General Principles of European Community Law, 25–34

European Community law and to adapt them to the problem to be settled. As a result, it is not always easy to establish the exact lineage of principles of law defined by the ECJ. The principle of proportionality provides an illustration. The ECJ frequently relies on this principle, which can also be found in the case law of the French Conseil d'Etat, the supreme court in administrative matters in France. The concept of proportionality is also important in German and Dutch administrative law.[4] It would be difficult to encounter the notion in English cases or in English law books. However, when discussing the practical application of proportionality with English lawyers, one cannot fail to notice that the same results are often achieved in English law on the basis of the concept of reasonableness.

The problem in Europe is not so much the dissimilarity of standards to be applied; the divergences concern rather the conceptual avenues by which similar solutions are to be attained. Consequently, the debate on general principles of law is largely a debate on concepts, not on problems of substance. For this very reason, it may be interesting to have a look at the way these principles developed in the framework of the national systems of law in which they originated.

1.2.2 Developments in France

The notion of general principles of law was probably coined by the French Conseil d'Etat: "principes généraux du droit". The expression itself appears for the first time in a 1945 judgment,[5] but commentators agree that this judgment merely gave a name to a phenomenon which existed already for nearly a century. As one observer put it: "la notion a précédé la terminologie".[6] In a first stage, the court considered that French legislation, for example the Civil code, was based on certain assumptions and that administrative bodies were not free to depart from them. The underlying assumptions were considered as principles: they did not bind the legislative institutions when enacting a statute, but other authorities could not disregard these principles. Decisions or regulations of the government, or the Prime Minister, or a city council, could be annulled when they failed to respect these general principles. One of the oldest examples of such a principle in French case law is the freedom of trade, which characterized, according to the Conseil d'Etat, French commercial and business legislation.

In a second stage, the Conseil d'Etat developed a series of procedural requirements, to be met by administrative authorities even if the applicable statute did not mention them. Most important among these requirements were the rights of the defence ("droits de la défense"). These rights include, in particular, the right to be heard. Even if the court has the feeling that the administrative decision was correct from a point of view of substance, annulment will follow when the administration did not give the interested person the opportunity to make his point of view

4. Under the names "Verhältnismäßigkeit" and "evenredigheid".
5. CE 26-10-1945, Aramu, Rec. 213.
6. Braibant and Stirn, Le droit administratif français (4th ed., Paris 1997), p. 218.

known.[7] That is also the case when the applicable legislation is silent on the matter. In the absence of statutory provisions to the contrary, said the court, administrative authorities are free to revoke an earlier decision, but they can not do so without due regard for the rights of the defence. Procedural requirements are particularly important in cases where the administrative body in question has wide discretionary powers, for example, when it can take certain decisions if there is a "threat" to public health, or if medicines are "dangerous", or if housing conditions are "insalubrious". The administrative courts traditionally respected the discretion granted to the administration by these words: but they insisted on the regularity of the decision making process and on strict compliance with the rights of the defence and other guarantees intended to protect the citizens, such as equal treatment in equal situations. This evolution increased the influence of general principles of law considerably. It also tended to transform these principles, inch by inch, into a general protection of citizens against arbitrariness of administrative behaviour.[8]

The third development brought the courts one step further into giving their own assessment of the work done by the administration. General principles of law helped the Conseil d'Etat to delimit the exact scope of the discretionary powers left to the administrative body in question. Whatever the wording of the legal provision according such a discretion, it cannot be taken to mean, said the Conseil d'Etat, that the administration can violate the principle of equality, a general principle of law to be upheld by the courts. A famous example occurred in 1954, when the Secretary of State at the Home Office had excluded some applicants from the list of students to be admitted to examinations for entry to the National School of Administration (Ecole Nationale d'Administration or ENA). These applicants alleged that, according to rumours, this had been done because they were communist activists. The Conseil d'Etat asked the Secretary of State to prove that he had not excluded the applicants because of their political opinions. The Secretary of State is free to admit or not to admit applicants, said the court, as the applicable statute does not put any limits to his powers; he can, therefore, look at behaviour of the applicants which he considers relevant for their aptitude for the public service. However, he cannot refuse admittance on the sole ground of their political convictions without violating the principle of equal access of all French citizens to the public service.[9]

Sometimes, therefore, general principles of law allow the administrative courts to impinge on the area of discretion of the government or of regional or local authorities. From this point of view, the principle of proportionality has a particular importance. An early example occurred in 1933, when the burgomaster of the city of Nevers had prohibited a public meeting, because left-wing organisations and trade unions had announced demonstrations against the main speaker. The Conseil d'Etat held that the burgomaster had the power to take the measures necessary for protecting

7. CE 5-5-1944, Veuve Trompier-Gravier, Rec. 133; CE 9-5-1980, Etablissements Cruse, Rec. 217.
8. See CE 1-4-1988, Bereciartua-Echarri, Rec. 135.
9. CE 28-5-1954, Barel, Rec. 308.

public order, but that he had to reconcile the exercise of this power with the freedom of assembly as guaranteed under French constitutional law. In the present case, it was shown that the burgomaster would have been able to maintain public order by ordinary police measures, so it was not necessary to prohibit the meeting.[10] Quite recently, the Conseil d'Etat annulled a declaration of the government that certain works were necessary for reasons of public interest, on the ground that the benefits to be achieved by the works (which concerned the construction of a motorway in the Alps) did not outweigh the grave disadvantages such as costs, noise, air pollution and damage to the landscape.[11] Here again, the discretionary power of the government to declare certain works in the public interest ("d'utilité publique"), which is the first step towards expropriation of the grounds, is limited by the application of general principles of law such as the principle of proportionality.

One of the major sources of general principles of law is the Declaration of the Rights of Man and of the Citizen of 1789 ("Déclaration des Droits de l'Homme et du Citoyen"). The present Constitution, the 1958 Constitution, refers to the Declaration in its preamble, by stating that the French people proclaims solemnly its devotion to it ("son attachement"); a similar statement had been included in the previous Constitution, the 1946 Constitution. Under that Constitution, the Conseil d'Etat considered already that general principles of law as implied by the preamble, or as defined in the Declaration, had to be observed by any administrative body, even in its regulatory activities, and even if legislative provisions were silent on the matter.[12] The Declaration and the Constitution are, however, by no means the only source of general principles of law. Sometimes, the court finds inspiration in legal traditions as laid down in statute law, as it did with regard to the freedom of trade. Violations of legal security or of the principle of proportionality are censured because these general principles result from legal traditions which span several centuries.

The way the Conseil d'Etat found general principles of law in the preamble to the Constitution and in the 1789 Declaration had an important collateral effect when the 1958 Constitution introduced a particular form of judicial review of legislation. The Conseil constitutionnel gives a final judgment on compatibility of new statutes with constitutional provisions when asked to do so, by some explicitly mentioned political institutions (not by citizens), before the statute is promulgated. From 1971 onwards, the Conseil constitutionnel developed the view that new legislation should not only respect the provisions of the Constitution but also the rights of the citizen laid down in its preamble and in the 1789 Declaration.[13] This view is particularly important since the 1958 Constitution itself, unlike most modern constitutions, does not refer to human rights and civil liberties; but the interpretation given to the preamble made the Conseil constitutionnel into the watchdog of

10. CE 19-5-1933, Benjamin, Rec. 541.
11. CE 28-3-1997, Autoroute du Chablais, Rec. 120.
12. CE 9-3-1951, Societé des Concerts du Conservatoire, Rec. 151; CE 26-6-1959, Syndicat des ingénieurs-conseils, Rec. 394.
13. Conseil constitutionnel 16-7-1971, loi d'associations, Rec. 29.

human rights.[14] Thus, the impact of the decisions of the Conseil increased. An example occurred in 1982, when the legislation on nationalisations in the industrial and banking sector, a fruit of the early Mitterrand years, was carefully scrutinised by the Conseil constitutionnel. The Conseil accepted that the possibility of nationalisation was recognised by the Constitution, but it held that this possibility should be reconciled with the protection of the right of property under the 1789 Declaration, and that it was the task of the Conseil to strike the balance.[15]

As far as the legal effect of general principles of law is concerned, a distinction should be made. For the Conseil d'Etat, whose jurisdiction is limited to review of administrative acts, general principles of law are binding upon administrative institutions, but the legislative bodies are free to depart from them (if they do so clearly and explicitly). For the Conseil constitutionnel, charged with review of legislation, the situation is not the same: some general principles such as human rights and the independence of courts are considered as fundamental principles of the Republic which cannot be disregarded by new statutes; but principles which are not moored to the Constitution, to its preamble or to the 1789 Declaration, for example the principle of proportionality, are not included in the Conseil's control of constitutionality of legislation. They are not part of what French constitutional lawyers call "le bloc de constitutionnalité".

Summarising, we can safely state that general principles of law are an important element of French constitutional and administrative law, that they have been developed over a period of more than a century and that their importance has been increasing over the last 25 or 30 years.

1.2.3 DEVELOPMENTS IN GERMANY

Since the birth of the Federal Republic of Germany in 1949, German legal evolution is very much influenced by the interpretation of the federal constitution, the Basic Law, by the federal constitutional court. The Basic Law is indeed characterised by the introduction of a sophisticated system of judicial review of legislation as well as by the prominent place it ascribes to human rights and fundamental freedoms. The combination of these two elements has the effect of giving a crucial role to the federal constitutional court, the Bundesverfassungsgericht. Its importance is further enhanced by the way the Basic Law affirms its attachment to certain values, by utilising relatively vague and general concepts, such as "Rechtsstaat" (the State governed by the rule of law), which do not have one clear and well-defined meaning. The choices to be made are often done by the courts, not by the government or the parliament. The framers of the Basic Law accepted this consequence, probably because of a certain distrust with regard to the political process, which may well have

---

14. See Jean Rivero, rapport de synthèse, in: Boulouis, Cappelletti and others, Le domaine de la loi et du règlement (2nd ed., Paris and Aix-en-Provence 1981), p. 261.
15. Conseil constitutionnel 16-1-1982, loi de nationalisations, Rec. 18.

been inspired by the sad experience with the dissolution of the Weimar Republic in the early thirties.[16]

One of the original features of the German constitutional system is the way in which ordinary courts, for example, in civil, criminal or tax matters, can refer problems of constitutionality of legislation to the constitutional court. And the litigants themselves can directly apply to the Bundesverfassungsgericht when they allege that one of their human rights, as defined in the Basic Law, has been disregarded by any public authority, courts included. As a result, the ordinary courts are very much inclined to follow the lead of the Bundesverfassungsgericht. Important chapters of constitutional jurisprudence thus find their way into, for example, private law. That is of particular significance because of the value-oriented method of interpretation employed by the constitutional court.

Some general principles of law are explicitly defined in the Basic Law. The principle of equality is, for example, embodied in a constitutional provision.[17] It has given rise to an elaborate case law, which had its repercussions on, among other things, family law, labour law, and tax law. Other general principles of law are extracted from constitutional concepts. According to the Bundesverfassungsgericht, the concept of "Rechtsstaat" embodies, for example, a certain number of values. One of these values is legal certainty, a general principle of law. The principle of legal certainty, in its turn, implies protection of legitimate expectations ("Vertrauensschutz"). Citizens should know what their legal position is, but they should also be able to rely on expectations they derive from statements or activities of public authorities. If the authorities have, for example, created the impression that they will follow a certain policy, they cannot adopt a different decision to the detriment of an individual citizen who had good grounds to believe that his case would be considered in the same way as previous cases. For similar reasons, legislation with retroactive effect is prohibited, unless it imposes no charges on the citizens.[18]

For the interpretation of the concept of "Rechtsstaat", vague though it may be, the courts can find their inspiration in legal history. Already in the early 19th century, legal literature in the German-speaking world devoted much attention to it, even, one might say, helped to create it. Moreover, the values of the "Rechtsstaat", such as legal certainty, are typically "legal" values. Similar considerations apply to the concept of "Bundesstaat" (federal state): the division of powers characterizing federalism is laid down in the Basic Law itself, and historical and comparative elements may help to define its particular features. The concept of "Sozialstaat" (social state), also mentioned in the Basic Law, presented more difficulties, as the principles or the standards it embodies do not seem very appropriate for judicial interpretation. Nevertheless, the Bundesverfassungsgericht found a certain number of guidelines to be respected by legislation in matters of labour law, education and welfare. Political

16. See David P. Currie, The Constitution of the Federal Republic of Germany (Chicago and London 1994), ch 1-II; Peter Badura, Staatsrecht (Munich 1986), ch A-3.
17. Article 3, s. 1-3, Basic Law.
18. BVerfGE13 nr. 19, Grunderwerbsteuergesetz Hamburg, 1962.

choices can only be made, said the court, within the limits of the guidelines inherent in the notion of "Sozialstaat".[19] The court brings some more certainty in its interpretation of these fluid terms by considering that there is some coherence between them: the exact contours of one of these concepts can only be determined in the light of the contours of the other concepts. This is so because the Basic Law is supposed to embody one system of values, with a consistency of its own ("objektive Wertordnung"). The text of the Basic Law lends some support to this legal construct, by evoking the concept of "constitutional order" as a general designation of the system of values laid down in the Basic Law.[20] It is difficult, however, to define the exact contents of this constitutional order, and a considerable amount of literature has been devoted to it.

When compared to the French experience, the position of German courts seems relatively strong because general principles of law find their basis in written texts, in particular of the Basic Law, and have a direct influence in the entire field of the law, private and criminal law included. On the other hand, however, there is a certain vagueness in the German approach, which is not present in French case law. One of the reasons may be the highly deductive style employed by the Bundesverfassungsgericht; it has a "top-down" method in the sense that its reasoning starts by formulating abstract concepts and slowly descends to the real world of facts. The French Conseil d'Etat, by comparison, has a much more case-oriented and inductive practice, and is in so far closer to the methods of common law courts.[21] It is only fair to add that the political impact of the decisions of the German constitutional courts has no equivalent in France, and certainly not in Great Britain, or in any of the Benelux or Scandinavian countries. In Germany the political process has been brought under a certain form of judicial control, as the constitutional courts determine the limits within which that process is allowed to play its role. This control exists at the level of the federated states, the "Länder", as well as at the federal level; occasionally the federal constitutional court will have to decide conflicts of jurisdiction.[22]

1.2.4 THE EUROPEAN COURTS

The European Court of Human Rights is in a position which bears some resemblance to that of the German constitutional courts. The concepts used by the European Convention embody certain values, but the terminology of many provisions of the Convention is vague and indefinite. The Court will have to specify the exact meaning of the different notions. The Convention refers, for example, to "inhuman" punishment, to a "fair" hearing and to an "effective" remedy.[23] What the European Court

19. BVerfGE 33 nr. 22, Numerus clausus Medizinstudium, 1972.
20. See Art. 9(2), 20(3) and 20(4) Basic Law.
21. On this parallellism: C. J. Hamson, Executive discretion and judicial control (6th Hamlyn lecture, London 1954) ch. II-III.
22. BVerfGE 99 nr. 18, Das bessere Müllkonzept, 1997.
23. Articles 3, 6 and 13 Eur. Conv. Human Rights.

does, in a way which is not unfamiliar to those who have studied the case law of the German Bundesverfassungsgericht, is to extract certain principles of law from the concepts used by the Convention; these general principles, in their turn, are supposed to embody specific rules of law to be respected by the Contracting States. The concept of "fair trial" mentioned in Article 6 provides an example: the European Court held that it embodies the general principle of "equality of arms" between the parties in litigation. Subsequently, the Court decided that equality of arms should also be observed in criminal proceedings, and that there was no reason, from this point of view, to reserve a special position to those systems of criminal procedure where the prosecution of the suspect is in the hands of a specialised public service such as a public ministry ("ministère public"). The question then arose whether witnesses in drugs cases could truly be heard in the presence of the suspect; some evidence suggested that these witnesses were only prepared to give reliable information if they were perfectly sure they could not be recognised by the suspect and his friends. The European Court found, however, that the rule of equality of arms applied, and it formulated strict requirements with regard to the hearing of anonymous witnesses.[24] Its way of reasoning is deductive: it derives general principles from concepts used in the Convention, and it then finds that these principles embody certain rules of law which are to be applied in specific cases.

A different method prevails in the case law of the ECJ and of its sister institution, the Court of first instance of the European Communities. Most general principles of law developed by these courts can be considered as principles common to the legal systems of the Member States; on this basis, the ECJ developed principles such as the principle of proportionality, the protection of legitimate expectations, and legal certainty. Sometimes, the court asks for comparative legal materials before actually deciding.[25] There is, however, a second category of general principles of law: they are the principles underlying the provisions of the EC-treaty. Thus, a general principle of equal protection was considered to be embodied in the treaties. One can find some of its "manifestations" in different Treaty provisions, such as the rule of non-discrimination on grounds of nationality, non-discrimination between producers, equal pay for male and female workers etc.[26] In a similar way, the ECJ relies on principles such as free movement of goods, which are set out among the aims of the European Community in the opening articles of the EC-treaty and then elaborated in a number of technical provisions on abolition of customs duties in intra-Community trade and on quantitative restrictions and measures of equivalent effect. At a certain moment, the ECJ began to found its case law concerning the admissibility of import restrictions directly on the general principle of free movement of goods.[27] A third category of general principles of law consists of the protection of human rights and

24. ECHR 20-11-1989, *Kostovski v. the Netherlands*, Series A Vol. 166.
25. Case 155/79, A.M. & S. [1982] ECR 1575.
26. Cases 75 and 117/82, Razzouk and Beydoun [1984] ECR 1509. See also Evelyn Ellis, EC Sex Equality Law (2nd ed., Oxford 1998), p. 168-190.
27. See Case 120/78, Rewe ("Cassis de Dijon") [1979] ECR 649.

fundamental freedoms; provisions of the European Convention of Human Rights, though not directly applicable in Community law, define the standards which are to be observed by Community institutions because they express general principles of law. An example is access to justice, which was, according to the Court, necessarily implied in the provisions of a Community directive (which were not very precise), as it must be considered as a general principle of law also expressed in Article 6 of the European Convention of Human Rights.[28]

For our purpose, the most interesting category of general principles of law is that of the principles common to the legal systems of the Member States. Sometimes, these principles are applied in exactly the same way as in their Member States of origin. Thus, the general principle of legal certainty prevents retroactive regulations in the same way as under German constitutional law. Similarly, the principle of proportionality is applied in the same way as in the legal systems of the Member States when excessive charges for producers are considered as incompatible with Community law. In one of these cases, the ECJ held that by virtue of the principle of proportionality, measures imposing financial charges on economic operators are lawful if they are appropriate and necessary for meeting the objectives pursued by the regulation in question; when, however, a choice has to be made between several appropriate measures, the least onerous method should prevail.[29]

We are in more uncharted waters when the principle of proportionality is used in situations which cannot occur in a Member State, because they concern the way of realising a common market. Exceptions to free movements of goods are, for example, allowed by the EC-treaty for protecting public health and the life of humans, animals or plants. The provision in question adds that the health measures should not constitute "a means of arbitrary discrimination or a disguised restriction on trade between Member States".[30] Even with this caveat, the exact boundary between health and trade, and between Member State powers and Community jurisdiction, cannot always be easily traced. In the German beer case, the import ban on foreign beers manufactured in accordance with other standards than those laid down in German legislation was considered incompatible with the principle of free movement of goods;[31] but the German government had a second line of defence which was based on its powers concerning the protection of human health. If beer is not manufactured according to German standards, they argued, it would be necessary to use certain additives, for example, colouring agents, preservatives or foam stabilisers; according to veterinary experts, the consumption of additives in very large quantities might be dangerous for public health. The ECJ solved this problem by applying the proportionality test. The main question was whether the total ban on imports did not go beyond the limits of

---

28. Case 222/84, *Johnston v. Chief* constable of the Royal Ulster Constabulary [1986] ECR 1651.
29. Case 265/87, Schräder [1989] ECR 2237; Case C-296/94, Pietsch [1996] ECR I-3409.
30. Art. 30 (ex 36) EC-treaty.
31. Case 178/84, *Commission v. Federal Republic of Germany* ("Reinheitsgebot") [1987] ECR 1227.

necessity; if, under certain conditions, some additives used in some foreign beers might present a health risk, that could not justify a total ban of all foreign beers. It is not difficult to recognise here some of the Conseil d'Etat's way of reasoning.

As the example of the German beer case shows, the principle of proportionality permits the courts to penetrate relatively far into the balancing of interests performed by the rule-giving institutions. It may, therefore, bring the courts into sensitive political areas. However, just as the French Conseil d'Etat did not stop at the frontier of the sensitive area of public order, the ECJ relies on the principle of proportionality in a similar way: it respects the discretion left to the political institutions, but it traces the boundary lines of the discretionary powers. In doing so, it attempts to find the point or points where a political or administrative decision stops being merely a matter of politics or administration and develops into a legal matter, to be dealt with by legal means.

1.2.5 EPILOGUE

It may be clear from the foregoing considerations that the emphasis on general principles of law is not only characteristic of European Community law. We find the same phenomenon in German law, in French constitutional and administrative law and in the case law of the European Court of Human Rights. It would not be difficult to find other examples as well.[32] The general principles are not, or not any more, used to patch gaps left between legal provisions duly enacted by the framers of laws, constitutions or treaties. On the contrary, they are an integral part of the conceptual tools judges employ nowadays for settling conflicts.

In so far, the development of general principles of law may correspond to a broader evolution. As the end of the 20th century is near, it becomes more and more obvious that the traditional law-making institutions, such as parliaments and governments, are not equal to the exigencies the performance of their task implies in present-day conditions. Technological progress, rapid processes of social change and the internationalisation of the economy raise new challenges, to which no satisfactory answer has yet been found. By the same token, courts will have to rely on other sources of law than their usual codes, statutes and regulations. From that point of view, the emphasis on general principles of law has a significance which goes beyond questions of legal techniques. This same emphasis has, however, a soothing effect for lawyers who keep to traditional ways of thinking. The fact is indeed that general principles of law, however new they may sometimes appear in their implementation, are also the very incarnation of legal traditions, as the values they represent find often their origin in the written or unwritten law of bygone ages. With some slight exaggeration, we can say that they constitute the accumulated wisdom of generations of lawyers. That makes them a safe instrument in the hands of courts.

---

32. See Walter van Gerven, The effect of proportionality on the actions of Member States of the European Community, in Evelyn Ellis (ed.), The principle of proportionality in the laws of Europe (Oxford 1999), p. 37.

1.3 On Legal Normative Dynamics and Jurisdictional Dialogue in the field of Community General Principles of Law

Hjalte Rasmussen

1.3.1 About the Article's Themes

The following, by necessity short, article brings into focus two of Community law's most sacred general principles of law: The rule of law and/or of legality, on the one hand, and on the other, Community law's human rights protection. As we know these general principles of law today, both are results of legal-normative dynamics. In essence, the European Court shaped their contents and went ahead showing how they were to operate in practice. The two relevant lines of case law are basically as old as the Community itself. I propose in what follows to take a brief look at these two general principles of law.

During the 1990s both these general principles of law were elevated to a special status in that they became the themes of a jurisdictional dialogue between the Community's legal order and, at least, two national legal orders. This dialogue was between Community law and national constitutional law. The main interlocutor on the side of the Community and its law was the European Court. National constitutional law was 'represented' by two national constitutional/supreme courts: The German Constitutional Court and the Danish Supreme Court who took up the issue in their *Maastricht-ratification* judgments which were rendered in 1993 and 1998, respectively.[1]

The two high national courts expressed critical views about the quality of these two general principles. They were critical of the European Court's operation in practice of the principles, which did not afford, as the two courts saw things, an acceptable level of protection of the interests or values they were meant to safeguard.

The thrust of the critical observations about the Court's handling of the principle of legality was that, when balancing legal protection and policymaking efficiency, the European Court had shown a tendency to yield too much weight to efficiency. More specifically, evidence of the European Court's tilt towards efficiency could arguably be found in cases dealing with situations where the validity of a Community legislative enactment has been challenged. According to the two high national courts, the

1. The German Maastricht-ratification judgment of 12 October 1996, is reported in Entscheidungen des Bundesverfassungsgerichts [1993] 89, p. 155. The Danish judgment is reported in UfR 1998.800 H.

Ulf Bernitz and Joakim Nergelius (eds.), General Principles of European Community Law, 35–46

European Court has failed ever to rule that an important legislative act had been adopted *ultra vires* by the Community legislature.[2]

In addition, in particular the German Maastricht-judgment aired doubts about the European Court's institutional commitment to develop and enforce a Community human rights protection matching the ideals of a modern body politic governed by the principles of democracy and rule of law.

The high national judges which in both instances spoke unanimously were concerned with what future course of action the Community's legal order ought to take in order to lay to rest remaining national quality-concerns.

The said approach draws into focus the question about the degree of autonomy over which the Community's legal order disposes for the purposes of defining its own general principles of law. Professor Henry Schermers apparently assumed that any legal order's autonomy is unabridged when he said that general principles of law are

> "[c]ompelling legal principles, stemming from the common legal heritage of Western Europe, and setting out binding rules. These are a form of natural law which should be obeyed irrespective of whether they form part of the written legal order or not. The question of which rules belong to this category depends on the society concerned. Each society subjectively decides what legal principles it considers to be compelling and each society changes this notion slowly but continuously. A definition of these principles is therefore very hard to give."[3]

When the two high national courts gave voice to their doubts about the genuinely protective qualities of the principles of rule of law and human rights protection in Community law, they seem to question that the Community's legal order enjoys such an unabridged autonomy. The questionmark is most pointedly formulated in those parts of the judgments where it is said that if by *national constitutional standards* the quality of the protection offered by the two general legal principles is too slack or unfocused, then it cannot help: Then, it is emphasised, it will be the national courts' national-law-bound duty to refuse to apply on national territory Community legal enactments which in the two respects are enacted below standard. These dicta presuppose, I submit, that competence to define Community law's general principles of law is a shared competence, shared between the Community's and the national legal orders.

This submission raises the far more consequential question whether competence-sharing in the area of general-principle-lawmaking is a mere reflection of a higher principle according to which the competence to rule in the last resort whether all Community norms are valid, is also a shared competence.

2. The 'legislature' used to be the Council of Ministers, i.e. acting upon a proposal from the Commission, etc., etc... In more recent years the EP and the Council share in more and more respects the role as the Community's legislature.
3. Henry Schermers *et al.*, Judicial Protection in the European Communities, 5th ed., 1992, Kluwer Law and Taxation Publishers, Deventer and Boston, at p. 27.)

Leaving aside for a moment the legal questions just raised, at issue is in this article the sociological question about what ought to be the European Court's jurisprudential reaction in the face of a situation as rich in its potentiality for conflict and confrontation? What ought, and what can, the European Court do in order to contribute, from its side of what more than anything else looks as a legal no-man's-land, to avoiding the worst scenario which will emerge if one or both of these courts[4] would one day decide to carry out the threat of non-application?

This article's fundamental issue is, in other words, about peaceful co-existence or confrontation between the legal orders of the Member States and that of the Union.

1.3.2 The Essentials of the National Judicial Findings

For the purposes of what follows, I take the view that the German and Danish *Maastricht-ratification* judgments grappled with essentially the same legal-constitutional problems; and that they solved these problems on their merits in largely identical ways. Of course, there are multiple shades and nuances in view and differences in emphasis between the two high courts' formulations of their national standpoints. Some of these may be theoretically important.

For the purposes of this article's analyses this is immaterial, however. At this place, where the dominant perspective is that of the relationship between Community and national law in the field of general principles of law, it is the conspicuous familiarities of views as expressed by the two high national courts which matter. Because details and nuances have no bearing on the lines of analysis of this article, I even propose to radically gloss over all differences of judgment between the two courts by explaining for the most part only what the *Danish Maastricht-ratification* judgment said.[5] The presentations of the article's main points should benefit from this simplification.

Which were the provisions that attracted so intensely the attention of the two national high courts? The constitutional provisions resistant of a potential supremacy take-over are, on the one hand, those which authorise transfer of powers from national authorities to Community institutions. It is, on the other, the constitutional provisions for the protection of fundamental rights or freedoms or, shorter, human rights.

---

4. Or, indeed, another high court of a Member State.
5. This judgment is discussed in Ole Due, The Danish ratification of the Maastricht Treaty before the Supreme Court, in Mélanges en hommage à Michel Waelbroeck, Bruylant, Brussels, 1999; Halte Rasmussen, Confrontation and Peaceful Co-Existence, in Liber Amicorum Lord Slynn of Hadley, Kluwer Publ., Holland, 2000. Sten Harck and Henrik Palmer Olsen, Decision Concerning the Maastricht Treaty, The American Journal of International Law, Vol. 93, No. 1, 1999, pp. 209-214; and Henning Koch, Dansk forfatningsret i transnational belysning, Juristen, 1999, pp. 372-412; Ole Spiermann, Hvad kommer efter tyve? En analyse af Højesteretsdommen i "Grundlovssagen", UfR 1998.B.325; I have subjected the problems regarding standing in Section 20 cases to a detailed analysis in Om tobaksreklamedirektivets anstrengte forhold til grundlovens § 20.

At the centre of interest stands the two high courts' dicta according to which national constitutional provisions such as these stand above every bit and piece of Community law, written or judge-made; they are immune to a Community take-over bid. The implied rationale to this proposition seems to be that immunity is legally indispensable because the relevant provisions are legal centrepieces of the constitutions of the two Member States. Because these Member States came into existence before the Community – which was set up by instruments of international law – and because the national constitutions existed before the treaties, constitutional provisions such as the ones in question can never, so the high courts stated, be permitted to give in to Community law's judge-invented claim to unconditional supremacy. The assumption seems to be that if stripped by the effect of Community law's supremacy rule of fundamental constitutional rules as the ones in question, the two states' inherent quality as states would be radically and unacceptably challenged and transformed.

Explaining in some more detail what the immunity means in legal terms, the Danish Supreme Court declared, first of all, as regards the provisions authorizing the transfer of national powers, that if a Community institution adopts a piece of legislation for which there is no legal basis in the Treaty the act will not be enforced. It will be left inapplicable on Danish territory. It should be stressed at this time that the Danish court took the radical view that it is ultimately for itself to rule on whether a proper legal basis is available. In performance of this duty, the court's test is this: The enactment should be upheld if the nationally operated transfer of powers granted the Community a competence to adopt it; if the Danish Judge handling the case feels sufficiently certain that the enactment is *ultra vires* the transfer of powers, it will be declared inapplicable. Thus, Community enactments must observe the national constitutional limitations to the transfers of competencies even if, on pure Community law grounds, the disputed Community enactment is considered to have a sufficient legal basis in the Treaty.

It is of no less importance that the Supreme Court further declared that in the event a Community institution proposes the adoption of a legal act off limits the invoked legal basis, Danish ministers, other Danish officials and, perhaps, even commissioners, judges and Community staff with a Danish passport cannot lawfully participate in the adoption of the *ultra vires* act.

As regards, specifically, the national constitutional provisions for the protection of human rights, the Danish court – again much in the same terms as its German counterpart-court, but more soft-spoken, had this to say: Since only powers vested in the ordinary national authorities can be transferred; and since these authorities cannot adopt acts contrary to the national constitution, neither can the institutions of an international organisation be entrusted with such powers.[6] In other words, a Community

6. Advocate-General Warner argued along the same lines in his conclusions in Case 7/76, *IRCA* [1976] ECR 1213. He was not followed by the Court which, as early as in Case 44/79, *Hauer* [1979] ECR 3727 explained that a Community enactment's validity was conditioned by its conformity with Community law only. Next, in *Foto-Frost*, the Court declared that national courts can under no circumstances declare a Community enactment invalid, Case 314/85 [1987] ECR 4199. The Supreme Court was not respectful of any of these commandments.

enactment, which with sufficient clarity violates one of, for example, the Danish constitutional provisions for the protection of human rights, will not be enforced on Danish territory.[7]

As regards the implications of its judgment, it is important to notice that the Danish Supreme Court assuaged its threat of non-application in two respects. The first is that the Supreme Court made it clear that a judicial finding of non-application can never precede a hearing of the European Court. The latter must have been given an opportunity to rule whether the act under attack is, in this court's view, *ultra vires* the Treaty.

Second, the Supreme Court added no less importantly that all Danish courts can as a rule base their decisions about the applicability in Denmark of Community law on that of the European Court's interpretations hereof. An exception to this applies only if a Danish court "with the required certainty" finds that an act upheld by the European Court is without a proper legal basis in the Treaty because the invoked power to act has not been validly transferred under the Danish Constitution's Section 20.

Both the German and the Danish court implied that the European Court had to be granted a considerable margin of discretion in respect of how to develop and handle in practice both the principle of legality and a high quality Community human rights protection. Also, both courts acknowledged that the European Court must enjoy such discretion in order to be able jurisprudentially to satisfy the public order needs of the Community's legal and political order. Yet, they implied nonetheless, if not postulated in express terms, that there were limits to this discretion.

1.3.3 Why National Judicial Threat of Rebellion?

The European Court is a highly imaginative institution. It has been acclaimed by most observers for its interpretative ingenuity and creativeness. More specifically, the European Court has over the years earned a reputation for never striking down an enactment of the Community's legislature of any political importance on *ultra vires* grounds. This is a remarkable record in a system of enumerated powers. There is an air about it that the rule of law principle was not strictly enforced. By *ultra vires* grounds I mean that the European Court was always able to explain away that the chosen legal basis was either too narrow or irrelevant for the adoption of the legal act

7. The 'Danish' threat of non-application, it ought to be said, may not be carried out soon. In fact, Danish courts, when performing constitutional review of national legislation, never earned a reputation for enforcing a particularly high-powered human rights protection *vis-à-vis* Danish parliamentary enactments. Potentially far more relevant from the point of view of a future downbreak of the Community-national jurisdictional dialogue will be the attitude of the German Constitutional Court which masterminded the creation of one of the Western World's finest judicial protections of fundamental rights and freedoms. The German Constitutional Court's threat of non-application for a human rights violation does not therefore invite complacency on the part of the Community's institutions.

under constitutional attack. In still other cases the Court has upheld such acts by side-stepping the legality-issue. Or following an expansive reading of the legal basis invoked by the Council. Here, it is not the place to argue this point in any detail. Therefore, let me, merely for the sake of illustration, point to the implied-powers-doctrine which, in the field of the Community's international competencies made it out for a lack of an express Treaty-power enabling the Council to act. Yet, the reader will notice a quite similar creative and imaginative interpretative pattern in all cases, including such where the plaintiff had laid before the Court evidence and legal arguments strongly suggesting that there was no legal basis in the Treaty to uphold the validity of the act.[8,9]

The Court and its members have over the years regularly explained that the tendency to expansive construction of legal basis was not a judicial invention. Instead, it was the spirit of the Treaty in combination with the methods of interpretation available to the European judges which dictated the interpretative outcomes. If

8. The Court has annulled Council enactments which have infringed against formal requirements (insufficient motivation, for example) or because it violated a human right protected by Community law. This is, however, an entirely different matter as compared to the one under discussion here.

9. Let me nonetheless briefly corroborate my submission: The Court will consider only whether the Community manifestly exceeded its powers or misused them: Case C-331/88, *Fedesa* [1990] ECR I-4023. Thus, for example, if a Community enactment's main policy objective falls outside the invoked (only) legal basis, the act will be upheld by the Court if the act incidentally pursues another policy-objective of minor importance which can be said to lay inside the legal basis; illustration: *UK v. Council* [1988] ECR 892. In Case C-295/90, *EP v. Council (Students' right to residence)* [1992] ECR 4193, the Court found another implied power. Moreover, in the field of social (etc) rights of migrant workers few will probably dispute that the Council legislated outside the powers vested in it by Article 42 (ex Article 51). Further, for years it was commonly assumed that it fell to the Council to determine – *i.e.* immune from judicial review! – what Article 308 (ex Article 235) could be used for; see for example judgment in Case 8/73, *Massey Ferguson* [1973] ECR 897. It is debatable whether the Court's opinion in 2/94, *EU/ECHR* [1996] ECR I-1759 modifies that picture. Also, when the Commission in Joined Cases 188-190/80, *France, Italy and UK v. Commission* [1982] ECR 2545, was under attack for having assumed a major policy making role, the one normally incumbant on the Council, the Court's reaction was the same, i.e. to find that there was a legal basis for the enactment in the Treaty.

   Admittedly, the Court in two instances actually invalidated major policy instruments for lack of a sufficient legal basis. Yet, with a minor retouche they fit into the main pattern of "finding" Community competencies: Opinion 1/78, *Natural Rubber* [1979] ECR 2871 and Joined Cases 281/85 and 283-285/85 and 287/85, *Germany et al v. Commission* [1987] ECR 3203. Indeed, the technique adopted by the Court was the same in both instances: It first substantially expanded the scope of Community competencies to issue the act only in the end to find a minor excess of powers on the ground of which to set aside the act. This was a three-steps-forward-and-one-step-back-and-everybody-happy technique: at the price of an invalidation – the political price of which was minimal for the Institutions – the Court massively reduced the scope of the Member States' residual powers in the two fields of public policy.

this explanation is not without merit, it is arguably not the whole explanation.[10] Indeed, with considerable likelihood the personal philosophies of the judges provided another powerful integrationist yardstick. Moreover, it is a normal phenomenon that institutions, once created, strive for more prestige, might and power for themselves. Hence, one should not be surprised to witness the European Court following a similar pattern.

I guess on the backdrop of these short observations that it could be less a matter of principle than of conjecture that the Court over a period of two to three decades came to the rescue of the Community lawmaker's *ultra vires* enactments. Therefore, I propose to explain (most of) the relevant judgments as brainchilds of the following three inarticulate premises.

The Court's first inarticulate premise was to assume that since the Community's political processes had decided that the EC ought to promulgate the act now under attack, the lawmaker must have been carried by his commitment to furthering political integration, alias the attainment of the Preamble's ever closer union – or, at least, enhancing the conditions of functioning of the pertinent policy-sector. The next premise was, it seems, that if the act in this meaning was good for integration there ought also to be a legal basis for its adoption.

A reasoning along this line, is of course, legally flawed. Placed in a broader context though, it may perhaps be politically defended. The ground of defence begins by taking notice of the decisionmaking processes of the Community's political branches of government which were, from approximately 1965 to 1985 more than cumbersome; sometimes they virtually came to a complete halt by being taken hostage of national special interests, big as well as small. These processes were, in other words, difficult enough without judicial interference for the safeguarding of a general legal principle the exact contours of which were, in the final analysis, difficult to stipulate with precision. The members of the Court may in these circumstances quite legitimately have felt that it would be awkward for them to strike down what appeared to be the exception to the rule, namely an important political initiative, painfully adopted and embedded in the act now under attack for the reason that it was without a proper legal basis in the Treaty.

The expansive-reading-approach may, thus, have occurred as justified and justifiable to the members of the European bench as long as the Community's political processes did not function as presumed. This was also the times when the Court successfully muted the high national courts' concerns about the quality of its human-rights protection.

10. Study after study has proven beyond reasonable doubt that the explanation that the methods of interpretation were responsible for the Court's pro-union activism is wholly unfounded in judicial fact and reasoning. Among the more recent, critical studies is Dr. Diarmuid Rossa Phelan's recently published, very fine analyses of a large number of competence-boundary cases in his book entitled 'Revolt or Revolution'. The book's subtitle is: Constitutional Boundaries of the European Community, Round Hall Sweet & Maxwell, Dublin, 1997.

However, by the end of the 1980s the political processes emerged as fully vital. I refer to the accomplishment on time of the 1992-programme, the rise to prominence and power of the EC's most visibly democratic branch of government, the conclusion of three intergovernmental conferences and all the rest. By then, part of the *acquis communautaire* was also the political processes' firm commitment to the values of democracy and rule of law.[11] No less important is that by the end of the 1980s several Member States noticed that the Court had been guzzling up big chunks of national sovereignty which the Member States had not transferred to the Community.

Former EC-judge T. Koopmans uttered in 1986 that

> "[i]n the past, the Commission often thought it could rely on the Court's help when its case was likely to strengthen European integration. In the future, perhaps it will only be able to do so when it can show a solid legal basis, as the Court's willingness to construct such a basis on its own initiative may diminish."[12]

Unfortunately, the judges who were appointed to the Court in the following years did not fully perceive things as Koopmans did. They failed, if not totally, to take judicial notice of the world outside the Court's judicial palace that was changing at a quick pace. This failure is the more remarkable considering that signs which could be interpreted as warnings about an imminent rebellion were at the time not in sparse supply.[13]

In this new environment of intellectual, political and legal doubts about the legitimacy and perhaps even legality of the European Court's action, it seems to me difficult to explain why the Court apparently continued to offer the Council's *ultra vires* enactments judicial protection. It is tempting to ask whether the European judges turned a deaf ear to the emerging quest for a more enlightened dialogue between them and the European and national polities which the Court was established to serve.

The preceding observations leads me to conclude with not much doubt in my mind that the European Court has been paying far too little attention to the societal necessity of a principled handling the principle of legality.

It is in my view the recognition by several high national courts of this lamentable state of the Court's art as the guarantor of the observance of one of Community law's

---

11. *Cf.* Preamble to Treaty on European Union and this Treaty's Article 6.
12. Italics original; The Role of Law in the New Stage of European Integration, 35, International and Comparative Law Quarterly, pp. 925 et seq.
13. I have reported a large number of these in my book entitled European Court of Justice, GadJura, Copenhagen, 1998, on pp. 329-333. Anthony Arnull reports about high-level political criticisms emerging from the British government, in: The European Union and its Court of Justice, Oxford EC-law Library, Oxford University Press, 1999, at pp. 2-3. Although written in Danish, it is also worth noting that the President of the Danish Supreme Court, Mr. N. Pontoppidan, found reason to express his concerns about the European Court's approach to judging, in Forord (preface) to Liber Amicorum Ole Due, GadJura, Copenhagen, 1994.

most sacred and fundamental legal principles, which has prompted them into a position threatening with defiance and perhaps even rebellion.

1.3.4 Not a Satisfactory Human Rights Protection

The history of the European Court's grappling with the issues of setting up a satisfactory human rights protection is almost as old as the Community itself. This history cannot be retold at this time which necessarily must focus on what happened at the terminus of that long jurisprudential avenue.[14]

The only exception to this analytical program is to remind the reader about the close kinship between the supremacy-principle and the Court's drive for the protection of human rights. It was indeed an attack, coming out of German court rooms, against the supremacy-principle which prompted the European Court to take human rights protection seriously for the first time. This happened in the *Nold II* judgment of 1974.[15] The attack was mounted in what later became known as the *First Solange* judgment rendered in 1974 by the German Constitutional Court.[16] According to *Nold II* this protection was designed to operate at a level above the lowest common denominator to the constitutional traditions of protection of the Member States. But how much above?

Nold II was a clever jurisprudential move. Similar in effect to the administration of an anaesthetic on national judicial EC-human-rights quality-concerns, the Court via this move managed to save time. Some of this time was spent on drafting the intellectually sophisticated and persuasive judgment in the *Hauer* case.[17] A direct line of influence can probably be traced between the *Hauer judgment* and the German Constitutional Court's retreat from the threatening postures it had taken in the *First Solange* judgment.

In the *Second Solange* judgment[18] the German Constitutional Court agreed to wait and see if and how the European Court really intended to take its protection-promises seriously. The emergence of the *Maastricht-ratification* litigation and the ensuing judgments show presumably that the invention of an EC-human rights protection did not eclipse the high German and Danish court concerns.

I have, as said, published elsewhere a detailed analysis of the European Court's human rights case law.[19] There, I concluded that the Court's commitment to a high quality protection of a wide catalogue of Community fundamental rights hardly merits much praise. When it comes to actually setting aside EC enactments, particu-

---

14. I have dealt comprehensively with the historical aspects in: European Court of Justice, Chapter Nine, 1998, GadJura Publishers, Copenhagen.
15. Case 4/73 [1974] ECR 491.
16. This judgment is reported in English in (1974) Common Market Law Reports, pp. 540 and following.
17. Case 44/79 [1979] ECR 3727.
18. The retreat came in the *Second Solange* judgment which is reported in English in (1987) Common Market Law Reports, pp. 225 and following.
19. See above note 13.

larly when they are of a general nature, the Court's courage notably shrinked. The reason, it may be argued, was that the Court, once again, recoiled from imposing duties on the institutions which would fetter the effectiveness of their actions.[20]

Due and Gulmann, the former Danish judge and president of the European Court and the latter the present Danish judge, have recently identified some barriers to more and better protection.[21] Summing up their unoptimistic reasoning, the following points can be made:

First, differences are notorious between Member States traditions of constitutional protection: Protection of ethnic or religious minorities v. freedom of expression; women's right to abortion v. protection of life. Second, rights are often not static over time but changeable both by constitutional amendment and dynamic interpretation. Third, comparative 'better-protection' and 'highest-protection-always-best' evaluations are suspect because of the lack of an agreed standard which cannot be construed because of societal differences of perspective due to different conditions rooted in the Member States' historic, cultural, religious and social conditions.

Due and Gulmann conclude, therefore, that the European Court should 'endeavour to develop a catalogue of fundamental rights adapted to what is specific to the Community, taking into account the particular relationship between Community law and the national legal orders.'

In my view, after the two *Maastricht-judgments* the Court does not seem to enjoy much of a discretion in this endeavour. The Court has, arguably, its back against the wall in these matters. If there are barriers to progress they have to be overcome. The real nub is that the Court must shift signals in the protection of the fundamental rights field of public policy: If it will not, by offering real and effective protection – even if the Community's regulatory processes may become more cumbersome – the Court and the Community run the risk of loosing the battle over effective national compliance with the supremacy principle. That battle is too important: It has to be won at almost any price.

If one day a Community enactment will be invalidated in a national court because of its human rights shortcomings, the principle of supremacy and thereby the integrity of the Community's legal order will have suffered great and the damage will be difficult to redress.

What can the European Court do about this? The easy answer it to say that the Court ought to increase the number of protected rights and enhance the quality of the protection actually on offer in its case law. Not solely for the sake of the protection of

20. This timidity is, it may be noted in an aside, remindful of the weak enforcement in its case on the Community's non-contractual liability, a kinship which may not be accidental considering that a duty to pay compensation for damages in case of illegal general enactments is conditioned by the showing of a 'sufficiently flagrant violation of a superior rule of law for the protection of the individual'. Needless to say that the higher-leveled is the protection of human rights, the more frequently will the said condition be met and a duty to pay damages result.
21. Community Fundamental Rights as Part of National Law, in: Scritti in honore di Guiseppe Federico Mancini, Volume II, Guiffrè Editore, Milano, 1998, pp. 405-422.

the principle of supremacy. But also because the actual state of affairs is not satisfactory all the way round.

A higher level of protection will yield a stronger legitimation of Community law in general. To provide the foundation for more legitimacy ought to be the Court's first priority. That an enhanced legitimation of the whole operation of the Community's legal order in the legal orders of the Member States will, as a reflex, reduce risks that the non-application threat will be carried out, should be seen as an important side-effect.

1.3.5 PROSPECTS FOR A FRUITFUL FUTURE JURISPRUDENTIAL DIALOGUE

Two of the most sacred Community law general principles of law have been the focus of attention in this article: The rule of law and/or of legality and the principle of human rights protection.

In the course of the presentations above it emerged that the European Court's application of these principles to concrete cases has been marked by a non-negligible tilt towards giving preference to institutional concerns about prestige, efficiency and political integration over the promotion of an intense legal protection of the individual company and person. The Court seems to have become a victim of a perhaps understandable but nonetheless dangerous inclination to avoid highjacking the institutions' policymaking efficiency in the name of the protection of the individual.

A German Constitutional Court and a Danish Supreme Court eventually objected to the European Court's priorities. This happened when the two courts gave voice to their anxieties a long time after other actors on the Community/national law- and policymaking scene had expressed their concerns over what Professor Shapiro characterised as

> "Constitutional law without politics [presenting] the European Community as a juristic idea; the written constitution as a sacred text; the professional commentary as a legal truth, the case law as the inevitable working out of the correct implications of the constitutional text and the [Court] as the disembodied voice of right reason and constitutional theology."[22]

What is lacking is, in other words, a qualified and openminded dialogue between the Court, which has sole authority on the part of the Community to define the contents of the general principles of law of the Community's legal order and interlocutors coming from other quarters of the Community and its Member States. The deaf-ear approach is no longer valid. The Court must send out new, strong signals that change is in the making. These must include a far more intensive review of politically important acts adopted by the Community's legislature to ensure the observance of the limitations entrenched in each individual legal basis.

---

22. Italics added; Martin Shapiro, Commentary, 53 Southern Californian Law Review (1980) 537-542.

Where to begin? At present, both the German government and the German Tobacco Industry have brought cases before the Court arguing that the Directive on the Ban of Tobacco Products is *ultra vires* the invoked legal bases. Exceptionally, sixteen EC-law specialists, several of them of distinguished professional reputation, have independently of each other concluded that the Directive is without a legal basis in the Treaty. Even more exceptionally, the legal service of the Council is known to have shared in this opinon.[23] The European Court's rulings in these cases will therefore be awaited with considerable interest.

This Court can help to avoid the looming crisis between the Community and several national legal systems which could explode into an actual confrontation if it invalidates the Directive. The sole alternative to this will be to thoroughly explain in the judgments why the experts and the legal service were all wrong in this case.

The Court ought not to reach its interpretative judgments without regard to their potential impact on national constitutions. National courts ought not to interpret laws or constitutions without regard to the resolution of their compatriots to take full part in European Union or European Community.[24] "If conflicts despite this come into being through judicial decision-making and interpretation, there will necessarily have to be some political action to produce a solution."[25]

23. See Schneider, Hans-Peter and Torsten Stein (eds.) The European Ban on Tobacco Advertising, Nomos Verlag, Baden-Baden, 1999.
24. Harck and Palmer Olsen discuss the potentiality for conflict or peaceful co-existence in their article cited in note 3, p. 214.
25. Neil MacCormmick, Democracy, Subsidiarity and Citizenship in the "European Commonwealth", in: Law and Philosophy (1997), pp. 331-356.

2. Human Rights

2.1 Leading by Example or Leaning on Supremacy? Some reflections on the Union, the Individual and the Protection of Fundamental Rights

*Hans Ragnemalm**

2.1.1 INTRODUCTION

The fundamental rights debate within the European Union – at times rather passionate[1] – has mainly focused on the national authorities' obligation to respect Community fundamental rights when implementing or applying Community law.[2]

Without any pretension of completeness, the Court of Justice has been criticised, among other things:

- for not taking rights seriously;
- for an instrumental use of its fundamental rights discourse;
- for expanding its jurisdiction, in the guise of fundamental rights protection, into areas previously reserved to the Member States – the "Trojan horse" argument;
- for applying double standards when it comes to protecting fundamental rights at national or Community level; and
- for placing the protection of economic and social rights on a different level than the protection of civil and political rights.

Faced with this vale of tears, this article will not engage the critics of the Court. As an academic, it is tempting to "add my piece of wood to the fire" – as it is said in Sweden – in order to nourish the debate and keep the braises alive. However, my years in Luxembourg have taught me caution: by common European standards, rather than keeping the fire burning, this is more frequently perceived as pouring oil on it or, alternatively, as stones being thrown in a glass house.

---

* Judge of the Court of Justice of the European Communities. The author is indebted to William Robinson for his review of the text from a linguistic point of view.

1. Coppel and O'Neill, *The European Court of Justice: Taking Rights Seriously?*, 29 CML Rev. (1992), 669-692; Weiler and Lockhart, *"Taking Rights Seriously" Seriously: The European Court and its Fundamental Rights Jurisprudence*, 32 CML Rev. (1995), 51-94 (Part I) and 579-627 (Part II).
2. See, for example, Due and Gulmann, *Community Fundamental Rights as Part of National Law*, in *Scritti in onore di Giuseppe Federico Mancini*, Vol. II (1998), 405-422.

Ulf Bernitz and Joakim Nergelius (eds.), General Principles of European Community Law, 49–59

Turning to the problem of divergent levels of protection of fundamental rights. Proposals for structural reforms or, alternatively, changes in judicial policy, include:

- the accession of the Community to the ECHR;[3]
- the adoption of a "pluralist approach", by which an autonomous (minimum) Community standard would be carved out;[4]
- the adoption of a "maximum standard approach", based on the sum total of relevant international and national fundamental rights standards binding upon the Member States, as the Community law standard;[5]
- the adoption of a "local maximum standard", founded on the principle of subsidiarity;[6] and
- the elaboration of a Charter on Fundamental Rights of the Citizens of the European Union.[7]

In order to stoke the fire, it should be noted, at the outset, that, in my opinion, the fundamental rights discussion sometimes tends to get a bit too theoretical and doctrinal. Judges are faced with the difficult task of guaranteeing rights that are practical and effective in everyday life.

The parameters of the study are the impact of general principles of Community law at the national level and how they are "transformed" into the national legal systems. As a prerequisite, it is essential, to my mind, to focus on the European Courts' recent case law on the *European institutions'* obligation to respect fundamental rights.

Under the new Article 6(1) EU (ex Article F), "the Union is founded on the principles of liberty, democracy, respect for human rights and fundamental freedoms, and the rule of law, principles which are common to the Member States". Article 6(2) EU provides what is already settled case law, namely that "the Union shall respect fundamental rights, as guaranteed by the European Convention for the Protection of Human Rights and Fundamental Freedoms (....) and as they result from the constitutional

3. Mancini and Di Bucci, *Le développement des droits fondamentaux en tant que partie du droit communautaire*, in *Collected Courses of the Academy of European Law*, Vol. 1, Book 1 (1991), 27-52.
4. Weiler, *Fundamental Rights and Fundamental Boundaries: On Standards and Values in the Protection of Human Rights*, in Neuwahl and Rosas, *The European Union and Human Rights* (1995), 51-76.
5. Besselink, *Entrapped by the Maximum Standard: On Fundamental Rights, Pluralism and Subsidiarity in the European Union*, 35 CML Rev. (1998), 629-680.
6. Idem.
7. *Leading by Example: A Human Rights Agenda for the European Union for the year 2000, European University Institute* (1998). See also Alston (ed.), *The EU and Human Rights* (1999). – According to European Council decisions in Cologne (3 and 4 June 1999) and Tampere (15 and 16 October 1999) a draft EU Charter of Fundamental Rights would now be elaborated by a body made up of representatives of Heads of State or Governments of Member States, the President of the Commission and members of the European Parliament and of national Parliaments.

traditions common to the Member States, as general principles of Community law." Since the entry into force of the Amsterdam Treaty, Article 46 EU (ex Article L) explicitly gives the Court competence to interpret Article 6(2) EU with regard to "actions of the institutions".

This article will examine three fundamental tendencies in the recent case law. First, European citizens' right of participation in an "effective political democracy"; second, principles of good administration within the Community institutions; and third, the general principle of Community law that everyone is entitled to a fair legal process.

2.1.2 SECURING EUROPEAN CITIZENS' RIGHT OF PARTICIPATION IN AN "EFFECTIVE POLITICAL DEMOCRACY"

In an effective political democracy, the idea of an informed citizenry, the free expression of opinion of the people in the choice of the legislature and the possibility to complain about one's government and administration must be secured as fundamental rights.

The Court has repeatedly held that due consultation of the European Parliament constitutes an essential formal requirement, the breach of which renders the measure concerned void.[8] Effective participation of the Parliament in the legislative process of the Community represents an essential factor in the institutional balance intended by the Treaty. This function reflects the *fundamental democratic principle* that the people should take part in the exercise of power through the intermediary of a representative assembly. In this respect, the Court did not wait for the new Article 6 (1) EU (ex Article F) – which it is not competent to interpret – in order to protect the principle.

In this context, the European Court of Human Rights recently handed down an interesting judgment in the case of *Matthews v. The United Kingdom.*[9] The Strasbourg Court held the United Kingdom responsible under Article 1 of the European Convention for securing the right to vote, guaranteed by Article 3 of Protocol No. 1, regardless of whether the elections were purely domestic or to the European Parliament.

To my mind, there is no dispute that the Convention provides the "minimum standard" of protection, "below" which neither the Member States nor the institutions of the European Union may fall. In that respect, the ECHR must be regarded as more than a mere "guideline" or an act with "special significance" in Community law.

Yet, the ECHR and the case law of the Strasbourg Court should never be "taken hostage" in order to deny the existence of a fundamental right within Community law. It is firmly rooted in the Strasbourg Court's case law that the Convention is a living instrument, which must be interpreted in the light of present-day

8. Case C-21/94, *Parliament v. Council*, [1995] ECR I-1827, para 17, and Case C-392/95, *Parliament v. Council*, [1997] ECR I-3213, para 14.
9. Judgment of 18 February 1999 in Case of *Matthews v. The United Kingdom* (application no. 24833/94).

conditions.[10] The fact that a fundamental right has not yet been recognised within the Council of Europe does not preclude its recognition within the European Union.[11]

Indeed, under Article 6(2) EU, the Union shall also respect fundamental rights, as they result from the *constitutional traditions common to the Member States*, as general principles of Community law. This is the very basis on which those rights were first recognised in Community law. The constitutional traditions may evolve more rapidly within the European Union than within the growing number of Member States in the Council of Europe.

Let me take the example of a fundamental right, which I have very much at heart: the right of individuals to have access to documents held by public authorities.[12] Indeed, the participation in an effective political democracy is not limited to the right to vote and the exercise of power through the intermediary of a representative assembly. It is this realisation – that people can form an independent opinion and eventually control the exercise of power – that is inherent in the *fundamental democratic principle.*

In the case of *Netherlands v. Council*,[13] the Court recalled that

> "the domestic legislation of most Member States now enshrines in a general manner the public's right of access to documents held by public authorities as a constitutional or legislative principle"

and that

> "at Community level, the importance of that right has been reaffirmed on various occasions."

Thus, the Court confirmed the existence of a

> "trend, which discloses a progressive affirmation of individuals' right of access to documents held by public authorities".

---

10. See, *inter alia*, the judgment of 23 March 1995 (preliminary objections) in Case of *Loizidou v. Turkey*, Series A No. 310, pp. 26-27, § 71, with further reference.
11. In Case C-249/96, *Grant v. South-West Trains*, [1998] ECR I-621, paras. 33–35, the Court relied, however, *inter alia* on a number of admissibility decisions from the European Commission of Human Rights and two judgments of the European Court of Human Rights in order to substantiate its findings that in the present state of the law within the Community, stable relationships between two persons of the same sex are not regarded as equivalent to marriages or stable relationships outside marriage between persons of opposite sex.
12. Ragnemalm, *Démocratie et transparence: Sur le droit général d'accès des citoyens de l'union européenne aux documents détenus par les institutions communautaires*, in *Scritti in onore di Giuseppe Federico Mancini*, Vol. II (1998), 809-830, and *The Community Courts and Openness within the European Union*, to be published in *The Cambridge Yearbook of European Legal Studies*, Volume 2, 1999.
13. Case C-58/94, *Netherlands v. Council*, [1996] ECR I-2169, paras. 34-37.

In its judgment, the Court called for general rules on the right of public access to documents held by the Community institutions. The Community legislature is now at work in order to adopt such rules on the basis of the new Article 255 EC, inserted by the Amsterdam Treaty.

In his opinion in that case,[14] Advocate General Tesauro stated, with reference to the individual's *right to information*, that "the basis for such a right should be sought in the democratic principle, which constitutes one of the cornerstones of the Community edifice (...)".

On this basis, and recalling its own case-law, the Court of First Instance recently held in *Hautala v. Council*[15] that the Council's internal measures on public access must be interpreted in the light of the *principle of the right to information* and of the principle of proportionality.

In contrast, in the *Guerra* case,[16] the Strasbourg Court reiterated its rather restrictive case law on freedom of information. *Freedom to receive information*, referred to in Article 10 (2) of the Convention, "basically prohibits a government from restricting a person from receiving information that others wish or may be willing to impart to him".[17] The Court held that this freedom cannot be construed as imposing on a State, in circumstances such as those of the *Guerra* case, positive obligations to collect and disseminate information of its own motion. However, in a concurring opinion, Judge Palm, joined by five colleagues,[18] strongly emphasised the factual situation at hand. She did not exclude that, under different circumstances, the State may have a *positive obligation to make information available* to the public and to disseminate such information, which by its nature could not otherwise come to the knowledge of the public.

The Court of Justice has in several cases and in different contexts confirmed that freedom of expression, enshrined in Article 10 of the ECHR, is protected in the Community legal order. Thus, in *Familiapress,*[19] the Court stated, with reference to *ERT,*[20] that when a Member State relies on overriding requirements, such as maintaining press diversity, in order to justify rules which are likely to obstruct the exercise of free movement of goods, such justification must also be interpreted in the light of fundamental rights such as the freedom of expression.

In the recent judgment in the case of *Economic and Social Committee v. E,*[21] the Court – concluding from its statement in *Oyowe and Traore v. Commission*[22] that the duty of allegiance to the Communities imposed on officials in the Staff Regulations

14. Point 19.
15. Case T-14/98, judgment of 19 July 1999 (not yet reported). The judgment has been appealed to the Court of Justice as Case C-353/99 P (pending).
16. Judgment of 19 February 1998 in Case of *Guerra and others v. Italy*, 1998-I, p. 223.
17. See the *Leander v. Sweden* judgment of 26 March 1987, Series A No. 116, p. 29, § 74.
18. Judges Bernhardt, Russo, Macdonald, Makarczyk and Van Dijk.
19. Case C-368/95, *Familiapress v. Bauer Verlag*, [1997] ECR I-3689.
20. Case C-260/89 [1991] ECR I-2925.
21. Case C-150/98 P, judgment of 16 December 1999 (not yet reported).
22. Case C-100/88 [1989] ECR I-4285.

cannot be interpreted in such a way as to conflict with freedom of expression – stressed that the respect of this fundamental freedom is particularly important when an official makes use of his statutory right to react on references given by his superiors. In such a case, only the use of expressions, which are profoundly abusive or demonstrate a grave lack of respect, could be considered as a breach of the duty to show temperance.

That freedom of peaceful assembly and of association, enshrined in Article 11 of the ECHR, is in the same way protected in Community law was recently confirmed in one of the Polypropylene judgments, namely *Montecatini.*[23]

2.1.3 Securing the principle of good administration within the Community institutions

As more and more citizens increasingly have direct contact with the European bureaucracy at both national and Community level, it is imperative to secure the quality of the administration within the Community institutions. When dealing with non-judicial proceedings of an administrative nature, it is preferable to say that public authorities are bound to comply with, what is best described as a *general principle of good administration*. The *right to a fair hearing*,[24] inspired by Article 6 of the ECHR, should in principle be reserved for judicial and quasi-judicial proceedings. Of course, this does not imply that a positive cross-fertilisation between administrative and procedural law should be ruled out, in particular in competition cases.

In *Lisrestal*,[25] the Court held that the observance of the *right to be heard* is, in all proceedings initiated against a person which may result in a "negative measure", a fundamental principle of Community law. That principle must be guaranteed even in the absence of any written rules governing the proceedings in question. It requires that any person against whom a decision may be taken adversely affecting his intentions should be placed in a position in which he may effectively make known his views on the evidence against him upon which the measure is based. Consequently, a decision to reduce assistance granted by the European Social Fund – adopted when the

23. Case C-235/92 P, *Montecatini SpA v. Commission*, judgment of 8 July 1999 (not yet reported).
24. As the Court, referring to Case 85/76, *Hoffmann-La Roche v. Commission*, [1979] ECR 461, recalled in Cases 100 to 103/80, *Musique Diffusion française v. Commission*, [1983] ECR 1825, para. 10, a fundamental principle of Community law requires the *right to a fair hearing* to be observed in all proceedings in which sanctions may be imposed, even if the proceedings are of an administrative nature. The undertaking concerned must have been afforded the opportunity, during the administrative procedure, to make known its views on the truth and relevance of the facts and circumstances alleged. This is also the case with the documents used by the Commission to support its claim that there has been an infringement of the Treaty.
25. Case C-32/95 P, *Commission v. Lisrestal*, [1996] ECR I-5373.

Commission had not heard the beneficiary – infringed the latter's rights of defence, irrespective of any practical difficulties for the Commission in consulting beneficiaries directly.

At the national level, a general principle of administrative and procedural law of fundamental importance is that a party must have a right to unrestricted *access to the file*, which the administrative authority or the administrative court uses as the basis for its decision. If a party is to conduct his case in a meaningful way, he must be able to obtain access – at the preparatory stage, i.e. before the adoption of a final decision – to all the material that has been introduced into the case, and which could thereby affect the outcome. Indeed, rules on access to the file are designed to ensure effective exercise of the rights of the defence, including the right to be heard.

After several invitations,[26] the Court explicitly recognised the *right of access to the Commission's file* as a "general principle of Community law" in *Baustahlgewebe*.[27] The Court also made clear that the general principles of Community law governing the right of access to the Commission's file do not apply, as such, to court proceedings. The latter are governed by the EC Statute of the Court of Justice and by the Rules of Procedure of the Court of First Instance.

The consequences of the breach of that principle in competition cases were recently developed in another of the Polypropylene cases, namely *Hercules*.[28] The Court held that such a breach in the procedure prior to the adoption of a decision can, in principle, cause the decision to be annulled if the rights of defence of the undertaking concerned have been infringed. The infringement committed is not remedied by the mere fact that access is made possible at a later stage, in particular during the judicial proceedings relating to an action in which annulment of the contested decision is sought. Indeed, belated disclosure of documents in the file allows the undertaking that has brought an action against a Commission decision to formulate arguments before the Community Courts. However, it does not put the undertaking back into the situation it would have been in, had it been able to rely on those documents in presenting its written and oral observations to the Commission. It is not therefore an adequate remedy for the infringement of the rights of the defence that occurred before the decision was adopted. The Court held that the undertaking concerned does not have to show that, had it been given access to the file, the Commission decision would have been different in content. It is only required to show that it would have been able to use those documents for its defence, which Hercules had failed to do in the particular case before the Court.

26. See, for example, Case 322/81, *Michelin v. Commission*, [1983] ECR 3461, para. 7, and Case C-310/93 P, *BPB Industries and British Gypsum v. Commission*, [1995] ECR I-865, para. 21.
27. Case C-185/95 P, *Baustahlgewebe v. Commission*, [1998] ECR I-8417, para. 90.
28. Case C-51/92 P, *Hercules Chemicals NV v. Commission*, judgment of 8 July 1999 (not yet reported). See paras. 75-83.

In *Sytraval*,[29] the Court recalled its settled case law[30] on the *obligation to state reasons* required by Article 190 of the Treaty, which enables the competent Community court to exercise its power of review. The "competent Community court" – in this case the Court of First Instance – had however confused the plea alleging infringement of Article 190 of the Treaty and the plea alleging manifest error of assessment. The Court recalled that these are distinct pleas, each of which may be raised in proceedings under Article 173 of the Treaty. The first plea, alleging absence of reasons or inadequacy of the reasons stated, relates to an issue of infringement of essential procedural requirements within the meaning of that article and, involving a matter of public policy, must be raised by the Community judicature of its own motion.[31] By contrast, the second plea, which relates to the substantive legality of the contested decision, is concerned with infringement of a rule of law relating to the application of the Treaty within the meaning of Article 173 and can be examined by the Community judicature only if it is raised by the applicant.

Revocation of favourable administrative acts is generally subject to strict conditions in Community law.[32] If a Community institution finds that a recently adopted measure is tainted by illegality, it has in principle the right to withdraw that measure within a reasonable period, with retroactive effect. However, in *De Compte,*[33] the Court repeated its constant case law that this right may be restricted by the need to fulfil the legitimate expectations of a beneficiary of the measure, who has been led to rely on the lawfulness thereof.

The Court held that legitimate expectations as to the legality of a favourable administrative act, once acquired, might not subsequently be undermined. The only exception is if there is a public-policy interest, which overrides the beneficiary's interest in the maintenance of a situation, which he is, in principle, entitled to regard as settled. The Court added that the operative time for determining whether the addressee of an administrative act has acquired legitimate expectations is not the date on which the act was adopted or withdrawn, but the date on which it was *notified*.

As indicated by these examples, the Court has enunciated a fairly complete set of general principles of Community law in order to secure good administration within the Community institutions. Others must judge whether these general principles have been consistently enforced in order to protect the rights of individuals.

---

29. Case C-367/95 P, *Commission v. Sytraval and Brink's France*, [1998] ECR I-1719.
30. See, in particular, Cases 296/82 and 318/82, *Netherlands and Leeuwarder Papierwarenfabriek v. Commission*, [1985] ECR 809, para. 19, Case C-350/88, *Delacre and others v. Commission*, [1990] ECR I-395, paras. 15 and 16, and Case C-56/93, *Belgium v. Commission*, [1996] ECR I-723, para. 86.
31. See, in particular, Case C-166/95 P, *Commission v. Daffix*, [1997] ECR I-983, para 24.
32. See Ragnemalm, *Confiance légitime et délai raisonnable. Quelques remarques sur le thème du retrait des actes administratifs favorables en droit communautaire*, in Rodríguez Iglesias, Due, Schintgen and Elsen (éd.), *Mélanges en hommage à Fernand Schockweiler* (1999), 511-522.
33. Case C-90/95 P, *Henri de Compte v. Parliament*, [1997] ECR I-1999.

2.1.4. ENFORCING THE GENERAL PRINCIPLE OF COMMUNITY LAW THAT EVERYONE IS ENTITLED TO A FAIR LEGAL PROCESS

Article 6(1) of the ECHR provides that in the determination of civil rights and obligations or of any criminal charge, everyone is entitled to a fair and public hearing within a reasonable time by an independent and impartial tribunal established by law.

It follows already from *Musique Diffusion Française*[34] that Community law contains all the means necessary for examining and, in an appropriate case, upholding the submissions based on alleged breaches of the applicant's right to a fair hearing. It should therefore come as no surprise that the general principle of Community law that everyone is entitled to a fair legal process, and in particular the *right to a legal process within a reasonable period*, is applicable in proceedings imposing fines on an undertaking for infringement of competition law.

In Baustahlgewebe,[35] the Court held that the reasonableness of the proceedings before the Community Courts must be appraised in the light of the circumstances specific to each case. In particular, the importance of the case for the person concerned, its complexity and the conduct of the applicant and of the competent authorities should be taken into consideration. This is a clear analogy with the case law of the European Court of Human Rights.[36]

Notwithstanding the relative complexity of the case, the Court of Justice held that the proceedings before the Court of First Instance, which lasted five and a half years, did not satisfy the requirements concerning completion within a reasonable time. In order to ensure an effective remedy, the Court set aside the judgment of the Court of First Instance in so far as it fixed the fine at 3 million ECU. The Court reduced those fines by 50,000 ECU, which was considered to be a reasonable satisfaction for the excessive duration of the proceedings before the Court of First Instance.

It should be noted that in competition cases, the structure of the proceedings implies that it is for the undertaking on which fines have already been imposed by the Commission to bring a case before the Community Courts. This reverses the roles of the parties in quasi-criminal proceedings, with the undertaking as applicant and the Commission as defendant before the Courts. It can at times complicate the issue of the compliance with the right to a fair hearing in Community law.

Nevertheless, in *Baustahlgewebe*, the Court held that where there is a dispute as to the existence of an infringement of the competition rules, it is incumbent on the Commission to prove the infringements found by it. It is for the Commission to

34. Above note 24, para. 11.
35. Above note 27, paras. 26-49 and 141-142.
36. See the judgments in the cases of *Erkner and Hofauer v. Austria* of 23 April 1987, Series A No. 117, § 66; *Kemmache v. France* of 27 November 1991, Series A No. 218, § 60; *Phocas v. France* of 23 April 1996, 1996-II, p. 546, § 71, and *Garyfallou AEBE v. Greece* of 27 September 1997, 1997-V, p. 1821, § 39.

provide evidence capable of demonstrating to the requisite legal standard the existence of the circumstances constituting an infringement.[37]

The Court drew the consequences of this reasoning in *Hüls*, yet another of the Polypropylene cases.[38] The Court held that the *presumption of innocence*, as it results especially from Article 6(2) of the ECHR, forms part of the fundamental rights, protected by the Community legal order. Having regard to the nature of the infringement, the degree and the severity of the sanctions, the principle of presumption of innocence is applicable in competition proceedings where fines and penalty payments may be imposed.

In this context, the occasionally quite cumbersome structure of the Community legal order is frequently put forward as an argument against applying "national" standards when protecting fundamental rights at the Community level. There is a general feeling that if the institutions were to be held accountable to such standards, their efficiency would be at risk.

This line of reasoning misses the point, when it comes to the protection of fundamental rights in Community law. The standards laid down by the Court are not "national". They are common to the Member States and to the European Union. Moreover, an administration and a judicial system unable to protect the most fundamental rights of its legal order are seldom efficient, at least in a democratic system.

2.1.5 Conclusion

As a closing remark, when it comes to the role of the Court in safeguarding fundamental rights, a clear tendency in recent case law can be discerned. Rather than continuing to *lean on the doctrine of supremacy* or primacy in order to ensure the compliance with general principles of Community law by national authorities, the Court has increasingly started to *lead by example*, in safeguarding the respect of fundamental rights by the Community institutions. This is, it is suggested, a condition *sine qua non* for the acceptance of general principles of Community law at the national level.

Finally, I cannot address the subject of the protection of fundamental rights without paying a tribute to Judge Federico Mancini, who died during the course of the summer of 1999.

He forcefully pleaded for the accession of the Community to the ECHR and for an external control of the Court's case-law on fundamental rights by the European Court of Human Rights. In his view, this would be a sign of maturity of the Community as such. As he pointed out, the time when the Court saw its primary task as that of

37. Above note 27, para. 58. See also Case C-49/92 P, *Commission v. Anic Partecipazioni SpA*, judgment of 8 July 1999 (not yet reported), para. 86.
38. Case C-199/92 P, *Hüls AG v. Commission*, judgment of 8 July 1999 (not yet reported), paras. 149-150. See also *Montecatini*, above note 23, paras. 175–176.

ensuring independence and freedom of action of Community institutions – sometimes to the detriment of the protection of fundamental rights – has long passed.[39]

With the possible forthcoming elaboration of a Charter on Fundamental Rights of the Citizens of the European Union, Judge Mancini's premonitory calls may at least be partially answered. However, as he often pointed out both in his writings and privately, what really matters, beyond general statements of principle, is the concrete application of those principles and the effective sanction of all violations of fundamental rights.[40]

It is clear that Federico Mancini's legacy to the protection of fundamental rights at both national and Community level, as in so many other areas of the law, will inspire academics, practitioners and judges for many years to come.

---

39. Mancini, *Safeguarding Human Rights: The Role of the Court of Justice of the European Communities*, in *Judicial Protection of Human Rights at the National and International Level*, Vol. I (1991), 497–517, at 504.
40. Mancini and Di Bucci, above note 3, at 52.

2.2 Human Rights as General Principles of Law

Henry G. Schermers

2.2.1 Definitions

Both general principles and human rights are rather vague notions. Some bring more under these headings than others.

There are two different kinds of general principles. (1) Regulatory principles of law, which are used to fill gaps if no other rule exists. They are a kind of law in reserve, subordinate to written legislation. (2) Compulsory principles of law which are fundamental principles of a higher level taking priority over written legislation and having to be applied irrespective of the question whether the legal system has rules of its own. Rules conflicting with these latter principles may not be applied.

The source of general principles of law may vary. Two-hundred years ago general principles were taken from the bible. Later, the interest of the fatherland took priority and whatever the fatherland, or the king, required, was a principle of law. In recent times human rights came to the foreground. The Western World promotes the respect for human rights throughout the world in much the same way as it promoted Christian religion in a previous era. This means that in present Western Europe the most fundamental rights are at the same time general principles of law. Whenever positive law lacks, principles of equity, fairness and proportionality may fill the gaps. Codified human rights, and in particular those incorporated in the European Convention on Human Rights are even compulsory principles which take priority over conflicting rules of the legal order.

To what extent European fundamental human rights take priority over conflicting domestic law also depends on the extent to which such rights have been accepted throughout Europe. In most fields the domestic laws on human rights are the same, or very similar, in all Member States of the European Union. In some fields, however, there may be variations. The right to change sex which for some people is an essential element of private life, is not accepted in all countries of the Union and has, so far, not been accepted by the European Court of Human Rights as being covered by the European Convention. In the American Convention on Human Rights life is protected as from conception, which means that abortion is murder. Some states in Europe take the same position, others see the right to have an abortion as part of the private life of the mother. The European Commission on Human Rights held that the right of life begins at birth and that therefore neither a prohibition of abortion, nor a right to have an abortion is covered by the Convention.[1]

1. *X v. United Kingdom*, application 8416/79, decision of 13 May 1980, DR Vol. 19, pp. 244–254.

Ulf Bernitz and Joakim Nergelius (eds.), General Principles of European Community Law, 61–71

2.2.2 BORDERLINES

Are all human rights general principles of law or are all general principles of law human rights?[2] Some classifications are clear. The prohibition of torture and the right of life are generally seen as fundamental human rights. However, were they not enumerated in human rights conventions, were they not part of any positive law, then a judge could well classify them as general principles of law. In European Community law, the rights enumerated in the European Convention on Human Rights are accepted as "an integral part of the general principles of law",[3] binding with priority over conflicting other rules. Other fundamental rights have also been accepted as general principles of law. As examples we mention a number of rights which the Court of Justice of the European Communities classified as general principles of law and which may at the same time be fundamental human rights.

2.2.2.1 Proportionality

The Court of Justice applied the principle of proportionality from the beginning. In its Fédéchar judgment of 29 November 1956 the Court expressly mentions the principle of proportionality as a general principle of law. Seven years later Mrs Schmitz was dismissed because of her bad behaviour. The Court of Justice annulled this decision of the Commission in its judgment of 19 March 1964 because it considered this dismissal disproportionate to the behaviour of Mrs Schmitz.[4] Much later, in 1979, the Court held that particular provisions of regulations could not be applied because they conflicted with the principle of proportionality.[5]

2.2.2.2 *Non bis in idem*

In *Gutmann* the Court held on 5 May 1966 that on the ground of *non bis in idem* it is prohibited, not only to impose two disciplinary sanctions for one mistake, but also to start two disciplinary procedures for the same set of facts.[6]

---

2. See also Deirdre Curtin & Ton Heukels (eds), *Institutional Dynamics of European Integration*, Vol. II, pp. 485-571.
3. *Stauder* case and *Second Nold* case, see below.
4. *Schmitz* case (18/63) 19 March 1964, [1964] ECR 85.
5. *Buitoni* case (122/78), 20 Feb. 1979, [1979] ECR 677; *Atalanta* case (240/78), 21 June 1979, [1979] ECR 2137, consideration 15 at p. 2151.
6. *Gutmann* case (18, 35/65), 5 May 1966, [1966] ECR 103.

2.2.2.3 The right of defence[7]

The right of defence is another general principle applied by the Court of Justice. See for example *Moli,*[8] *or Transocean Marine Paint.*[9] *In Third Hoffmann-La Roche* the Court referred to the right of defence as a fundamental principle of Community Law.[10]

2.2.2.4 Legal certainty

Legal certainty is another legal principle applied by the Court. The *Second Defrenne* case hinged on that legal principle.[11] Also the organisers of this conference considered legal certainty so important that they invited Mr. Temple Lang to devote a separate chapter to this principle. I refer to that chapter.

2.2.2.5 Right to receive information

Judge Ragnemalm, to whose chapter I may refer, already mentioned this principle of law.

2.2.2.6 Non-discrimination[12]

Also the principle of non-discrimination was applied by the Court of Justice in a number of cases. See for example *Frilli*[13] or *Ruckdeschel.*[14]

2.2.2.7 Vested rights

The protection of vested rights is an interesting principle of law as it illustrates the development of the role of such principles in Community law. In 1960 the Court of Justice held: "Community law, as it arises under the ECSC Treaty, does not contain any general principle, express or otherwise, guaranteeing the maintenance of vested rights".[15] Nine years later in *Klomp* the Court referred to continuity of the legal system, which comes close to vested rights as "a principle common to the legal

---

7. See also R.H. Lauwaars, *Rights of Defence in Competition Cases*, in Curtin-Heukels (*cit.* note 2), pp. 497-509.
8. *Moli* case (121/76), 27 Oct. 1977, [1977] ECR 1971.
9. *Transocean Marine Paint* case (17/74), 23 Oct. 1974, [1974] ECR 1063.
10. *Third Hoffmann-La Roche* case (85/76), 13 Feb. 1979, [1979] ECR 461, at 511.
11. *Second Defrenne* case (43/75), 8 April 1976, [1976] ECR 455.
12. See also René Barents, *The Significance of the Non-Discrimination Principle for the Common Agricultural Policy*, in Curtin-Heukels (*cit.* note 2) pp. 527-548.
13. *Frilli* case (1/72), 22 June 1972 [1972] ECR 457, at 466.
14. *Ruckdeschel* case (117/76, 16/77), 19 Oct. 1977, [1977] ECR 1753 at 1769.
15. *Geitling, Nold and others* case (36, 37, 38 and 40/59), 15 July 1960, 1960 ECR 423 at p. 439.

systems of the Member States, the origins of which may be traced back to Roman law".[16]

Are these principles also human rights? Only some of them are incorporated in human rights treaties, such as the right to receive information, the prohibition of discrimination, the right of defence and *non bis in idem*. Under the European Convention of Human Rights the prohibition of discrimination has only partly been accepted in Article 14. *Non bis in idem* is expressly mentioned in Article 4 of Protocol 7. The right of defence, though only expressly mentioned for criminal law, is understood to be part of the fair trial rule of Article 6. Most – if not all – of the other rights mentioned could also be incorporated in the notion "fair trial" which is accepted as part of Article 6 of the Convention.

2.2.3 HUMAN RIGHTS BEFORE THE COURT OF JUSTICE

The development of the protection of human rights by the Court of Justice can be illustrated by the story of Nold. Nold was a limited partnership carrying on a business as a wholesaler in coal. It bought coal directly from the German mines and sold to consumers a total amount of less than 60.000 tons a year. In 1956 the High Authority of the Coal and Steel Community ruled that only those wholesalers could be maintained who sold more that 75.000 tons a year. In 1957 the amount was lowered to more than 60.000 tons a year but still, Nold was no longer entitled to buy directly from the mines. This meant the end of its business and a serious interference with its property.

Article 14 of the German Constitution protects private property. The German Constitutional Court had ruled that this protection also extended to commercial undertakings. Therefore, Nold invoked the right of protection of its property before the Court of Justice, considering that the limitations of government power imposed by the German Constitution must also apply to international institutions which obtained their powers, at least in part, from the German government. No government can transfer to an international organisation more powers than it has itself.

In reply to Nold, the Court of Justice held:

> "It is not for the Court, whose function is to judge the legality of decisions adopted by the High Authority ..... to ensure that rules of internal law, even constitutional rules, enforced in one or other of the Member States, are respected."[17]

Though the human rights claim was rejected the Court annulled the decision on other grounds of a procedural nature. Therefore, Nold could continue to operate as a wholesaler.

The reasoning of the Court was heavily criticised by German authors. As the German government is bound by the German constitution, and the human rights provisions of that constitution may not be amended, the German government should

16. *Klomp* case (23/68), 25 Feb. 1969, [1969] ECR 43, at 50.
17. *Geitling, Nold and others* (36, 37, 38 and 40/59), 15 July 1960, [1960] ECR 423, at 438.

have taken care that the human rights protection under the Coal and Steel Treaty would not be less than under the constitution. Nobody can transfer more rights than he has. The Community, therefore, should respect the fundamental human rights enumerated in the German constitution.

The unhappiness of the German constitutional lawyers was later reflected in the first *Solange* case in which the German constitutional court held:

> "As long as the integration process has not progressed so far that Community law also receives a catalogue of fundamental rights decided on by a parliament and of settled validity which is adequate in comparison with the catalogue of fundamental rights contained in the Constitution, a reference by a court in the Federal Republic of Germany to the Bundesverfassungsgericht in judicial review proceedings, following the obtaining of a ruling of the European Court under Article 177 of the Treaty, is admissible and necessary if the German court regards the rule of Community law which is relevant to its decision as inapplicable in the interpretation given by the European Court, because and in so far as it conflicts with one of the fundamental rights in the Constitution".[18]

Even though the first *Solange* case was never actually applied it was severely criticised by Community lawyers as it opened a possibility that the application of Community law in Germany would be blocked by the German Constitutional Court.

Undoubtedly, the criticism in Germany influenced the case law of the Court of Justice. In 1969 it held in an *obiter dictum* in *Stauder* that fundamental human rights are enshrined in the general principles of Community law and protected by the Court of Justice.[19]

This gave new hope to Nold. When in 1972 the High Authority made a new decision depriving Nold of its right to act as a wholesaler Nold challenged this new decision again with the argument that it infringed a fundamental right which was guaranteed to it by the German constitution.

This time, the Court of Justice anwered Nold's submission in greater detail. It held:

> "As the Court has already stated, fundamental rights form an integral part of the general principles of law, the observance of which it ensures.
> In safeguarding these rights, the Court is bound to draw inspiration from constitutional traditions common to the Member States, and it cannot therefore uphold measures that are incompatible with fundamental rights recognized and protected by the Constitutions of those States.

18. *First Solange* case (Handelsgesellschaft) Bundesverfassungsgericht 29 May 1974, [1974] 2, CMLR 548-554. For a further discussion of this case see chapter 1.1.2.2 of this book.
19. *Stauder* case (29/69), 12 Nov. 1969, [1969] ECR 419 at 425.

Similarly, international treaties for the protection of human rights on which the Member States have collaborated or of which they are signatories, can supply guidelines which should be followed within the framework of Community law".[20]

The ruling of this case was confirmed in many later cases.[21] In 1977 its content was confirmed by a formal declaration of the European Parliament, the Council and the Commission,[22] in 1986 in the preamble of the Single European Act and in 1992 in Article F (now Art. 6) of the Treaty on European Union. The series of cases finally also convinced the German Constitutional Court that human rights were sufficiently protected in the Community legal order. In October 1986 it changed its position of the first *Solange* case in the following reasoning:

"In view of those developments it must be held that, so long as the European Communities, and in particular in the case law of the European Court, generally ensure an effective protection of fundamental rights as against the sovereign powers of the Communities which is to be regarded as substantially similar to the protection of fundamental rights required unconditionally by the Constitution, and in so far as they generally safeguard the essential content of fundamental rights, the Federal Constitutional court will no longer exercise its jurisdiction to decide on the applicability of secondary Community legislation cited as the legal basis for any acts of German courts or authorities within the sovereign jurisdiction of the Federal Republic of Germany, and it will no longer review such legislation by the standard of the fundamental rights contained in the Constitution; references to the Court under Article 100(1) for that purpose are therefore inadmissible".[23]

2.2.4 Extent of the control by the Court of Justice

In the previous paragraph we noticed that the Court of Justice now considers fundamental human rights as part of the general principles to be applied by it. Does this mean that we have a second court, next to the European Court of Human Rights controlling the application of human rights in Europe? So far, there is no basis for this submission. In controlling whether Community acts are in conformity with fundamental human rights the Court of Justice does for European Community law what each national supreme court does for national law. It verifies the legality of Community acts. The situation will be different when the Court of Justice supervises

20. *Second Nold* case (4/73), 14 May 1974, [1974] ECR 491 at 507.
21. See *inter alia Hauer* case (44/79), 13 Dec. 1979, considerations 17-19, [1979] ECR 3745, 3746; *Rutili* case (36/75), 28 Oct. 1975, consideration 32, [1975] ECR 1232; Kirk case (63/83), 10 July 1984, consideration 22, [1984] ECR 2718. For further details see Schermers-Waelbroeck, *Judicial Protection in the European Communities*, 5th ed. pp. 37-42.
22. Joined declarations of 5 April 1977, OJ 27 April 1977, No. C 103/1.
23. *Second Solange* case, Bundesverfassungsgericht, 22 Oct. 1986, [1987] 3 CMLR 225, at p. 265.

whether rules of national law are in conformity with human rights. In doing so it may enter into the field in which of the European Court of Human Rights is competent. So far, the Court of Justice has refused to accept a general competence of controlling whether domestic legislation is in conformity with fundamental human rights. It held:

> "Although it is the duty of the Court to ensure observance of fundamental rights in the field of Community law, it has no power to examine the compatibility with the European Convention on Human Rights of national legislation lying outside the scope of Community law."[24]

This limitation of its own competence was not absolutely necessary. In the case of *Konstantinidis* Advocate-General Jacobs suggested that any infringement of human rights, even if not at all related to Community law, would at the same time be an infringement of Article 48 on the freedom of movement of workers and Article 52 on the freedom of establishment. Workers would not like to move into a country where their human rights were not protected. Neither would persons want to establish themselves in such a country. The *Konstantinidis* case also demonstrates that such cases could easily come before the Court of Justice. Mr. Konstantinidis complained that his private life was not respected because the German administration forced him to change his name in an unacceptable way. This should be seen as an infringement of Article 8 of the European Convention of Human Rights. At the same time, however, Article 52 of the EC Treaty was involved, as Mr. Konstantinidis was a Greek national who had established himself in Germany. In order to be allowed to bring an application to Strasbourg Mr. Konstantinidis had to exhaust all domestic remedies. However, he did not get any further than the German Court of First Instance as that court asked a preliminary ruling under Article 177 of the EC Treaty which brought the case to Luxemburg. Through the system of preliminary rulings the road to Luxemburg is shorter than the one to Strasbourg which means that cases which could be handled by both courts are most likely to end up in Luxemburg. In the *Konstantinidis* case the Court of Justice first considered that nothing in the EC Treaty precludes the transcription of a Greek name in Roman characters and that Member States may adopt rules for such transcription. The Court then goes on:

> "Rules of that kind are to be regarded as incompatible with Article 52 of the Treaty only in so far as their application causes a Greek national such a degree of inconvenience as in fact to interfere with his freedom to exercise the right of establishment enshrined in that article".

---

24. *Demirelle* case (12/86), 30 Sept. 1987, consideration 28, [1987] ECR 3719, at 3754. Similar decisions were rendered in the *ERT* case (C 260/89), consideration 42, [1991]. ECR I, 2925; *Cinétèque* case (60 and 61/84), consideration 26, [1985] ECR 2605, at 2627.

The Court finally holds:

> "Article 52 of the Treaty must be interpreted as meaning that it is contrary to that provision for a Greek national to be obliged, under the applicable national legislation, to use, in the pursuit of his occupation a spelling of his name whereby its pronunciation is modified and the resulting distortion exposes him to the risk that potential clients may confuse him with other persons".

Even though the Court of Justice will not exert control over national legislation which does not relate to Community law it does exert control over national laws which are made in the execution of Community obligations. In 1980 Germany introduced a new law which subjected the renewal of a resident permit to members of the family of migrant workers to the condition that appropriate housing was available to them. The Commission considered this law contrary to Article 48 of the EC Treaty on the free movement of workers and to regulation 1612/68 which was made in the execution of this article. The Commission therefore started proceedings under Article 169 against the German Federal Republic. In those proceedings the question arose whether the forced separation of guest workers from their families, which could follow from the German law, infringed Article 8 of the Convention which guarantees respect for family life. In this case the Court of Justice held:

> "Regulation No 1612/68 must also be interpreted in the light of the requirement of respect for family life set out in Article 8 of the Convention for the Protection of Human Rights and Fundamental Freedoms. That requirement is one of the fundamental rights which, according to the Court's settled case-law, restated in the preamble to the Single European Act, are recognized by Community law.
>
> .....
>
> The German legislation is therefore incompatible with the obligations arising under Community law in so far as it provides for non-renewal of a residence permit or a reduction *a posteriori* of the period of validity of a residence permit for a member of the family of a migrant worker by virtue of the fact that the family's housing can no longer be regarded as suitable according to the criteria applied in that regard in the place of residence, whereas sanctions of comparable severity are not provided for in regard to German nationals".[25]

In a later case on the requirements of the protection of fundamental rights in the Community legal order the Court held:

> "Having regard to those criteria, it must be observed that Community rules which, upon the expiry of the lease, had the effect of depriving the lessee, without

25. *Konstantinidis* case (C168/91), 30 March 1993, [1993] ECR I 1218,1219

> compensation, of the fruits of his labour and of his investments in the tenanted holding would be incompatible with the requirements of the protection of fundamental rights in the Community legal order. Since those requirements are also binding on the Member States when they implement Community rules, the Member States must, as far as possible, apply those rules in accordance with those requirements".[26]

The category of national laws implementing rules of Community law may lead to overlap. Assume such national law infringes the European Convention on Human Rights. Assume further that the victim of these infringements wants to bring the case before the European Court of Human Rights. He has to exhaust domestic remedies which often means that he has to bring his case before three instances of national jurisdiction. Each of these instances could refer the case to the Court of Justice for a preliminary ruling. The Court of Justice could then rule on the question whether the European Convention has been respected or not. After having received this preliminary ruling the national court can decide the case. If the applicant is unhappy with the outcome he may have to exhaust further domestic remedies before finally bringing an application to the European Court of Human Rights. That court would then render the final decision on the interpretation of the Human Rights Convention, possibly overruling the judgment of the Court of Justice. In principle this seems acceptable as the interpretation and application of the Human Rights Convention is the domain of the Strasbourg Court. However, the road to Strasbourg, which is a very long one anyway, will then have been extended with some two years.

One may raise the question whether the domestic remedies are properly exhausted when the national court does not request the preliminary ruling of the Court of Justice. Especially when Community law leaves little discretion to the national authorities in the way of executing a Community rule, responsibility for the infringement of the Convention may lie more with the Community authorities than with the national ones. The Court of Justice may then be the only court who can properly remedy the situation and prevent that the national state infringes the Human Rights Convention by executing the Community rule in the way as required by the Community itself. In such a situation the preliminary ruling may be an essential element of the exhaustion of domestic remedies. However, individuals have no power to force national courts into requesting preliminary rulings. Therefore, the applicant cannot be blamed when no ruling has been asked. This makes it extremely unlikely that the European Court of Human Rights would declare the application inadmissible for non-exhaustion. In its case law so far the European Court of Human Rights has always taken a reasonably mild attitude with respect to exhaustion of domestic remedies. Only those remedies that are effective have to be exhausted; extraordinary remedies do not have to be invoked.

---

26. *Wachauf* case (5/88), 13 July 1989, consideration 19, [1989] ECR 2609, at 2639, 2640.

2.2.5 THE TREATY ON EUROPEAN UNION

Article 6 § 2 of the Treaty on European Union provides: "The Union shall respect fundamental rights, as guaranteed by the European Convention for the Protection of Human Rights and Fundamental Freedoms signed in Rome on 4 November 1950 and as they result from the constitutional traditions common to the Member States, as general principles of Community law." This reduces the formula used by the Court in *Nold II* because it limits the respect for fundamental rights to the European Convention whilst in *Nold* all international treaties for the protection of human rights were taken into account. This is particularly important for the Protocols added to the European Convention. Some of these Protocols are irrelevant as they just changed the procedure of the supervisory organs of the Convention and are subsequently incorporated in it, but Protocols Nos. 1, 4, 6 and 7 add new rights to the Convention. The position of at least three of these protocols differs from that of the Convention as Protocols Nos. 4, 6 and 7 have not been ratified by all Members of the Union. This makes it difficult to consider it self-evident that the Protocols belong to the Convention and require the same respect within the Union. Other conventions, such as the International Covenant on Civil and Political Rights are not at all mentioned in the Treaty on European Union. In other respects the Treaty on European Union is stronger as it requires respect for the fundamental rights of the Convention whilst the formula of the Court of Justice mentioned human rights treaties only as potential guidelines which should be followed. It is not quite clear whether the provision in the Treaty on European Union that the European Convention shall be respected "as general principles of Community law" contains a weakening of the text in the sense that only the general principles of the Convention have to be followed or whether these last words are added just to make clear that the Union is not a party to the Convention, and that therefore the Convention itself is not applied.

An important enforcement of the protection of human rights in the European Union is Article 7 of the Treaty on European Union which provides that sanctions can be taken against Member States which commit a serious and persistent breach of the principles of liberty, democracy, respect for human rights and fundamental freedoms and the rule of law. It is not likely that such sanctions will ever be used but the possibility strengthens the position of fundamental rights in the legal order of the Union. As the Union is not bound by any treaty on human rights the source of the rights to be applied will be the general principles of law.

2.2.6 CONCLUSION

We may conclude that in theory conflicts and overlapping between the two European Courts are possible. In practice they are rather unlikely. Many human rights, such as the right of life and the prohibition of torture and slavery, can be committed only in fields that are outside the competence of the Communities. When human rights may be at stake, both the Council and the Commission will take care that their acts will not infringe them. However, conflicts and overlapping are possible. So far, the Court of

Justice has applied the European Convention on Human Rights as part of the general principles of Community law, and it interprets the Convention in conformity with the interpretation given by the European Court of Human Rights. It is only when no ruling by the latter court has been given that the Court of Justice may interpret the Convention in a way that is later not supported by the European Court of Human Rights. As long as there is no formal link between the two courts this risk must be accepted. Serious problems could not be expected. When a wrong interpretation of the Convention by the Court of Justice is later overruled by the European Court of Human Rights nobody will deny that the later ruling is decisive for the future interpretation of the law.

2.3 Human Rights as General Principles of Law, in the Past and in the Future

*A.G. Toth**

2.3.1 Introduction

Article 6(2) [F(2)] of the Treaty on European Union[1] provides that:

> "The Union shall respect fundamental rights, as guaranteed by the European Convention on Human Rights and as they result from the constitutional traditions common to the Member States, as general principles of Community law."

Thus, almost half a century after the setting up of the first European Community, human rights are still protected within the European Union only as general principles of law. In spite of the fact that Community law is a codified legal system, human rights themselves have never been codified and fully integrated into this system. They have been, and still are, linked only indirectly to the main body of Community law by the instrumentality of concepts such as "common constitutional traditions" and "general principles of law".

The purpose of this paper is to examine the question whether human rights can truly be regarded as general principles of law, and whether their treatment as such in the Community's legal system ensures their adequate protection. In the course of my investigations, I intend, first, to look back in time to deal briefly with the origins, nature and function of general principles of law, and then to look forward to the future to see, if the present protection of human rights in the European Union is found to be unsatisfactory, what could be done to make it better. However, I do not intend to rehearse the development of the protection of human rights within the European Community, since other papers cover this.

2.3.2 The origin, nature and function of general principles of law

Although the general principles of law play a fundamentally important part in the jurisprudence of the European Court of Justice, the concept of general principles of law itself was not "invented" by the Court. Long before the European Communities

---

* Professor of European Law, University of Strathclyde, Glasgow.

1. In this paper, the Articles of the Treaty on European Union and of the EC Treaty are referred to by the new numbers introduced by the Treaty of Amsterdam, followed by the old numbers in square brackets.

Ulf Bernitz and Joakim Nergelius (eds.), General Principles of European Community Law, 73–92

came into existence, that concept had already been known and used in the broader context of public international law. In that context, the general principles of law as a source of law made their first appearance shortly after the First World War in Article 38(1) of the Statute of the Permanent Court of International Justice, which expressly directs the Court to apply, in deciding disputes submitted to it, in addition to treaties and custom, "the general principles of law recognised by civilised nations." The inclusion of this provision in the Statute of the Court was nothing short of a revolutionary innovation in the field of contemporary international law. No wonder it attracted the attention of most commentators of the 1920s and 1930s. Several and in part greatly differing views were put forward as to what the precise meaning of the phrase "general principles of law" was. Without going into detail, suffice it to say that there was a considerable body of opinion which welcomed the concept as signifying the end of rigid legal positivism which had dominated public international law throughout the 19th century and in the early part of the 20th. Some writers looked at the general principles of law as a sign of the re-emergence of natural law in the field of international law. They believed that at least some of those principles involved inherently necessary principles of natural law causing that law to be a formal source of law.[2] These were principles which were so deeply rooted in the legal consciousness of mankind that no legal system could exist without them.

The inclusion of the general principles in the Statute of the Permanent Court, and subsequently of the present International Court of Justice, had an enormously liberating effect on the future development of international law. The very existence of the concept refuted the positivist view, propounded mainly by 19th century German philosophers, in the first place by Hegel, that international law was not a "law above States" but derived from the "will" of the sovereign, omnipotent and over-glorified State. Surely, if international law could be deduced, at least in part, from these general principles, which formed a distinct source in addition to treaties and custom, and which therefore existed even in the absence of any positive act, consent or acceptance by the sovereign State, this must have meant that international law was a legal order standing above States and not entirely subordinated to their "will".

However, while the appearance of the general principles had a revolutionary effect on the way in which international law came to be perceived, interestingly these principles failed to make a significant mark on the jurisprudence of the two International Courts. While individual judges, and the Courts themselves, have not infrequently referred to such principles, no majority decision of either Court has been expressly based on a general principle of law. In international law, treaties and custom remain the primary sources of the law to this day.

When the European Court of Justice (ECJ) came into existence in the 1950s and started relying, with increasing frequency and importance, on general principles of law, its judges could not have been unaware of, and uninfluenced by, the

2. See *e.g.* Sir Gerald Fitzmaurice, "Some Problems Regarding the Formal Sources of International Law" in *Symbolae Verzijl* (La Haye, 1958), p. 153 at p. 174.

developments which had taken place in the field of international law. Yet, to my knowledge, no decision of the ECJ (as opposed to opinions of Advocates-General) has ever referred to the Statute or case-law of the International Courts in connection with the general principles of law, thus giving the (false) impression as if the ECJ had itself "invented" or developed this concept in its case-law. This is the more surprising as the origins, or basis, of Community law are to be found in international law, the founding Treaties themselves being (at least when they were concluded) treaties governed by international law. This was recognised by the ECJ itself when in the famous *Van Gend en Loos* case it described the Community as " a new legal order of international law".[3]

Nevertheless, in Community law the respective role and importance of custom and general principles came to be reversed as compared with international law. Custom, understood as constant and uniform practice accompanied by the *opinio juris*, has never really become a source of Community law. Nor could it. As the ECJ has repeatedly held, the practice of the Member States or of the institutions, however constant and uniform, cannot depart from the rules laid down in the Treaties and therefore cannot lead to the emergence of new rules. The Treaties can only be modified by means of the formal amendment procedure laid down in them. As the Court has said, resolutions and practices, which express the political will of the Council or of the Member States, cannot prevail over the rules contained in the Treaties.[4] This simply follows from the very nature of Community law as a codified legal system. Thus, to give an example, the infamous Luxembourg Compromise has never become a binding rule of Community law in spite of some 20 years of constant and uniform practice, and has at least on two known occasions[5] simply been departed from when it no longer served the interests of the majority of the Member States, before its final demise following the Single European Act.

By contrast, the general principles of law have become a genuine source of Community law as a result of the jurisprudence of the ECJ. This is quite in contrast with their position in international law.[6] As sources of Community law, the general principles may be resorted to by the ECJ for a number of purposes, of which the following are the most important:

---

3. Case 26/62 [1963] ECR 1 at p.12.
4. Case 43/75 *Defrenne* [1976] ECR 455 at p. 478; Case 59/75 *Manghera* [1976] ECR 91 at p.102; Case 68/86 *United Kingdom v. Council* [1988] ECR 855 at p. 900.
5. In 1982 and 1985, see *Bulletin of the EC* 5-1982, pp.7-8 and 6-1985, pp.13-14.
6. This is not the time and place to compare the respective roles of the general principles in international law and in Community law. But it would be fascinating to examine, for example, to what extent the two legal systems rely on the same or on different principles; what are the common principles which necessarily underlie them both; from what sources these principles are derived in each system; whether the same principle has exactly he same or a different meaning and effect in international law and in Community law, and so on.

- to review the legality or the validity of the acts of the institutions: an act infringing a general principle recognised by the Court as part of Community law will be annulled or declared invalid;[7]
- to review the compatibility with Community law of the legislation or administrative practice of the Member States: a national law or practice infringing a general principle will be held incompatible with Community law;[8]
- to interpret provisions of written Community law;[9]
- to supplement the provisions of written Community law, that is to say, to fill gaps in the body of the law;[10]
- to establish the non-contractual liability of the Community and of the Member States.[11]

Since general principles can override the acts of the institutions, they stand higher in the hierarchy of the sources of Community law than secondary legislation. Whether they stand higher than the Treaties themselves, will be considered below.

Unlike primary and secondary legislation, which fall within the competence of the Member States and the political institutions, respectively, the general principles of law can only be defined and applied by the Court of Justice. They fall entirely within the province of the judiciary. The reason for this is that only a process of interpretation can establish them, and the ECJ has exclusive power to interpret the law with final binding authority. Neither the Member States nor the other institutions can do that.

This exclusive power puts the ECJ in a unique position. By relying on the general principles, the Court can develop Community law in a way in which neither the Member States nor the other institutions can. This is what lends to Community law its robust, dynamic character, what ensures its natural evolution between two Intergovernmental Conferences. It enables the Court to fill obvious gaps in the body of the

---

7. See *e.g.* Case 4/73 *Nold v. Commission* [1974] ECR 491 at p. 507; Case 114/76 *Bela-Mühle* [1977] ECR 1211 at p. 1221; Case 122/78 *Buitoni* [1979] ECR 677 at pp. 684-5; Case 224/82 *Meiko Konservenfabrik* [1983] ECR 2539 at pp. 2548-50, etc.
8. See *e.g.* Case 203/80 *Casati* [1981] ECR 2595 at p. 2618; Case 222/84 *Johnston* [1986] ECR 1651 at pp. 1682-3, etc.
9. See *e.g.* Case 13/61 *Bosch* [1962] ECR 45 at p. 59 *per* Advocate-General Lagrange; Case 15/63 *Lassalle v. Parliament* [1964] ECR 31 at p. 54 *per* Advocate-General Lagrange; Case 53/81 *Levin* [1982] ECR 1035 at p. 1049, etc.
10. See *e.g.* Case 11/70 *Internationale Handelsgesellschaft* [1970] ECR 1125 at p. 1134 *per Curiam,* pp. 1146-7 *per* Advocate-General Dutheillet de Lamothe; Case 7/72 *Boehringer v. Commission* [1972] ECR 1281 at pp. 1293 et seq. *per* Advocate-General Mayras; Case 64/74 *Reich* [1975] ECR 261 at pp. 274-5 *per* Advocate-General Warner; Case 155/79 *AM & S v. Commission* [1982] ECR 1575 at pp. 1610-12 *per Curiam,* pp. 1648-50 *per* Advocate-General Slynn, etc.
11. Article 288(2) [215(2)] EC. See, in particular, Cases C-6 and 9/90 *Francovich* [1991] ECR I-5357 at pp. I-5413-15; Cases C-46 and 48/93 *Brasserie du Pêcheur and Factortame* [1996] ECR I-1029 at pp. I-1143-4.

law, two of the most important examples of which are the protection of human rights themselves and the principle of State liability for damage caused to individuals as a result of a breach of Community obligations.

This being the case, the question then arises: where does this considerable power of the Court come from? Unlike Article 38(1) of the Statute of the International Court of Justice, neither the Treaties nor its Statutes expressly authorise the ECJ to apply general principles of law in deciding disputes submitted to it. (The only exception is Article 288(2) [215(2)] EC, which provides that the non-contractual liability of the Community shall be determined in accordance with the general principles common to the laws of the Member States.) What is the legal basis for the Court's applying unwritten general principles in a codified legal system? This question is the more relevant as it is a fundamental rule of the Community legal order, stated in Article 7 [4] of the EC Treaty, that

> "Each institution shall act within the limits of the powers conferred upon it by this Treaty."

Since the ECJ in one of the five institutions listed in Article 7 [4], it, too, must act under a power conferred upon it by the Treaty.

As is well known, the Court itself derives its power to apply general principles of law from Article 220 [164] EC, which provides that

> "The Court of Justice shall ensure that in the interpretation and application of this Treaty the law is observed."

There are, of course, numerous examples of the Court relying on Article 220 [164] when it applies general principles, but perhaps the following passage from the *Brasserie du Pêcheur and Factortame* cases,[12] in which the Court dealt with the principle of State liability, may be cited as a classic example:

> "Since the Treaty contains no provision expressly and specifically governing the consequences of breaches of Community law by Member States, it is for the Court, in pursuance of the task conferred on it by Article 220 [164] of the Treaty... to rule on such a question in accordance with generally accepted methods of interpretation, in particular by reference to the fundamental principles of the Community legal system and, where necessary, general principles common to the legal systems of the Member States."

In other cases, the Court simply refers to its "general function as custodian of the law, as laid down in Article 220 [164] of the Treaty".[13]

12. Note 11 above, at p. I-1144.
13. See *e.g.* Case 294/83 *Les Verts v. Parliament* [1986] ECR 1339 at p. 1364.

Thus, while the general principles of law may be derived from a number of different sources,[14] the power of the Court to apply those principles is ultimately derived from the abstract concept of "the law", or "the rule of law", which governs the interpretation and application of the Treaties. Thus, it may be said that the general principles occupy a status in Community law which is necessarily superior even to that of the basic Treaties. Otherwise, how can it be explained that the Court invoke these principles not only to interpret the written provisions of the Treaties, but also to supplement them and in extreme cases even to amend them in order to make them comply with a general legal principle. This is what happened, for example, in the *Les Verts*[15] and *Chernobyl* cases[16] where the Court virtually amended Article 230 [173] of the EC Treaty in order to ensure that the European Parliament has both a passive and an active right of action for annulment, as required by the fundamental principles of the rule of law and institutional balance, respectively.

It may be argued, therefore, that the notion of general principles of law has introduced into Community law, just as it has into international law, an abstract concept of law which cannot always be derived from the written rules laid down by the Member States or institutions and is superior to those rules, and which may ultimately be regarded as an emanation of the notion of natural law.

This being the case, the next question is whether the ECJ has unlimited power to draw upon these general principles or whether there is a limit beyond which these principles cannot be used. In this respect, a major difference exists between international law and Community law. Unlike international law, Community law is based on the fundamental principle of conferred powers, which is now stated in Article 5 [3b] of the EC Treaty in the following words:

> "The Community shall act within the limits of the powers conferred upon it by this Treaty and of the objectives assigned to it therein."

Thus, the limits of the Community's powers are more or less precisely determined by the objectives pursued by the Treaty, and the general principles can only be resorted to within those limits. This means that even a general principle cannot be utilised, however superior it may be, if this would result in extending the Community's activities beyond the stated objectives. We shall return to this point in the next part.

---

14. In the *Brasserie du Pêcheur* case, note 11 above, the Court itself distinguished between "fundamental principles of the Community legal system" and "general principles common to the legal systems of the Member States". In other cases, the Court or its Advocates-General derived principles from public international law and Roman law.
15. Note 13 above.
16. Case C-70/88 *Parliament v. Council* [1990] ECR I-2041.

2.3.3 Are human rights adequately protected as general principles of law?

Having looked briefly at the origins, nature and function of the general principles of law, it is now time to apply the findings made so far specifically to human rights, and to consider the question whether they are adequately protected as general principles of law.

Ever since the *Stauder* decision of 1969, [17] the basis for the protection of human rights in the European Community has been that:

> "Fundamental rights form an integral part of the general principles of law whose observance the Court must ensure."[18]

The treatment of human rights as general principles of law has undoubtedly been one of the most ingenious solutions ever devised by the Court. Coupled with references to the common constitutional traditions of the Member States and to international treaties on human rights, it has enabled the Court to fill a rather embarrassing major gap in Community law, without the need to wait for assistance from the Community legislator, which has been less than forthcoming to this day. The Court's solution has been generally accepted without questioning, and has not only been endorsed by the political institutions but has found its way into the Community Treaties.[19] However, upon closer analysis in the light of some recent developments, this solution shows a number of weaknesses and flaws, which may be summarised as follows.

First, the very basis of the Court's solution has been considerably undermined by Opinion 2/94,[20] in which the Court held that as the law now stands the Community has no competence to accede to the European Convention on Human Rights. Three statements made by the Court in support of this conclusion are particularly relevant to the present discussion. First, relying on Article 5 [3b] EC, mentioned above, the Court states that the Community "has only those powers which have been conferred upon it" (para. 23). Secondly, the Opinion goes on, "no Treaty provision confers on the Community institutions any general power to enact rules on human rights or to conclude international conventions in this field" (para. 27). Thirdly and most importantly, such power cannot even be derived from Article 308 [235] since this would mean "widening the scope of Community powers beyond the general framework created by the provisions of the Treaty as a whole and, in particular, by those that define the tasks and activities of the Community" (para. 30). Since these latter provisions to which the Court refers are those which determine the Community's objectives, it follows that to enact rules on human rights would go beyond the objectives of the Community.

---

17. Case 29/69 [1969] ECR 419 at p. 425.
18. See *e.g.* Opinion 2/94 [1996] ECR I-1759 at p. I-1789.
19. See Article 6(2) [F(2)] TEU, cited above.
20. Note 18 above.

This view has been recently confirmed in the *Grant* case[21] where the Court said that "human rights cannot in themselves have the effect of extending the scope of the Treaty provisions beyond the competences of the Community".

The problem here is that all these considerations apply with equal force to the Court itself. According to Article 7 [4] EC, the Court is one of the five institutions, which must, like the others, act "within the limits of the powers conferred upon it by this Treaty". Read in conjunction with Article 5 [3b] EC, this means that the Court must act within the limits of the competences conferred on the Community itself and within the limits of the objectives assigned to it by the Treaty. Therefore, everything that the Court says in its Opinion about the institutions' lack of power to act in the human rights field seems to apply, in principle, also to the Court itself. How can the Court do by way of general principles that, which the other institutions cannot do by legislation, i.e. incorporate rules on human rights into the corpus of Community law? As seen earlier, the power of the Court to apply general principles of law ends where the competences and objectives of the Community end. Those competences and objectives can only be added to by Treaty amendment, as the Opinion itself concludes, but cannot be extended by the use of the general principles of law any more than by secondary legislation.

The power of the Court to introduce new principles into Community law has been expressly challenged in a different context by the German Government in the *Brasserie du Pêcheur* case[22]. In that case, the German Government argued that a general right to reparation for individuals could be created only by legislation, but not by judicial decision. This would be incompatible with the institutional balance established by the Treaty. However, the Court simply dismissed that objection by saying that the existence of State liability is a question of Treaty interpretation, which falls within the jurisdiction of the Court by virtue of Article 220 [164].

There can be no doubt that the reasoning of the Court in the *Brasserie* case was correct. There is, however, a world of difference between developing and applying general principles of law in areas which are covered by the Treaty (i.e. non-contractual liability) and developing and applying them in an area (human rights) which is now stated to be outside the scope not only of specific Treaty provisions but also of the general Treaty framework and objectives. The Court could only do this by arrogating to itself a power, which does not seem to have been conferred upon it by the Treaty. The explanation that this is simply a question of Treaty interpretation which falls within the jurisdiction of the Court, given in the *Brasserie* case, does not hold good here. Clearly, the Court cannot interpret into the Treaty that which it itself has declared not to be in it.

Therefore, to my mind, there is a contradiction, or at least a paradox, in saying, on the one hand, that human rights fall outside the scope of the general framework and objectives of the Treaty and, on the other hand, that they form an "integral part" of the general principles of Community law. That paradox is not resolved by Article

21. Case C-249/96 [1998] ECR I-621 at p. I-650.
22. Note 11 above.

6(2) [F(2)] TEU. Although that provision was already in force at the time when the Court delivered Opinion 2/94 and is, in fact, referred to in it, it was apparently found by the Court to be insufficient to serve as a legal basis for Community legislative and treaty-making action in the human rights field, or to bring human rights within the scope and objectives of the EC Treaty.

The second problem with the present system is that the protection of human rights is based exclusively on the ECJ's case-law, and therefore suffers from the inherent weaknesses of any uncodified legal system. That case-law develops in a piece-meal and haphazard manner, with the Court having no control over the types of cases that come before it. Thus, important issues may remain unclarified for long periods of time. The Court's decisions can only operate *ex post facto*, after a violation has been committed, and this does nothing to ensure legal certainty, another fundamental principle of Community law.

Thirdly, and more importantly, unwritten general principles are, by their very nature, entirely unsuitable to afford adequate legal protection in an area like human rights which requires precise, detailed, meticulously drafted rules. In this respect, clearly, human rights are not even remotely comparable to other general principles, such as legal certainty, proportionality, legitimate expectations, confidentiality, equality, etc., which can be easily defined by case-law and applied to a great variety of factual situations. It may even be said that while the notion itself that human rights should be protected is a general principle of law, the particular rights themselves which are the subject of protection, and the method (procedure) of protection, cannot be derived from general principles but must be laid down in a codified form.

It was obviously for this reason that the Court has relied, right from the beginning, on two additional sources: the constitutional traditions common to the Member States and international treaties for the protection of human rights which the Member States have ratified, in the first place the European Convention. It thus appears that in the absence of written rules, the protection of fundamental rights is based on extraneous, i.e. non-Community, sources. This has, however, created certain problems, which have not been fully resolved to this day.

As regards, first, the constitutional traditions, the question arises whether, in order that the Court may protect a particular right, it is necessary for that right to be enshrined in the Constitutions of *all* the Member States, or whether it is sufficient if it is guaranteed by any one or some of them. While the Court has never expressly answered that question, it appears that in all the relevant cases the Court has consistently referred to the constitutional traditions "*common to the Member States*". And in the *Hauer* case,[23] in dealing with the right to property, the Court expressly mentioned the "constitutional rules and practices of the nine Member States". This is in contrast with the approach which the Court adopts when recognising other general principles of law as part of Community law, even if they have not been generally accepted in *all* the Member States.

23. Case 44/79 [1979] ECR 3727 at p. 3746.

As regards, secondly, the European Convention on Human Rights, its precise status in Community law has never been clearly established. In a formal sense, it is not binding on the Community since the Community has never acceded to it. Nevertheless, in several cases[24] the Commission put forward the argument that following its ratification by all the Member States, the Convention became an "integral part" of Community law and was legally binding upon the Community. The Commission based its view on the so-called "substitution theory", according to which the Community, having acquired legislative and executive powers, had been substituted for the Member States. However, this view has never been expressly endorsed by the ECJ. In this respect, therefore, the Convention is in a different position from GATT and certain other Conventions dealing with customs matters, in respect of which the ECJ accepted that they became binding on the Community on the grounds that the Community had replaced the Member States upon acquiring competences in the areas governed by them.[25] The ECJ has never said that the European Convention on Human Rights is binding on the Community: it only supplies "inspirations" and "guidelines" for the Court, which must be followed within the framework of Community law.

This unclarified relationship between two distinct legal orders, those created by the Convention and by the European Treaties, is one of the major drawbacks of the present system. Thus, it is not at all clear whether in applying the "principles", "guidelines", "standards" supplied by the Convention, the ECJ is bound by interpretations given to those principles and standards by the Convention organs, and in particular by the European Court of Human Rights (ECHR). The co-existence of two supranational Courts, the ECJ and ECHR, each having independent power to interpret and apply the same text, the Convention, carries with it the possibility of conflicting interpretations, which is bound to undermine legal certainty and confidence in the system. Such discrepancies and divergences in the Convention's interpretation have already come to light in several well-known cases.[26] They are virtually unavoidable in the present system where the ECJ is not only not bound by the rulings of the ECHR (which is the primary custodian of the Convention) but, in the absence of an appropriate mechanism, is unable to seek any preliminary advice or opinion before interpreting a provision which the ECHR has not interpreted previously.

In addition to the European Convention, the Court also sometimes refers to international treaties on human rights. However, this may cause potentially even more problems. At least, in the case of the European Convention it may be said that since the Convention represents a "common denominator," a common standard of

24. See *e.g.* Case 48/75 *Royer* [1976] ECR 497 at pp. 506-7; Case 118/75 *Watson and Belmann* [1976] ECR 1185 at p. 1194.
25. See Cases 21 to 24/72 *International Fruit Company* [1972] ECR 1219 at p.1227; Case 38/75 *Nederlandse Spoorwegen* [1975] ECR 1439 at p. 1450.
26. Compare *e.g.* Cases 46/87 and 227/88 *Hoechst v. Commission* [1989] ECR 2859 paras. 17-18 with *Niemitz v. Germany,* Series A, No. 251-B, 16 EHRR 97, para. 31, or Case 374/87 *Orkem v. Commission* [1989] ECR 3283 para. 30 with *Funke v. France,* Series A, No. 256-A, 16 EHRR 297, para. 44.

protection acceptable to all the Member States, which has been reasonably clarified by the case-law of the Convention organs, this standard can be applied also in Community law as forming a general principle of law. However, in the case of international treaties and conventions, it is very difficult to say with any degree of certainty whether and under what conditions a particular right protected by them, as interpreted sometimes with non-binding effect by a body set up to implement those conventions, has attained that level of general acceptance by the international community as a whole, and by the Member States of the EC in particular, which is a necessary prerequisite for regarding it as embodying a general principle of law binding on the Community.[27]

Thus, the conclusion may be drawn that even with the addition of two extraneous sources, the constitutional traditions and international treaties, the concept of general principles of law is not suitable to provide a clear-cut, unambiguous, predictable protection of fundamental rights.

The fourth, and final, unsatisfactory feature of the present system is the way in which Community law protects individuals against human rights violations committed by the Member States. Several problems arise in this context.

In a long line of cases, the ECJ has recognised that it has some control over the observance of human rights by the Member States. Thus, in the *Wachauf* case [28] the Court said that:

> "...the requirements of the protection of fundamental rights in the Community legal order... are also binding on the Member States when they implement Community rules... [therefore] the Member States must, as far as possible, apply those rules in accordance with those requirements".

In *ERT,* [29] the Court has further stated that:

> "... where [national] rules ......fall within the scope of Community law, and reference is made to the Court for a preliminary ruling, it must provide all the criteria of interpretation needed by the national court to determine whether those rules are compatible with the fundamental rights the observance of which the Court ensures and which derive in particular from the European Convention on Human Rights".

27. See *e.g.* Case C-249/96 *Grant,* note 21 above at pp. I-650-1, concerning the interpretation of the International Covenant on Civil and Political Rights of 1966 by the Human Rights Committee, according to which "sex" is to be taken as including "sexual orientation" in the context of the prohibition of sex discrimination. This interpretation was not accepted by the ECJ as not reflecting a generally accepted interpretation of the concept of sex discrimination.
28. Case 5/88 [1989] ECR 2609 at pp. 2639-40.
29. Case C-260/89 [1991] ECR I-2925 at p. I-2964.

The first problem here is that in order to provide "all the criteria of interpretation", the Court must first interpret fundamental rights which "derive in particular from the European Convention on Human Rights", that is, it must interpret the Convention itself. However, according to the Court's established case-law, in preliminary ruling procedures brought under Article 234 [177] EC, the Court can only interpret the EC Treaty and the acts of the institutions, but has no jurisdiction to interpret international agreements concluded by the Member States outside the framework of Community law.[30] It is, therefore, not clear on what legal basis the Court can interpret the European Convention in preliminary ruling proceedings in order to assist national courts in determining the compatibility of national rules with the Convention. This is another aspect of the problem, discussed earlier, arising from the uncertain legal status of the Convention in Community law.

The second difficulty is that, by contrast, the Court has repeatedly held that

> "...it has no power to examine the compatibility with the European Convention on Human Rights of national rules which do not fall within the scope of Community law".[31]

Thus, the Court has created a highly artificial distinction between national rules which do, and those which do not, fall "within the scope of Community law". As a result, individuals are subject to two different systems of protection at the supranational level: in matters falling within the scope of Community law they are able to use the remedies available before the ECJ, but in other matters they must seek protection of their fundamental rights from the ECHR. This situation is very confusing and unsatisfactory, the more so as in many instances it is by no means certain whether a matter falls within or outside the scope of Community law. The problem is exacerbated by the fact that with the progress of integration (not to mention the possible application of the principle of subsidiarity) the precise scope of Community law is subject to constant change and reinterpretation. Thus, in situations where they have been unable to obtain redress in the national courts, individuals may not be in a position to know before which higher forum the remedy lies, and this is clearly contrary to the principle of legal certainty.

Deciding whether a matter falls within the scope of Community law or of national law is creating more and more difficulties both for the national courts and for the ECJ. One group of cases in which this question has arisen concerns compensation for damage arising from the application of national measures implementing Community rules. Thus, in the *Bostock* case,[32] which concerned compensation for a milk quota, Advocate-General Gulmann pointed out that this issue is

30. Case 130/73 *Vandeweghe* [1973] ECR 1329 at p.1333; Case 44/84 *Hurd* [1986] ECR 29 at pp.76-7.
31. Case C-260/89 *ERT*, note 29 above.
32. Case C-2/92 [1994] ECR I-955.

> " of fundamental significance because it is determinative for the division of powers between the Court of Justice and national courts as regards the protection of basic rights and the question is a difficult one to answer ..... Similar questions may arise in the most diverse situations..."[33]

In that case, the Advocate-General came to the conclusion that the issue of compensation did not fall within the scope of Community law and that Member States were not required to respect fundamental rights in that context as part of Community law.[34] By contrast, the ECJ's approach seems to imply that the Court regarded the question of compensation as falling in principle within the scope of Community law and thus covered by the fundamental right to property, although the Court denied compensation in the particular circumstances of the case.[35]

The problem has most recently come before the Scottish Court of Session, Inner House, in *Booker Aquaculture Ltd. v. The Secretary of State for Scotland*.[36] This case raised the question whether compensation for destroying fish because of a viral infection, ordered under a United Kingdom regulation implementing a Community directive, was a matter falling within the scope of Community law (in which case compensation would, in principle, be available in accordance with the right to property protected under Community law according to the European Convention on Human Rights), or whether it was governed by United Kingdom domestic law (under which compensation was not payable at all). After reviewing the relevant case-law of the ECJ, the Lord President found that he had "real doubt" about the question, which he was unable to resolve and therefore proposed to refer the matter to the ECJ for a preliminary ruling.

How paradoxical results this artificial division may produce may be illustrated by the following example. In the *Maurin* case,[37] criminal proceedings were brought against Mr Maurin who was charged with selling food products after the expiry of their use-by date contrary to French law. During the course of the proceedings, some procedural irregularities occurred and the French court asked the ECJ whether these were compatible with the rights of the defence as protected by the European Convention on Human Rights. At the relevant time, there was in force a Community directive, which required the indication of the use-by date on the labelling of foodstuffs but did not regulate the sale of foodstuffs complying with this requirement. The directive therefore did not impose any obligation on Member States to start criminal proceedings where, as in the present case, there was a sale of products, which complied with the directive in respect of labelling but were sold after the

33. Ibid. at p. I-972.
34. Ibid.
35. Ibid. at pp. I-982-4. See also Case C-315/93 *Flip and Verdegem* [1995] ECR I-913 at p. I-935, where the Court held that compensation for the slaughter of pigs under Community measures to control classical swine fever fell within the competence of the Member States.
36. Opinion of 12 August 1999, unreported.
37. Case C-144/95 [1996] ECR I-2909 at pp. I-2918-19.

expiry of the use-by date. In these circumstances, the ECJ held that the offence with which Mr Maurin was charged involved national legislation falling outside the scope of Community law and that the Court therefore did not have jurisdiction to determine whether the procedural irregularities amounted to a breach of the right of the defence.

It would seem to follow from this case that where procedural or other irregularities are committed in criminal proceedings which were brought by a Member State in implementation of a Community obligation, the Court would have jurisdiction to determine whether those irregularities are in breach of the provisions of the European Convention. There are a number of situations in which Member States are under an obligation to start criminal proceedings in implementation of Community rules. Thus, Article 280(2) [209a(2)] EC requires the Member States to take the same measures to counter fraud affecting the financial interests of the Community as they take to counter fraud affecting their own financial interests. Under Article 194(1) Euratom, Member States are required to prosecute under their laws anyone within their jurisdiction who illegally discloses classified Euratom information. Article 27 of the ECJ's Statute requires Member States to treat any violation of an oath by a witness or expert in the same manner as if the offence had been committed before their own courts and to prosecute the offender according to their laws.

If in these proceedings an irregularity occurs which involves an alleged breach of the European Convention (most likely Article 5 or 6), the ECJ would have jurisdiction to deal with the case under a preliminary reference, while if the very same irregularity occurs in a *Maurin*-type situation, the Court would have no such jurisdiction. Where is the logic in this system? However, this example also shows that, contrary to the general belief that criminal law does not fall within the scope of Community law, certain criminal proceedings do, and this may put the Court in the extremely difficult position of having to interpret not only a substantive but also a procedural/technical rule of the Convention which has not so far been clarified by the ECHR. For example, would the Court be prepared to go so far as to decide what is the proper time-limit within which a person arrested in implementation of one of the above-mentioned Community provisions must be brought before a judge or other officer so as to comply with Article 5(3) of the European Convention? This provision only requires that such a person is brought "promptly" before a judge, and in the *Brogan* case[38] the ECHR refused to set a precise time-limit, saying that each case must be assessed according to its special features.[39]

But the greatest weakness of the status quo is that Community law can only protect individuals *vis-à-vis* the Member States if they rely on human rights in exercise of a right granted by the EC Treaty. It cannot protect against human rights violation *per se*. Since most Community rights can only be exercised by EC nationals, particularly in areas in which human rights violations by Member States are most likely to occur, such as the free movement of workers, the right of establishment, and the freedom to provide or receive services, human rights protection is practically – or to a great extent – restricted to EC nationals (and the members of their families). Thus, ultimately, the

38. Series A, No. 145-B, 11 EHRR 117.

39. In the *Brogan* case, even 4 days and 6 hours did not comply with Article 5(3).

individual is only protected under Community law as a "Market citizen", not as a human being. The exclusion of non-EC nationals from human rights protection is clearly illustrated by the *Demirel* case,[40] in which the Turkish wife of a Turkish worker lawfully living and working in Germany could not rely on Article 8 of the European Convention to avoid expulsion from Germany (and thus separation from her husband) because there was no provision of Community law permitting the family reunification of Turkish workers. Thus, her case fell outside the scope of Community law.

Moreover, even EC nationals are not fully protected by Community law against infringements of their fundamental rights by Member States. This is because an individual can only invoke the Treaty (and Community law in general) if he is in one of the situations envisaged by the Treaty. It is established case-law that the Treaty cannot be relied on in "purely internal situations", i.e. those which exist within a single Member State. Thus, Treaty rights cannot be claimed by an individual who is a national of a Member State but has always lived and worked in that Member State and has never exercised the right to freedom of movement. If a Member State infringes one of the fundamental rights of that individual, Community law is powerless to protect him; he must look elsewhere, to another system, which operates outside the framework of Community law. His only remedy lies before the ECHR.[41]

One final weakness of the system is that Article 6(2) [F(2)] TEU, which proclaims that "The Union shall respect fundamental rights", remains judicially unenforceable *vis-à-vis* the Member States. The amendments introduced into Article 46 [L] TEU by the Treaty of Amsterdam only confer jurisdiction on the ECJ over Article 6(2) [F(2)] "with regard to action of the institutions", but not with regard to that of the Member States.

In the light of the above considerations, the conclusion seems inescapable that human rights are not adequately protected in the European Community as general principles of law. Even in combination with extraneous sources, such as the constitutional traditions of the Member States and international treaties, they are too vague, general and indeterminate to provide a reliable and effective protection against both the Community institutions and the Member States. It is, on the whole, unacceptable that there are no written, binding and enforceable rules on human rights in the Treaty on European Union other than these vague references to other international instruments, which are not part of Community law. It may be said that at the beginning of the 21st Century the citizen has every right to expect more of a Community or Union based on the rule of law than mere "inspirations" and "guidelines"; that he is entitled to see his fundamental rights set out in black and white in terms that he may enforce in a court of law.

So, what is the solution?

40. Case 12/86 [1987] ECR 3719 at p. 3754.
41. For a recent example, see Case C-299/95 *Kremzow* [1997] ECR I-2629 at pp. I-2645-6.

2.3.4 THE FULL INTEGRATION OF HUMAN RIGHTS INTO THE COMMUNITY LEGAL SYSTEM

Clearly, the solution lies in the codification of human rights and their full and direct (as opposed to indirect) integration into the Community legal order. As is well known, two main proposals have been put forward over the years as to how this could be achieved. The first is the drawing up of a separate catalogue of fundamental rights specifically designed for the requirements of the Community. The second is accession to the European Convention on Human Rights. This is not the time and place to deal with these proposals in detail. Suffice it to say that neither is wholly satisfactory.

A separate catalogue for the Community/Union would create three main problems. First, it would set up a dual system of human rights protection in Europe: one for the Community and one for other States. Such a splitting up of the present single system would undermine the authority of the Convention. Secondly, the drawing up of the catalogue would present almost insurmountable difficulties. What rights should be included? Civil and political rights only, or also economic and social rights? What criteria should be used for the inclusion of rights? Thirdly, what legal status should such a catalogue have? Clearly, it would carry very little weight unless it was fully integrated into the Treaties themselves.

Accession to the European Convention is, of course, ruled out for the time being by Opinion 2/94. This is not an insurmountable difficulty since the Member States can, in theory, always amend the Treaty to confer the necessary competence on the Community. (It is another question whether they would want to do this.) It is, however, not clear whether and, if so, how the Union could accede to the Convention since only the Community, and not the Union, has the necessary legal personality and treaty-making power. In the case of accession by the Community only, the Convention would not apply to the second and third pillars of the Union.

Accession would have undoubted advantages. There would be a written catalogue of rights, already interpreted by copious case-law, which would enhance legal certainty. There would be a firm legal basis for the Court's decisions, instead of the present vague notions of "guidelines" and "inspirations". The Convention would be incorporated, albeit indirectly, in the Community legal order.

However, there are a number of disadvantages in this proposal. Probably the main objection is that it would subject the ECJ to the jurisdiction of the ECHR, and the Court might find this unacceptable. In a new Opinion, the Court would probably veto accession as being incompatible with the EC Treaty. Accession would also raise a number of institutional/technical problems, as yet unresolved, and would necessitate the amendment of the Convention itself, which would require the unanimous consent of all the Signatory States, which might not be forthcoming.

Finally, it is not at all clear what would be the effect of accession on the status of the Convention within the legal order of the Community and of the Member States.

The Commission[42] and some commentators[43] have expressed the opinion that accession would have implications solely within the field of application of Community law. According to this view, the Convention would impose additional obligations on the Community institutions only, but its status and effects within the national legal systems would not change. Outside the scope of Community law, the protection of human rights would remain entrusted to the Member States, as at present, without any Community involvement.

It is, however, difficult to see how this view can be reconciled with the EC Treaty and the case-law of the ECJ. According to Article 300(7) [228(7)] EC, "agreements concluded under the conditions set out in this Article shall be binding on the institutions of the Community and on Member States". The case-law of the ECJ[44] confirms that both the institutions and the Member States must comply with obligations arising from agreements concluded by the Community; that such agreements may produce direct effect within the Member States; that the Court has jurisdiction to give preliminary rulings on their interpretation and generally to ensure their uniform application throughout the Community. It follows from this case-law that the Convention would be binding not only on the institutions but also on the Member States (which would be bound both as Contracting Parties and as a matter of Community law), and that the Convention as a whole would become an integral part of the Community legal system, possibly producing direct effect in the Member States. This is confirmed by Opinion 2/94, in which the Court has stated that:

> "Accession to the Convention would entail…integration of all the provisions of the Convention into the Community legal order" (para. 34).

Thus, the Court would have jurisdiction to give preliminary rulings on the interpretation of any provision of the Convention, and thereby control the compatibility of national law with the Convention, irrespective of whether that law falls within the scope of application of Community law or not.

Given all these uncertainties, difficulties and problems, neither a catalogue of fundamental rights nor accession to the Convention would provide a satisfactory solution.

A far simpler and more effective way of integrating human rights into the Community legal system would be the incorporation of all the substantive provisions (Articles 1-18) of the European Convention into the Treaty on European Union as a

42. See the Commission's Memorandum on the accession of the European Community to the European Convention on Human Rights of 4 April 1979, *Bulletin of the EC*, Suppl. 2/79, p. 7 at pp. 8-9 and 19-20.
43. See Gaja in 33 CML Rev. (1996), p. 973 at p. 985; Schermers in "The Human Rights Opinion of the ECJ and its Constitutional Implications", University of Cambridge, Centre for European Legal Studies, Occasional Paper No. 1 (1996), p. 15.
44. See, in particular, Case 104/81 *Kupferberg* [1982] ECR 3641 at pp. 3662-3 and 3665; Case 12/86 *Demirel*, note 35 above at pp. 3750-2; Opinion 1/91 [1991] ECR I-6079 at pp. I-6105-6, and the cases cited in these cases.

new Title, together with the annexation of the substantive Protocols to the Treaty as Protocols, and the insertion of a new clause into Article 2 [B] TEU and Article 2 [2] EC, stating that the objectives of the Union and of the Community shall include the protection of human rights and fundamental freedoms as provided in this new Title (with the simultaneous repeal of Article 6(2) [F(2)] TEU). At the same time, the jurisdiction of the ECJ under the EC Treaty would be extended to this new Title and related Protocols.

The direct incorporation of the Convention into Community law would at a stroke resolve all the problems discussed so far. In particular, it would have the following main advantages.

Firstly, in contrast to accession, it would create a clear-cut and predictable situation. The Convention would be fully and directly integrated into the Community legal order. There would be a single, uniform system of human rights for the whole of Europe, binding on the European Union/Community, the Member States and non-member countries alike; a set of clearly defined and familiar rules, backed up by a large body of case-law developed by the ECHR. These rules would have constitutional status in the Union; there would be no longer a need to rely on the concept of "general principles of law", nor on the artificial device of treating the Convention as an "act of an institution", which would be the case in the event of accession. The European Union would finally catch up with the modern democracies of the world, which all have provisions on the protection of fundamental rights written in their Constitutions. Those rules would have the same status and binding force for the Community institutions as for the Member States.

Secondly, the incorporation of the Convention would ensure that fundamental rights are protected without regard to nationality, since under its Article 1 the Union/Community and the Member States would be obliged to secure to "everyone within their jurisdiction" the rights and freedoms in question. The individual would be protected as a human being, not merely as a Market citizen. Since the Convention would form part of the EU and EC Treaties, any human rights violation covered by it would come within the (enlarged) scope of application of Community law and would therefore ultimately be subject to control by the ECJ. The artificial distinction between national rules falling within the scope of Community law and those falling outside it would become irrelevant.

Thirdly, the Convention would be fully integrated into the Community system of remedies also. Its provisions would be interpreted and enforced in the same manner as those of the EC Treaty, through the system of direct actions and preliminary rulings. This would have a number of important consequences. In the first place, it might be expected that in due course the ECJ would confirm that all the substantive provisions of the Convention (Articles 2 – 14) are capable of producing direct effect in the national legal systems. They all seem to meet the requisite conditions since they impose clear, precise and unconditional obligations and are drafted in peremptory terms. Some provisions, such as Article 8, might even be capable of producing "horizontal" direct effect and thus of being invoked by one individual against another. This would considerably extend the scope of the Convention.

In the second place, the provisions of the Convention would enjoy supremacy over national law in the same way as the provisions of Community law. National courts would be obliged to protect the rights which it confers on individuals and set aside any provision of national law which may conflict with the Convention, whether earlier or later in time.

The combined application of the principles of direct effect and supremacy would enormously enhance the effectiveness and efficiency of the enforcement of the Convention's provisions. The long, complicated, time-consuming and expensive Convention machinery would be replaced by the much faster and simpler proceedings before the domestic courts. Individuals would be able to invoke the Convention at the earliest possible opportunity in both civil and criminal cases, instead of having to go all the way to Strasbourg. There would be no longer a need to exhaust all domestic remedies and to comply with a multitude of admissibility requirements. This would result in a truly decentralised system of protection, in which the national courts would be playing the leading role, subject to the final interpretative authority of the ECJ under the preliminary ruling procedure. This would be perfectly in line with the philosophy of the ECHR itself that it is in the first place for the national authorities and courts to safeguard human rights, with the international judge having only a supervisory role. Such a system would also be in accordance with the spirit of subsidiarity. By virtue of direct effect, the protection in the domestic courts would become uniform throughout the whole Community, unlike the present position where the status of the Convention varies from Member State to Member State. This would lead to the creation of a genuine *Jus Commune Europaeum* in the human rights field.

A final major advantage would be that, unlike accession, incorporation would not lead to the jurisdictional subordination of the ECJ to the ECHR and could therefore be more easily achieved. In fact, since the Convention would become fully enforceable under Community law not only against the institutions, but also against the Member States, there would be no longer any need for the Member States to remain subject to the Convention's enforcement machinery. In order to avoid the simultaneous application of the two enforcement procedures, and thus the possibility of conflicting decisions being given by the two Courts operating independently of one another, the best course of action for the Member States of the Union would be to withdraw from the Convention. Thereby, the protection of human rights in the European Union and its Member States would be brought within a single system of enforcement under the final authority of a single Court. Since the Community has a complete system of remedies and procedures, there is no reason why the supervision exercised by the ECJ over the institutions and the Member States should be subject to further review by another Court which is of equal, but not of higher, status and calibre. Both Courts consist of equally highly qualified judges; they use similar methods of Treaty interpretation; they exercise supranational jurisdiction; and their decisions enjoy the same high respect and authority. In short, the ECHR could be replaced by the ECJ without any concern that the protection of fundamental rights would thereby diminish in any way. On the contrary, that protection would become more effective and more easily available to the individual.

Thus, the incorporation of the Convention into Community law would ultimately lead to the complete merger of the two distinct but partly overlapping supranational legal orders that currently co-exist in Europe. The present dual system came about as a result of purely historical factors, and there is no inherent reason why it should continue indefinitely. Initially, this merger would affect only the European Union and its Member States. However, as a result of successive enlargements of the Union which are already in progress or envisaged, more and more countries in Europe, comprising the large majority of the Signatories to the Convention, would in due course come within the scope of this single supranational legal order. In the meantime, the unity of human rights protection in the whole of Europe would be preserved since both the Union, its Member States and non-member countries would be subject to the same substantive provisions.

It might be thought that such a far-reaching extension of the competence of the Union/Community in the human rights field would be unacceptable to the Member States. However, there are signs that at least some steps in that direction might not. At the Cologne Summit of 3 and 4 June 1999, the European Council adopted a Decision to establish an *EU Charter of Fundamental Rights* "in order to make their overriding importance and relevance more visible to the Union's citizens". This Charter is to contain the fundamental rights and freedoms guaranteed by the European Convention, while also taking account of economic and social rights contained in the European Social Charter and the Community Charter of the Fundamental Social Rights of Workers. It is envisaged that a draft document will be presented prior to the European Council meeting in December 2000, on the basis of which a European Charter of Fundamental Rights will be solemnly proclaimed by the European Parliament, the Commission and the Council. It will then be considered whether and, if so, how the Charter should be integrated into the Treaties.[45]

Although it is too early to speculate at this stage, it is very much hoped that the Charter will be more than a mere declaration without legally binding force. It is hoped that it will fully, and not only selectively, incorporate the rights and freedoms guaranteed by the European Convention and that it will be so integrated into the Treaties so as to become legally binding and fully enforceable before the ECJ.

That would be a major step towards achieving what has been proposed in this paper: the codification of human rights by turning them from unwritten general principles of law into written and binding legal norms. Such codification seems inevitable if Community law is to develop into a fully-fledged legal system.

45. Conclusions of the Presidency of 3-4 June 1999, points I.18.44-45 and Annex 4, *Bulletin of the EU* 6-1999, pp. 13 and 35. See also the Conclusions of the Presidency at the Tampere European Council of 15-16 October 1999, Annex, *Bulletin of the EU* 10-1999, pp. 7 and 13.

3. Institutional Principle

3.1 Proportionality and Subsidiarity as General Principles of Law

Grainne de Búrca

3.1.1 Introduction

Within the framework of a conference on the General Principles of EC law, the principle of proportionality seems a natural choice for discussion. It was one of the earliest legal principles articulated by the European Court of Justice as a general principle of EC law. Further, some version of this principle is to be found within both the ECHR legal system and the legal systems of many of the Member States, from which in fact it was originally derived.[1] Thus the proportionality principle can be said, relatively uncontroversially, to apply to the actions of the Community and its institutions as well as to those of the Member States within the field of Community law. The same cannot however be said of the subsidiarity principle, to the extent that some would question whether the relevant provisions of the EC Treaty on subsidiarity can really be said to articulate a 'principle' at all.[2] In two recently published books on the general principles of EC law, written by John Usher and Takis Tridimas respectively, subsidiarity is not formally classified as such, and is discussed mainly in the context of its relationship to the proportionality principle proper.[3] This fact presents an interesting challenge in the context of a conference (out of which this book has emerged) which aims to consider how the general principles of EC law 'travel back' to the national legal systems and what kind of impact they have there. If subsidiarity, as opposed to proportionality, has not yet achieved the formal status of a general principle of law, which applies to the actions of the Member States within the field of EC law, its relevance for the legal systems of those states remains unclear.

One of the features of what have become known as the general principles of law is that they are normally derived by the ECJ from at least some of the legal systems of the Member States. This then tends to make their "re-transplantation" as general principles of EC law somewhat easier. If they are principles, which originate in some form from within a national legal system, it seems easier for that system to accommodate

1. See generally E. Ellis (ed) *The Principle of Proportionality in the Laws of Europe* (Oxford: Hart Publishing, 1999).
2. See *e.g.* the question posed by Bruno de Witte in his contribution to this volume, concerning whether subsidiarity can in fact be seen as a legal principle which embodies more than the particular rules of institutional behaviour contained in Article 5 EC and the Protocol to the EC Treaty.
3. J. Usher *General Principles of EC Law* (London: Longman, 1998) and T. *Tridimas The General Principles of EC Law* (Oxford: OUP, 1999).

Ulf Bernitz and Joakim Nergelius (eds.), General Principles of European Community Law, 95–112

them, even when they have been shaped by the ECJ and moulded to fit the EC's different legal and constitutional framework. This is true of human rights principles, proportionality, legitimate expectations, legal certainty and so on. It is not, however, true of a federal concept like the subsidiarity principle, which had been given prior recognition in relatively few national legal systems. This is probably at least one reason why it is not normally classified as a general principle of EC law. A second and more important reason, however, is that there is little so far to suggest, either in the jurisprudence of the ECJ or in any other institutional documents or legislation, that the Member States are "bound" even in a relatively soft legal sense, by the principle of subsidiarity when they are acting within the scope of EC law.

A further distinction between the subsidiarity and proportionality principles is that whereas subsidiarity, in so far as it is considered to be a legal principle, is perceived to be constitutional in nature, proportionality is generally described as a principle of administrative law. Yet given the blurred nature of the line between the administrative and constitutional law domain in the EU context, this distinction loses some of its significance.

Why, then, include discussion of the subsidiarity principle in the context of a conference and a book on this subject? One major reason is that it is a principle which has exerted considerable influence within EC law over much of the last decade. Despite the suggestions that it would be a 'busted flush'[4] or a 'fig-leaf',[5] little more than a temporarily useful label whose practical relevance would disappear when the Maastricht Treaty bargain gelled, the concept has endured and is increasingly rather than decreasingly evident not only in legislative texts but also within the Treaties themselves. And as a legal principle whose influence continues to grow rather than wane within EC law, its relevance for the Member States seems likely to develop even if it is not clear at present. More practically, given the linkage of subsidiarity and proportionality within Article 5 (ex 3b) of the EC Treaty and following the annexation of the Protocol on Subsidiarity and Proportionality to that Treaty by the Amsterdam Treaty, the two are being ever more closely connected – even blurred – in a way which suggests that they should be discussed together.[6]

---

4. Mackensie Stewart "Subsidiarity: A Busted Flush?" in D. Curtin and D. O' Keeffe, *eds Constitutional Adjudication in European Community and National Law* (Dublin, Butterworths, 1992)
5. N. Emiliou 'Subsidiarity: Panacea or Fig-leaf?' in *Legal Issues of the Maastricht Treaty* (London: Chancery, 1994) 65.
6. In relation to the general principles as principles of law, the tendency is to focus on their use by courts, and whether courts are drawing on these principles when interpreting national law, when reviewing measures adopted within the field of EC law etc. The Protocol, on the other hand, focuses on a different aspect of proportionality (and subsidiarity) which is less Court-centred in that it concerns primarily the relevance of these principles for the other EC institutions. However, this is certainly as important as their subsequent use in litigation before the Court, and determines their influence in practice at least as much.

This chapter will therefore proceed with a short discussion of the proportionality principle, as a more classic administrative law principle which is clearly recognised as one of the general principles of law binding both the EC and its institutions as well as national courts and institutions within the sphere of EC law. I will comment briefly on the use of the proportionality principle by the Court of Justice, adding to an earlier survey published in the Yearbook of European Law,[7] and also on its use by the national courts of one particular Member State, the UK, adding similarly to an earlier survey on this topic which was published in European Public Law.[8] The chapter will then go on to consider briefly the subsidiarity principle, which is not yet recognised as a general principle of law, and to examine how the proportionality principle has been consciously linked with the subsidiarity principle in the Treaties and elsewhere, and what implications this linkage has for both principles and their influence on national law.

3.1.2 PROPORTIONALITY AS A GENERAL PRINCIPLE OF LAW

3.1.2.1. Application by the ECJ and CFI

From a detailed survey carried out in 1993/4 of ECJ case law and the use of the proportionality principle, a number of conclusions were drawn.[9] The first was that proportionality was essentially a balancing principle, used in order to consider whether some legally recognised or protected interest or right was being excessively restricted. Its application generally consists of a number of stages: first, identifying what legally protected right or interest is at stake; secondly, identifying the extent to which this right or interest has been interfered with or restricted; thirdly, identifying the reason (the purported justification) for its restriction, whether for the protection of another right or public interest etc., and if so what weight is to be given to that other interest. Ultimately the question is whether, in the light of this balancing of interests, the interference with the protected legal interest is excessive or not. It became evident from examining a broad range of EC case law, including cases where Community actions were challenged for being disproportionate, cases where Member States were alleged to have acted disproportionately in limiting Treaty freedoms, and cases where Member States were argued to have acted disproportionately in implementing Community law, that there was no single 'way' in which the proportionality test was applied. Rather, it appeared as a sliding scale of scrutiny whose intensity altered considerably depending on the range of variables: on the importance and clarity of the legal right restricted, on the importance and nature of the public or other interest for which the right was being limited, and a range of other considerations. Where the

7. G. de Búrca 'The Principle of Proportionality and its application in EC law' (1993) 13 YBEL 105.
8. G. de Búrca 'Proportionality and Wednesbury Unreasonableness: the Influence of European Legal Concepts on UK Law' (1997) European Public Law 561.
9. N. 7 above.

right was not such a clearly defined or important one, and where the reason for restricting it entailed a broad matter of public interest involving the weighing of many political and economic factors, the proportionality scrutiny became relatively 'loose'. In such cases it appeared to be enough that the restrictive action was not manifestly inappropriate (even if there were many less restrictive ways of achieving a similar end). In other cases, however, especially where the measure being challenged was not a broad policy decision, but merely *e.g.* an individual penalty or decision without wider public consequences, and where the right infringed (*e.g.* personal liberty) was a clear and strong one, then the Court of Justice was more likely to apply a rigorous proportionality test, by asking whether there was no less restrictive means of achieving this end.

I identified a number of differences, however, when it came to ECJ consideration of Member State (rather than Community) action which was alleged to be disproportionate, whether in an Article 234 (ex 177) reference or in an Article 226 (ex 169) action. In such cases, if the Member State was restricting one of the core Treaty freedoms in a clear way, the ECJ seemed inclined to apply a strong proportionality test (the 'no less restrictive means' test). Unless the public interest reason for doing so was a complex and multi-faceted one (as, for example, in the Sunday Trading cases, where it was not clear, in any event, that the Treaty freedom of interstate trade really was being restricted in a significant way)[10] there appeared to be a greater number of findings of disproportionality against Member States than against the EC institutions. However, in cases involving Member States which were implementing rather than attempting to restrict Community policies, where the method of implementation was challenged by other actors as being excessive or disproportionate, the Court of Justice tended to leave this issue – partly, but not only, on account of the division of functions within the preliminary reference mechanism – for the national court to decide.

Having more recently conducted an up-to-date survey of ECJ case law involving the proportionality principle for the purposes of this chapter, it appears to me that the trends identified in the previous survey are continuing. In other words, the Court of Justice and the Court of First Instance appear still to be broadly protective of general Community legislative policy which is alleged to breach the proportionality principle, and seem reluctant to apply a particularly strict or rigorous proportionality test. The series of so-called 'mad cow disease' cases related to the ban on British beef are an instructive example.[11] Here, the protection of public health in the context of a difficult risk-assessment situation was the subject at issue and the European Courts were evidently unwilling to apply a strict or interventionist standard of scrutiny. On the other hand, the Court continues to be somewhat readier to declare Member State legislation, which infringes the Treaty's economic

10. See cases 145/88 *Torfaen B.C. v. B & Q* [1989] ECR 3851 and C-306/88, 304/90 & 169/91 *Stoke-on-Trent B.C. v. B & Q* [1992] ECR I-6457.

11. See, for example, case T-76/96R *NFU, ITF et al. v. Commission* [1996] ECR II-815.

freedoms to be disproportionate.[12] In the situation where a Member State has been implementing a Community measure, however, the trend continues to be such that the proportionality issue is generally left to the national court to decide, in particular where the measure leaves room for the Member State to choose different methods of implementation.[13]

3.1.2.2 Application by the English Courts

The application of the principle of proportionality by national courts is evidently something which, varies from state to state. In the case of states such as Germany, which have a fully developed, pre-existing doctrine of proportionality, the requirement under EC law to apply the proportionality principle does not pose particular problems (other than, for example, in its determination of the outcome of particular cases, such as the notorious banana litigation). However, in the UK, the position has been complicated by the fact that judicial review of legislative acts was virtually impossible due to the premises of national parliamentary sovereignty, and judicial review of administrative acts was limited to challenges on specified grounds of 'legality' which could not, in theory, enter into the substance or merits of the original decision, which review on grounds of proportionality was thought to entail. The closest ground of review was a ground of unreasonableness in English law known as *Wednesbury* unreasonableness, but there was considerable judicial and academic resistance to 'proportionality review' on the basis that it would involve an improper review of the merits and not only the legality of the decision taken.

I will not spend long on this point, since much has been written in the English literature about the relationship between proportionality and reasonableness as grounds of review, and specifically about how the UK courts have responded, under the influence of the general principles of EC law, to the doctrine of proportionality. I will summarise briefly what I concluded on this subject following the survey conducted a few years

12. Two relatively recent examples are Cases C-348/96 *Calfa* , judgment of 19 January 1999, concerning restrictions on the free movement of persons, and an Austrian advertising case involving public health restrictions on the free movement of goods, C-77/97 *Osterreicher Unilever GmbH v. Smithkline Beecham Markenartikel GmbH*, judgment of 28 January, 1999.
13. See *e.g.* the environmental Directive on nitrates in water C-293/97 *R v. Secretary of State for Environment & MAFF ex parte Standley and Metson* [1999] ECR I-2603, in which the ECJ said that the provisions of the Directive were deliberately flexible enough to enable Member States to observe the proportionality principle, so that it was for the national courts to ensure that was observed. See also case C-103/96 *DG des Douanes et Droits Indirect v. Eridania Beghin-Say* [1997] ECR I-1453, and the case concerning residence requirements for farmers in Sweden, C-9/97 & C-118/97 *Joleka & Pittaranta* [1998] ECR I-6267 where the ECJ ruled that the limits of discretion left by the Directive to the Member State was deliberately broad so that the limits of legal certainty and proportionality were similarly flexible.

ago,[14] and then go on to discuss a recent and important decision of the House of Lords, in the *International Ferry Traders (IFT)* case.[15] Essentially, the position adopted in English law is extremely mixed, and depends as much on the openness, ability and awareness of the judge involved as anything else. Some courts and certain judges have proven resistant to any kind of proportionality 'weighing', refusing to go much further than to say that a decision must not be so unreasonable than a reasonable decision-maker could not make it. Others, without expressly acknowledging that proportionality as a legal ground of review is part of English law, have adapted the idea of Wednesbury unreasonableness so that it is not as lax a standard as it sounds, but is used much more like a sliding scale, becoming a quite rigorous test, for example, where the right being restricted is a fundamental human one such as the right to life or personal freedom. However, even within the sphere of application of Community law, where most courts by now accept that they are required, in accordance with the case law of the ECJ, to conduct a proportionality examination, there has been a tendency on the part of many courts to conflate the two by saying that proportionality involves very little alteration to the traditional UK unreasonableness test, and that it merely requires a stronger reasonableness standard to be applied. Indeed, it is evident that some members of the House of Lords are hostile to the application of a proportionality doctrine, and it is possible that unwillingness to apply such a balancing test leads to erratic reasoning in their opinions on related questions.[16] And the difficulty with the approach which does not take the proportionality principle as a structured inquiry requiring identification of the competing interests (the right being restricted and the public or other interest which justifies the restriction) is that it leads to a far more impressionistic, often circular, less careful and certainly less reasoned judgment.[17] Further, it seems likely that following the coming into force of the Human Rights Act in the UK, courts there will have to confront the proportionality principle increasingly frequently since it is an integral part of adjudication under the ECHR, and not only "within the scope of EC law" but across the whole field of law and policy. However, if domestic judges continue to treat proportionality as a slightly amended version of the traditional unreasonableness test, there is the danger of continued confusion and inadequately reasoned decisions which do not address the fundamental weighing of interests in a fair and thorough way. Something of this confusion can be seen in the recent, important House of Lords judgment in the *ITF* case, mentioned above, in which the principle of proportionality was at issue.

In *ITF*, the applicant ferry company argued that the action of the Chief Constable of Sussex in refusing to continue financing the cost of daily policing of ferry

14. See n. 8 above.
15. *R v. Chief Constable of Sussex, ex parte International Trader's Ferry Ltd* (1998) 3 WLR 1260.
16. See the judgment of Lord Hoffman in the *ITF* Case, ibid. pp 1278-1287, and his extra-judicial opinion published in E. Ellis (ed) *The Principle of Proportionality in the Laws of Europe* (Oxford: Hart Publishing, 1999).
17. See also the note by C. Barnard and I. Hare , (2000) M.L.R forthcoming.

operations on cross-channel ferries which carried livestock cargo, in the face of strenuous protests at the port by animal rights protesters, had amounted to a quantitative restrition on exports in breach of Article 29 (ex 34) of the EC Treaty. The Chief Constable had decided to discontinue the level of financing of policing on the ground that it was detracting from the ability of the police force to provide adequate policing elsewhere, by diverting too many resources to this one area. *ITF*, whose business suffered heavily as a result, challenged this decision by arguing that it amounted to a disproportionate restriction on freedom to trade. Having succeeded before the High Court but lost in the Court of Appeal, the applicants ultimately lost their challenge before the House of Lords, which decided that, on the assumption that his actions could be described as a restriction on the freedom to export under EC law, the Chief Constable had not acted disproportionately. However, the various judgments demonstrate the confusion which continues to exist within the British judiciary in relation to the proportionality test, in particular as a result of the legacy of the so-called *Wednesbury* test, even in its modernised or re-formulated guises. They reveal a lack of understanding of the basic difference between a carefully structured proportionality test entailing the careful articulation and weighing of different rights and interests, as developed within EC law and in other jurisdictions, and the apparently common-sense but often conclusory 'reasonableness' test of English law.

Lord Slynn gave the main judgment, and began by considering the matter under English law. He declared that it was clear that the Chief Constable had taken into account a whole range of issues, including the right of IFT to trade, the right of protesters to demonstrate, the rights of the public and their protection, and the resources and means available to the police force, in deciding that his decision to discontinue policing was justified, but Lord Slynn did not question how the Chief Constable had weighed up those factors, concluding instead that the approach taken was open to the police chief "if there was evidence reasonably to support it".[18] In other words, there was sufficient evidence to suggest that the Chief Constable's decision was reasonably taken after a balancing exercise, but the judge did not himself investigate the justifiability or proportionality of the decision, nor did he consider and weigh the relative importance of the various rights and interests at stake. He ruled that the decision was "not shown to be unreasonable in a Wednesbury sense".[19] Moving on then to consider the argument under EC law, and specifically the argument that the decision, even if not unreasonable, was nonetheless a disproportionate restriction of the right to trade, Lord Slynn took the view that the distinction between the EC proportionality test and the Wednesbury unreasonableness test "is in any event much less than is sometimes suggested". He considered that a margin of discretion or appreciation would be allowed to the Chief Constable in the case of either standard of review, and in the light of this discretion, the decision taken was proportionate, as being a "suitable and necessary way of dealing with potentially violent demonstrators". Again, however, the judge noted that the Chief Constable had

18. (1998) 3 W.L.R. 1260 at 1269.
19. Ibid., 1272.

considered a range of interests, including the right to export and the other police duties he had to carry out within finite resources, but without assigning weight to the various interests nor asking what weight the Chief Constable had assigned, and indeed, without mentioning the freedom of expression of the protesters. In comparing the reasonableness test and the proportionality test as standards of judicial review, Lord Slynn seems to have partially conflated them, rather than engaging himself in the structured balancing required by the proportionality ground. The result he reached might well – and indeed would probably – have been the same, but the review could have been carried out in a more careful, reasoned and rigorous way.

Lord Hoffman in his judgment took the view that the Chief Constable's decision was not a 'measure' for the purposes of Article 29 (ex 34) so that there was no need to apply the proportionality test in reviewing the validity of a public policy exception under Article 30 (ex 36). However, having declared that the decision was certainly 'not unreasonable',[20] and that the considerations which would have to be taken into account in deciding on the proportionality of a restriction under Article 29 EC were quite different from the 'domestic' considerations which the police chief should take into account in balancing the interests of the traders with the policing needs of the county, he concluded very briefly, without any further argument, that if the EC question had to be answered, "the degree of restriction on exports cannot be shown to be disproportionate". He did not seem to countenance any difference between the domestic 'reasonableness' standard of review and the EC proportionality review, although he suggested – somewhat confusingly, given that they seem to amount to essentially the same thing in the specific circumstances of the case – that the interests being balanced could be said to be different because in the former they would involve the interests of ITF versus the policing demands of Sussex County, whereas in the latter they would involve the Community interest in the free movement of goods versus the public policy interest of the UK.

The third member of the House of Lords to give a judgment was Lord Cooke, who, like Lord Slynn, argued that both in the case at hand, and in many other cases "the European concepts of proportionality and margin of appreciation produce the same result as what are commonly called the *Wednesbury* principles".[21] He describes the *Wednesbury* test as being whether a particular decision was one which a reasonable authority could reach, and in this specific case it was whether the Chief Constable had struck a balance which was fairly and reasonably open to him. Having looked at the high cost of police protection and the kind of trade which ITF was seeking such protection for, he concluded that the police chief's response was reasonable and proportionate. Once again, while we may agree that this is a conclusion which could equally have been reached on a loose and impressionistic 'reasonableness' test, as well as on the basis of a structured proportionality test, the two legal principles cannot themselves be equated, and it is clear that the nature of the judicial inquiry is required to be considerably more rigorous and more careful in the case of the latter. The various

20. Ibid., 1281.
21. Ibid., 1288.

rights and interests must be articulated distinctly, and the extent of restriction of one should be identified, before the relative importance of that right and of the public policy or policies in whose interest it is being restricted are compared and balanced. The reasonableness test, by comparison, is much more fluid and unstructured, and its formulation does not encourage the judicial branch to do any more than ask, in what can often be a rather circular way, whether the decision was broadly reasonable.

Perhaps this example of the UK's reception of the proportionality principle through the channel of EC law is instructive in highlighting the difficulties of transplantation of a concept, even in the context of a reasonably open-minded judiciary which is attempting to integrate EC legal principles into domestic adjudication. Pre-existing legal standards and judicial perspectives and roles necessarily condition the nature and shape of the legal principle, which is being integrated, and the 'travel back' is not as smooth as European legal doctrine on the general principles of law might suggest.

3.1.3 The Principle of Subsidiarity

One can argue over whether the subsidiarity concept should even be called a legal principle, given that its existence in EC and EU law is primarily governed by a fairly detailed set of Treaty provisions, rather than expressing a more general kind of legal guideline or norm.[22] Indeed, it tends to be a characteristic of most of what are considered to be the 'general principles of EC law' that they are not in fact listed or defined in the Treaties, but are developed through the case law by the ECJ which draws on common national constitutional and administrative legal principles and internationally recognised norms. Subsidiarity on the contrary did not emerge within the EC legal order in this way, but rather was formally introduced in 1993 by the Maastricht Treaty into what was then Article 3b (now 5) of the EC Treaty.

Nonetheless, the introduction of this admittedly complex and ill-defined notion was evidently intended to signify a change in the EC's political and legal culture, and to suggest more restraint on the Community's part in law and policy making. And it is to this extent, particularly in view of the more general expression of subsidiarity in the provisions of the Treaty on European Union rather than the EC Treaty, as a broader value indicating that decisions should be taken "as closely as possible to the citizen", that it can be argued to be a general principle designed to guide decision-making at all levels within the EU. There is a vast legal literature on subsidiarity but it will not be discussed in any detail in this chapter,[23] which is concerned primarily

22. See n. 2 above

23. For some of the general literature on the subject, see A.G. Toth "A Legal Analysis of Subsidiarity", J. Steiner "Subsidiarity under the Maastricht Treaty" and N. Emiliou "Subsidiarity: Panacea or Fig Leaf?" all of which are published in D. O' Keeffe and P. Twomey, eds., *Legal Issues of the Maastricht Treaty* (London: Wiley, 1994), also K. Lenaerts and P. Van Ypersele "Le Principe de Subsidiarité et son Contexte" (1994) 30 CDE 3, and for more policy-specific discussions see W. Wils, "Subsidiarity and EC *Contd.*

with one specific aspect of the subject, namely its possible status as a general principle of European law.

3.1.3.1 Subsidiarity before the Court of Justice

In examining how the principle has fared since 1993 before the Court of Justice in those cases in which it has been invoked, we see that so far it has figured very little, so that little can be said with any certainty about its current status – as opposed to its future development – as a general principle. Although it has been cited and argued in different ways before the ECJ on quite a number of occasions,[24] the Court has only rarely addressed itself directly to the subject, and on the two occasions on which it has considered subsidiarity as a principle of review, it has not treated the concept as a

---

Contd.

Environmental Policy: Taking People's Concerns Seriously", [1994] JEL 85, G. Cross "Subsidiarity and the Environment" (1995) 15 YBEL 107, Brinkhorst "Subsidiarity and EC Environmental Policy: a Panacea or a Pandora's Box?" (1993) 2 EELR 17 and T. Jeppesen "Subsidiarity: A Janus Head?" European Studies Discussion Paper No. 11/95, Odense University, but also in many other sectors: *e.g.* "L'applicabilité du Protocol social à l'art 118a du Traité" (CEEP, Bruxelles, Opinion of 6 January 1995), P. Santos "Industrial Policy, Subsidiarity and Cohesion" (ECU, Bruxelles, No. 30 1995/1) pp. 54-58, A. Cox "Derogation, Subsidiarity and the Single Market" (1994) 32 JCMS 127, S. Smith "Subsidiarity and the Co-ordination of Indirect Taxes in the European Community" (1993) 9 Oxford Review of Economic Policy 67, P Spicker "The Principle of Subsidiarity and the Social Policy of the European Community" (1991) Journal of European Social Policy 3, J. Sun & J. Pelkmans "Why Liberalisation needs Centralisation: Subsidiarity and EU Telecoms" (1995) 18 World Economy 635, K. Lenaerts "Subsidiarity and Community Competence in the field of Education" (1994)1 Columbia Journal of European Law 1.

24. In C-278/94 *Commission v. Belgium* [1996] ECR I-4307, the Belgian Government challenged the Commission's claim that its programme for unemployed young people fell within the scope of access to employment and Regulation 1612/68. Although the ECJ in paragraph 35 mentioned that the Belgian Government had invoked the principle of subsidiarity, it did not expressly address that argument nor indicate whether its reasoning was based on or affected by the subsidiarity point. And in case C-11/95 *Commission v. Belgium* [1996] ECR I-4115, the government again argued, in response to the Commission's claim that Belgium was in breach of Article 2 of the Broadcasting Directive 89/552 in maintaining a system of prior authorisation for cable retransmission of TV broadcasts from other Member States, that according to the principle of subsidiarity in Article 3b, it was at liberty to intervene in cultural matters provided it did not fail to observe Community law obligations. The ECJ replied simply by stating that a Member State could not escape a specific obligation under a Directive by relying on the principle of subsidiarity. In C-91/95P *Tremblay v. Commission* [1996] ECR I-5574 the Commission's decision not to take action on the basis of certain complaints in the field of competition law on the basis that they could more appropriately be dealt with by the national authorities, was challenged as being a misapplication of the subsidiarity principle, but the challenge was unsuccessful before the Court.

particularly stringent standard of judicial review.[25] Most recently in *Kellinghausen,* the ECJ ruled that it has no retroactive effect in relation to measures which were adopted before the principle was expressly added to the EC Treaty,[26] and in *Dubois*,[27] concerning the question of liability to customs officers whose profession was severely affected by changes introduced by the Single European Act, the Court of First Instance (CFI) said the case could be decided "without even raising the question of subsidiarity" on the basis that it was primarily incumbent on the Member States to take any compensatory measures which were needed. Similarly in the challenge to the parental leave Directive before the CFI, *UEAPME* argued that the legislation was in breach of the subsidiarity principle because of the non-involvement of certain organisations representing small and medium sized enterprises in the negotiations, but once again the Court avoided ruling on the issue by dismissing the challenge on *locus standi* grounds.[28]

The two cases in which the ECJ did actually address – albeit in a less than satisfactory way – the subsidiarity claims which were explicitly made, were the Working Time Directive case and the Bank Deposit Guarantee Scheme case.[29] In the first case, the UK sought the annulment of the Working Time Directive, which amongst other things laid down a maximum weekly working time.[30] As part of one ground of challenge, the UK argued that Article 118a (now 138) of the EC Treaty, on which the Directive had been based, should have been interpreted in the light of the subsidiarity principle. The government argued that the Community legislature had not considered a whole series of factors (largely those which are now set out in the Amsterdam protocol) relevant to whether this action should have been adopted at Community or at national level. It was also argued that the Directive breached the proportionality principle, in going further than was necessary to protect the health and safety of workers.

Although the ECJ did this time address the subsidiarity argument, it did so very briefly, stating that the principle concerned only "the need for Community action", rather than the nature or intensity of that action. Once the Council had simply considered, under Article 118a, that there was a need to improve the existing level of health and safety of workers by harmonising working hours, that was sufficient to satisfy the Court's inquiry as to subsidiarity and the Council did not actually need to

25. See the Working Time Directive Case C-84/94, *United Kingdom v. Council* [1996] ECR I-5755, and the Bank Deposit Guarantee Scheme case C-233/94, *Germany v. Parliament and Council* [1997] ECR I-2405, discussed further below.
26. C-36 & 37/97, *Kellinghausen v. Amt fur Land- und Wasserwirtschaft Kiel* [1998] ECR I-6337.
27. T-113/96, *Dubois* [1998] ECR II-125.
28. T-135/96 *UEAPME v. Council* [1998] ECR II-2335.
29. N. 25 above. For further analysis of these cases see G. de Búrca "The Principle of Subsidiarity and the Court of Justice as an Institutional Actor" (1998) 36 J.C.M.S. 214.
30. Council Directive 93/104/EC concerning certain aspects of the organisation of working time, O.J. 1993 L 307, p. 18.

demonstrate anything.[31] The Court did not ask for any of the reasons behind the Council's conclusion that levels of health and safety in this field needed to be raised across the Community, nor did it engage with the more detailed arguments of the UK government asking whether certain considerations (those now contained in the post-Amsterdam protocol) had been addressed by the Council. The case could be taken to suggest that the Court is not willing to use the principle of subsidiarity as a thorough or substantive standard for review of Community legislative action, given that it simply accepted the Council's assessment that the aims were best achieved at Community level and that the measure did not go beyond what was necessary for the aims, without actually requiring any "qualitative or quantitative" indicators to support the assertion. On the other hand, the Court did not deny that the subsidiarity principle was relevant to the lawfulness of EC measures – at least as far as assessing the initial "need" for Community action is concerned.

In the second case mentioned above, in which the annulment of a Council and Parliament Directive on deposit-guarantee schemes was sought, the German Government argued that the Community legislature had not adequately set out the reasons why it considered the legislative action to be compatible with the subsidiarity principle.[32] The Directive provided for the compulsory participation by all credit institutions in guarantee schemes providing a minimum level of cover, and one of Germany's objections was that the Directive would prevent a branch of a credit institution in a host Member State (whose head office was in a different home Member State) from offering a higher level of protection than the maximum level offered by the particular scheme operating in the host State. This "prohibition on exportation" was, in Germany's view, contrary to the supposed minimum harmonisation and mutual recognition aims of the Directive. However, even though the preamble to the Directive did not make any express reference to the subsidiarity principle,[33] the Court

31. In defence of the Court's perfunctory treatment of the subsidiarity principle in this case, it must be said that the Treaty article in question specifically confers on the Community a power of harmonization in the field of health and safety, so that once the Council concluded that "health and safety" included the number of hours worked, and that levels of health protection in relation to the number of working hours should be raised across the Community, the fact that the aim of harmonization could be better achieved at Community rather than at national level could hardly be questioned.
32. Case C-233/94, *Germany v. Parliament and Council* [1997] ECR I-2405.
33. Even though a requirement of subsidiarity-specific reasoning has been criticised as formalistic, it may actually be important in that it is designed at least to encourage the institutions – particularly the Commission – to reflect self-consciously about whether a given kind of Community action on a given issue is appropriate, and to force them to articulate more openly how and why they have reached that conclusion. It is a significant transparency-type requirement, since even if a "subsidiarity justification" is tacked on *ex post facto* in a largely self-serving and cosmetic way to the preamble or explanatory memorandum to a measure, that very fact and the unconvincing nature of the reasoning may provide evidence of the failure to take the subsidiarity questions seriously and could also be helpful if a subsequent challenge to the measure were to be mounted.

ruled that certain of the recitals provided a sufficient indication of the Parliament's and the Council's reasons for considering that the Directive was in conformity with the principle.[34] The Court however, by comparison with Advocate General Léger, accepted that the subsidiarity principle was in fact applicable and thus that the regulation of the activities of credit institutions and their freedom of establishment did not fall within the Community's exclusive competence. The ECJ then itself "extracted" from some of the recitals to the Directive a justification for compatibility with the subsidiarity principle, although these were not expressed as such by the Council or Parliament.[35] It also accepted the statement in the recitals that the action on guarantee schemes which had been taken by the Member States alone, in response to an earlier Commission Recommendation, had not been sufficient to achieve the desired result, but without asking – as the German Government argued was required by the subsidiarity principle and indeed as the subsidiarity Protocol would now appear to require – for any details as to why the standards of protection achieved by the Member States were insufficient.

Both cases suggest that as a standard of review of EC legislative action, the subsidiarity principle is not being treated by the Court as a strong standard of intervention and scrutiny. In each case the Court treated it as sufficient for the Council or the Council and Parliament to assert that they had considered there to be a need for Community action in the field in question without (in the Working Time case) the Court looking behind that assertion or (in the deposit-guarantee case) requiring the legislator to provide its own fully reasoned and detailed justification for that conclusion. Yet even if we accept that the highly political nature of the questions underlying the subsidiarity principle as expressed in Article 1 TEU, Article 5 of the EC Treaty, and also the protocol to that Treaty make them inappropriate for the Court rather than the political institutions ultimately to decide, the institutions must surely be obliged to provide something more by way of reasoning and justification than a simple assertion that they consider the legislation they adopt to be compatible with that principle. To this extent, the subsidiarity principle could be developed by the European courts as a more serious legal standard of review, in conjunction with the requirement to give reasons.

On the other hand, the approach of the Court in these two cases does not necessarily mean that subsidiarity is being treated by it as a non-legal or entirely non-

34. See also more recently in case C-150/94 *UK v. Council* [1998] ECR I-7235, the ECJ ruled that, as it had held in the case of subsidiarity in the deposit guarantee case, there was no need for the Council to make express reference to the proportionality principle in the preamble to its legislative measures – in that case Regulation 519/94 on the import of toys from China.

35. It concluded this from a number of statements such as that the measure was "indispensable to ensure a harmonized minimum level of deposit protection wherever deposits are located in the Community" and that the insolvency of certain credit institutions would have repercussions outside the borders of the Member State in which its head office was located, that the legislature had considered that action could best be achieved at Community level.

justiciable principle. It is clearly not, as yet, a strong principle of review, but it is nonetheless a principle which the Court considers to be relevant to the legality of Community action, and relevant in guiding the lawmaking institutions in their role. The general lack of success in use of the principle in litigation so far does not necessarily mean that subsidiarity is not a legal principle nor that it might not develop – as indeed the 'principle' of transparency can be argued to be in the gradual process of doing[36] – general principle of law. It remains a significant legal principle with potentially important ramifications more generally for the EU legal order and consequently for the Member States, even if it has not at this stage attained formal status as a general principle of EC law or as a strong principle of substantive judicial review of EC action.

3.1.3.2 Subsidiarity as a broader principle

The fact that subsidiarity is dealt with across a number of different parts of the EU Treaties, and that it is dealt with rather differently within these various provisions exacerbates its complexity. The preamble and Article 1 TEU express a broader, political idea about the appropriate level of decision-making, which is not expressly restricted to the Union and Member State levels alone. The democratic tones of "closeness to the citizen" suggest that subsidiarity in the EU context is not merely concerned with the division of competence between the Community and the Member States on the basis of practical efficiency. However, Article 5 EC expresses a narrower and more legalistic idea which has been described by the Commission as a test of "comparative efficiency",[37] and which centres on whether action is "better" taken, in terms of scale or effects, at Community or Member State level. The Amsterdam protocol sets out further details intended to guide the application of the Article 5 criteria, but makes reference both to the "closeness to the citizen" idea and to the efficiency-related "scale or effects" criteria, as well as setting out requirements for institutional consultation and reporting, and about the types and forms of legislation which should be adopted.

The legal conception of subsidiarity in Article 5 therefore seemed intended to assist in identifying appropriate areas for Community action on the one hand, and for Member State action on the other, in situations where competence is not 'exclusive' to either, despite its broader expression in the TEU provisions more as a general normative preference for action to be taken more closely to the citizen – implying the subnational as well as national level. In contrast, the predominant legal conception of proportionality, as set out above, is that action should not impinge any further on a protected interest/right than is necessary for achieving the legitimate aims of that action. And this principle is expressed in a particular context in the third paragraph of Article 5 of the EC Treaty, where the protected interest in question is the policy

36. See P. Craig & G. de Búrca, *EU Law: Text Cases and Materials* (Oxford, OUP 2nd edition, 1998), pp. 368-371.
37. Commission communication on the principle of subsidiarity, Bull EC 10-1992 2.2.1.

autonomy of the Member States. Thus, Community action should go no further, in restricting the Member States' freedom to act, than is necessary to achieve its aims.

In the Protocol added to the EC Treaty by the Amsterdam Treaty (which was based on the previous "Edinburgh guidelines" and inter-institutional agreement), however, these two concepts have been linked much more closely together. The protocol articulates a number of somewhat more detailed guidelines for assessing when the Community should take action on a given issue, but then goes on to prescribe a number of shared approaches to lawmaking which combine the subsidiarity-related concerns of how to respect the role of the states and the Community respectively in the context of a field of joint competence, and the proportionality concern of ensuring that Member State autonomy is not being excessively restricted by Community action. The various suggestions made in the protocol entail ways in which policy action can be spread across a number of levels, so that although the Community may adopt action of some sort, it will nonetheless leave room for input at lower levels also. Thus the form of Community action is to be 'as simple as possible', directives are to be preferred to regulations and framework directives are to be preferred to detailed measures, and overall Community measures should leave as much scope for national decision as possible.

Since directives are instruments which leave more room for – and indeed which positively require – national intervention and action in implementing their aims than most other types of binding Community legal instrument, it is clear from this paragraph that the intention is to encourage the Community, where possible, to set the general outline for action and to leave the Member States to choose their different ways of carrying this through in detail. The Protocol here is imposing certain constraints on the types of Community action which are appropriate, and although those constraints relate to the form rather than the substance of action, it is of course apparent that the type of instrument chosen is very likely to affect the nature, substance and degree of detail of any given measure. The terms of paragraph 7 of the protocol make this even more explicit, providing that Community action is to leave as much scope for national decision as possible, respecting well-established national arrangements and the organisation of the national legal systems, and permitting alternative ways for Member States to achieve the objectives of the action in question. In this way, the Protocol's procedural guidelines as to the form of Community action, which are partly phrased in the language of proportionality – in that "the Community shall legislate only to the extent necessary" – offer an alternative way of conceptualising the subsidiarity issue. Rather than pursuing the impossible attempt to divide general areas of policy into blocks of 'exclusive Community competence' and 'exclusive Member State competence', or seeking to provide hard legal guidelines for determining whether the Community should act at all, or seeking to confine action on a given issue to one level of government only, this approach focuses instead on the kind of action the Community could take, which leaves room for other levels of government to develop and articulate that policy further. This emphasis on mutual co-operation in the sharing of a common sphere of potential authority is evident also in paragraph 8 of the Protocol, in which reference is made to the duty of solidarity in Article 10 EC, to encourage the Member States, in the absence of Community action, to refrain from acting in any way which would jeopardise Treaty objectives.

This linking of subsidiarity and proportionality[38] has to some extent moved the notion of subsidiarity beyond the circular guidelines in Article 5 EC, and is also more specific than the 'closer to the citizen' expression in the TEU, by suggesting a number of ways in which law-making should be shared between different levels of government. A limited attempt is made to address issues of process and participation in decision-making by specifying various procedural obligations (consultation, publication, reasoning) on the EC institutions. However, no procedures for the national level of implementation are prescribed, so that it is more difficult to see how these aspects of the subsidiarity concept would be applied to Member States when they are acting within the sphere of Community policy. In this sense, the specific requirements of subsidiarity and proportionality as articulated in the Protocol and in Article 5 EC – whether or not they become standards of review, as opposed to general principles or guidelines – are undoubtedly primarily directed towards shaping the behaviour of the Community and its institutions, rather than that of the Member States or any other levels of government. And this is true even though the proportionality principle, as we have seen above, has always been treated by the EC as an administrative principle, which is relevant both to national authorities within the scope of Community law as well as to Community authorities.[39]

There are also some indications that the values expressed in the various parts of the protocol are relevant not only to the Community but also to the Member State levels of government. The Commission, for example, is required to ensure that any financial or administrative burden, whether on the Community, national governments, local authorities or on economic operators or individuals, is not excessive.

---

38. Note the European Parliament's opposition to the conflation or linkage of the subsidiarity and proportionality principles (See the Report of the Committee on Legal Affairs and Citizens Rights and the Parliament's Resolution on the Commission reports to the European Council, A4-0155/97, O.J. 1997 C 167/34). Rather than seeing these as alternative ways of respecting the notion of subsidiarity, by developing complementary roles for different levels of governmental authority and encouraging the input of different actors into the policy-making process through consultation, the Parliament instead perceives such moves as creating uncertain forms of softer law which are insufficiently binding and which might not be adequately transposed at national level (See Debates of the European Parliament No. 4-500/6-12, 12 May 1997). Parliament considers that the Commission and other Community actors need to show why Community action is necessary and would be more effective than national action in the first place, but that having done this that it should then act strongly and autonomously, rather than using softer forms of framework law or seeking to share decision-making with the Member States, or diluting its energy and commitment to introducing concrete legislation by engaging instead in widespread consultative processes.
39. See C-293/97, *R v. Secretary of State for the Environment, ex parte Standley*, [1999] ECR I-2603.

More significantly, however, even though it has no formal legal status as such, is the understanding of the scope of the subsidiarity principle, which is expressed by three of the Member State governments in a Declaration annexed to the Amsterdam Treaty:

> "It is taken for granted by the German, Austrian and Belgian governments that action by the European Community in accordance with the principle of subsidiarity not only concerns the Member States but also their entities to the extent that they have their own law-making powers conferred on them under national constitutional law".[40]

Their interpretation, in other words, is that subsidiarity does not only concern the EC level and the national level of government, but also lower levels of government which share in the exercise of power. Whether this understanding is shared by other Member States, or whether it or indeed the norm expressed in Article 1 of the TEU will over time be accepted and developed by the Court of Justice remains to be seen. Certainly in the past, the UK was seen as a Member State whose vision of subsidiarity reflected a clear desire for the retention of national sovereignty, and one which pertained only to central governmental authority rather than to regions or other units of governance. However, governments change, as do their legal visions, and it can hardly be argued that the constitutional vision and framework in the UK at present is the same as that which animated the arguments of the Conservative government which first argued for the insertion of the subsidiarity principle in 1992. Given the extent of devolution which has occurred since that time, and the many other interesting constitutional developments within the UK, there is clearly room – even on the part of that most 'awkward partner' – for a development of subsidiarity as a principle which is more relevant not just to the EC and national governments, but to the EU as a whole and all of its constituent parts and sub-parts, and to all levels of governance throughout.

3.1.4 CONCLUSION

If we focus on the 'general principles of EC law' in terms of their development as concrete legal principles by the Court of Justice, the degree of success in their use as standards of review by which to challenge Community measures, and perhaps most significantly, the extent to which they are legally binding on Member States acting within the scope of Community law, then although the proportionality principle clearly qualifies as such, the same could not be said of the subsidiarity principle. But if, on the other hand, our focus is not so much on the judicial arena, but rather on the political and legal influence of norms, their capacity or their potential to guide the making of policy within the EU, and the extent to which the values they express seem in practice to be taken into account, a different assessment of the significance

40. See 1997 OJ C 340/143.

of subsidiarity as a principle would be likely to result. However, as far as the influence of that principle in filtering down throughout the various levels of authority within and across the EU is concerned, it is true that to date the influence of subsidiarity within and below the level of central government is difficult to assess and unlikely to be significant, other than for those states which already have some form of federal division of power within which a subsidiarity-type norm has been established. Nonetheless, the potential for future development of subsidiarity as a more general legal principle, capable of influencing also the extent to which Member States, acting within the broad sphere of European law, respect the various levels of authority and governance within each of their constitutional systems should not, in my view, be overlooked. The EC and EU legal framework is not a static but a dynamic one, and has shown itself to be constantly capable of evolution to match the changing political realities within which it operates.

3.2 The Development of General Principles of Law Within Article 10 (ex Article 5) EC

*Laurence W. Gormley**

Article 10 EC, as we must now get used to calling the old Article 5 EC, has formed perhaps the single most dynamic provision in the Treaty in the hands of the Court. It meets sins of omission and commission and its obligations, like ancient Gaul, are divided into three parts. The literature on Article 10 is extensive,[1] but from among that vast array, the work of Due,[2] Durand[3] and Temple Lang[4] has been particularly useful in clarifying the scope of that provision, and giving concrete form and structure to the working out of its effects. It is impossible to seek to do justice to their work in the limited space available. Instead, this paper seeks to highlight a number of points in order to offer some pointers in what to some appears a minefield of prestigitation.

A minefield of prestidigitation, because that is how some of the reasoning must have appeared to a number of Member States when they were confronted with spectacular developments in case-law. But it is not only the Member States who have found themselves affected by conclusions apparently plucked like rabbits out of a judicial hat, or even out of thin air, often on the basis of alluring analogy. The Community Institutions have found themselves not merely the beneficiaries of Article 10, but also, no doubt to their bemusement, subject to it. Despite the fact that it is very clearly addressed to the Member States as such, the Court has been able to use it to prevent one Community Institution simply frustrating the decision-making process willy-nilly. Thus in a number of judgments the Court has derived from Article 10 a duty on the Community Institutions to conduct the inter-institutional dialogue in terms of sincere cooperation. This concept of mutual co-operation is revisited presently.

---

* Barrister; Professor of European Law and Jean Monnet Professor, Rijksuniversiteit Groningen (Jean Monnet Cenre of Excellence); Visiting Professor, University College, London & Universität Bremen. The style of the oral presentation has been largely preserved.

1. See also Kapteyn & VerLoren van Themaat (ed. Gormley), *Introduction to the Law of the European Communities* (3rd. ed., London, 1998) 148-162 and authors cited there. The present approach follows the discussion there.
2. (1992) SEW 355.
3. In Mégret *et al.* (eds.), *Commentaire Mégret Le Droit de la CEE* Vol. 2 (2nd Ed., Brussels, 1992) 25 et seq.
4. *Inter alia* (1987) Fordham Int'l. L.J. 503; (1990) 27 CMLRev. 645 and in Gormley (ed.), *Current and Future Perspectives on EC Competition Law* (London, 1996) 41.

Ulf Bernitz and Joakim Nergelius (eds.), General Principles of European Community Law, 113–118

Article 10 at first sight appears to be little more than an expression of the general principle *pacta sunt servanda.* It must not be forgotten that Article 10 has an essentially supplementary effect. It can be used to cajole, oblige or develop compliance with Community law, but non-compliance with Article 10 on its own seems to provide scant fruitful terrain for development. Thus the Commission may well join an Article 10 complaint to a substantive complaint in infringement proceedings, where, for example a Member State has refused to reply to correspondence, but will not take action solely on the basis of the refusal to reply, as all a Member State would have to do would be to send a reply, no matter how uncooperative the content of that reply.

Although it is at first sight tempting simply to look at the three obligations expressed in Article 10, as Due and Durand have demonstrated, that would be to obscure their true range in view of the principles developed from them. The first obligation, expressed in Treaty terms, is to take all appropriate measures, whether general or particular, to ensure the fulfilment of the obligations arising out of the EC Treaty or resulting from action taken by the Community Institutions. This obligation on the Member States can itself be analysed in three component parts:

- the obligation to take all appropriate measures necessary to ensure the effective application of Community law
- the obligation to ensure the protection of rights stemming from primary and secondary Community law, and
- the obligation to act (themselves) to achieve the objectives of the Treaty, particularly where the competent Community Institution has failed to act.

The first of these really refers to ensuring that the substantive rights and obligations are applied: it affects all levels of the public apparatus, including therefore the judiciary, and legislative and executive organs at whatever level. Indeed, a national court against whose judgment there is no appeal, which goes off on a frolic of its own, for example by suddenly inventing new rule of reason justifications in relation to the free movement of goods or public undertakings, without making a reference to the Court of Justice will cause a Member State to be in breach of Article 10 EC in conjunction with the breach of the obligation to make a reference. However, in view of the sensitivity of the Commission to arguments about the independence of the judiciary and the need not to endanger cooperation between the decentralised judges of Community law and the central Community judiciary, the attitude of the Commission in tackling judicial infringements has been somewhat reticent. Although in so far as it applies to the legislative and executive branches, this obligation is distinct from the second obligation relating to judicial protection, in its applicability to the judiciary it merges into that second obligation.

That second obligation was the joint basis for the development of liability of the Member States in damages for breach of Community law. Yet it is often forgotten that the availability of damages in national law for breach of a Community law obligation was recognised by the Court many years ago in the context of the

Commission's interest in continuing infringement proceedings in Case 39/72 *Commission v. Italy*.[5] Significantly in *Francovich,* the Court chose to found liability not simply on Article 10 but also on the ground that it was 'inherent in the system of the Treaty'. Article 10 was also the basis in *Factortame*[6] for the requirement that the national courts had to create a new remedy (*in casu* suspending the operation of legislation) unknown to national law, in order to ensure the full and immediate application of directly applicable and directly effective Community law. Article 10 was only relatively lately invoked to support right of individuals to invoke unconditional and sufficiently clear provisions of unimplemented directives.[7] While primarily directed at the judiciary, it is also now evident that this obligation applies to the legislative and executive branches in so far as is necessary to ensure proper access to appeal or review procedures.

The third obligation under this heading has two facets. On the one hand it involves obligations of mutual recognition, and to this extent ties in with the third major heading of mutual cooperation. On the other hand it has also been expressed as rendering the Member States trustees for the benefit of the Community: 'trustees of the common interest'.[8]

The second major heading flowing from Article 10 is the negative obligation to abstain from any measure that could jeopardise the attainment of the objectives of the Treaty. This heading has been identified by Durand as also having three aspects:

- The obligation to abstain from measures which could impede the effectiveness of Community law;
- The obligation to abstain from measures which could hinder the internal functioning of the Community Institutions, and
- The obligation to abstain from any measures which could hinder the development of the Community integration process.

Taking these one by one, the first finds particularly concrete expression in the obligation not to jeopardise the proper functioning of common organisations of the various agricultural markets or of Community harmonisation measures which only partly occupy the field concerned. It has also, as Due has noted, been the subject of judicial interpretation in relation to the corporatist activities of various Member States. Once again, though, there must always be a concrete link to specific obligations or infringements.

The second obligation, though important for the Institutions, and in particular for the Commission and the Parliament, is of less interest for the present discussion.

5. [1973] ECR 101 at 112.
6. Case C-213/89 *R. v. Secretary of State for Transport, ex parte Factortame* [1990] ECR I-2433 at 2473-2474.
7. Case 190/87 *Oberkreisdirektor des Kreises Borken et al. v. Handelsonderneming Moormann BV* [1988] ECR 4689 at 4722.
8. Case 804/79 *Commission v. United Kingdom* [1981] ECR 1045 at 1075-1076.

The third obligation is perhaps the most interesting. When in the context of the implementation of a common policy (such as agriculture, fisheries or transport), a Commission proposal is being discussed in the Council,[9] or where the Commission has given notice of its intention to present a proposal for harmonisation under the powers conferred upon it by Directive 98/34,[10] a Member State must abstain from acting. Outside those areas, though, the mere commencement of preparation of a Commission proposal or the submission of a proposal does not give rise to an obligation under Article 10.[11] If, though, a Directive has been adopted but has not yet entered into force, Member States are under an obligation to refrain from adopting 'any measures liable seriously to compromise the result prescribed'.[12] Following Durand, it is interesting to wonder whether Article 10 might be infringed by a Member State blocking decision-making in the Council on a matter where there is an existing legal obligation to act by a prescribed date. She acknowledges, though, that an action for failure to act would probably be more effective in these circumstances. The key may well lie in the reference in Article 10 to 'objectives of the Treaty' rather than to concrete legal obligations. Thus in this respect it may well be possible to invoke Article 10 in relation to political inactivity frustrating the achievement of the objectives of the Community, and not merely concrete infringements. On the other hand, this approach would be at variance with the other uses of Article 10 in conjunction with specific obligations, to which reference has already been made. It would also be the legal equivalent of the impact of The Queen of the Night appearing to arise from the depths of Lake Constance during a performance of The Magic Flute: prestigitation confounding even the most supreme architect.

The third heading of obligations emerging from Article 10 itself which Temple Lang and Durand rightly identify as a *leitmotif* in the case-law is the general principle of mutual cooperation. Durand identified three specific elements in this duty:

- an obligation on the national authorities and the Community authorities to co-operate with each other;
- a mutual assistance obligation on the Member States, and
- an obligation on the Community Institutions to cooperate sincerely with the Member States.

There is, though, a fourth specific element, not identified in Article 10, but derived from it by the Court: the duty on the Community Institutions to conduct the inter-institutional dialogue in terms of sincere cooperation.[13] As has already been implied, this element is particularly novel and of far-reaching institutional importance. However,

9. Ibid. at 1075.
10. O.J. 1998 L 204/37, as amended by Dir. 98/48 (O.J. 1998 L 217/18), see Art. 9(3).
11. Case 174/84 *Bulk Oil (Zug) AG v. Sun International Ltd. et al.* [1986] ECR 559 at 592-593.
12. Case C-129/96 *Inter-Environnement Wallonie ASBL v. Région wallonne* [1997] ECR I-7411 at 7449.
13. Case 204/86 *Greece v. Council* [1988] ECR 5233 at 5359 and Case-65/93 *European Parliament v. Council* [1995] ECRI-643 at 668.

the imposition on the Community Institutions of obligations which the Treaty places on the Member States is nothing new: thus the Council may not create new obstacles to the free movement of goods in the absence of a clear and specific authorisation in the Treaty.[14] Application of obligations by analogy may even be becoming commonplace: thus the Court found it had the power to determine which effects of a directive which it annulled should be declared definitive, even though the Treaty expressly confers such a power on it only in relation to regulations.[15] The legal foundation for such a conclusion was not Article 10, of course, but it is a useful illustration of the Court's willingness to prestidigitate. The mutual nature of these obligations under Article 10 between the national authorities, between them and the Community Institutions, and between the latter is certainly not readily apparent from the wording of Article 10, but it becomes logical once Article 10 is itself seen as a specific expression of the principle of a more general duty of mutual cooperation. This general duty has not always been specifically linked to Article 10 by the Court. The concepts of mutuality and equivalence in responsibilities also lie behind the approach to the conditions under which Member States may incur liability for damage caused to individuals through breaches of Community law for which they are responsible.[16]

The first of Durand's elements finds specific expression in the obligations to cooperate *bona fide* with Commission inquiries, to inform, and to consult. It leads also to an obligation to work together to surmount unforeseen and unforeseeable difficulties in giving effect to Community legislation, whilst fully observing the Treaty provisions concerned.

Her second element, the mutual assistance obligation on the Member States most famously operates in relation to the four freedoms, as has been observed above. In the celebrated judgment in *Matteucci v. Communauté française of Belgium et al.*[17] Article 10 was found to require Member States to facilitate the application of Community law and thus not to give effect to a bilateral agreement falling outside the field of application of the Treaty where giving effect to it would impede the application of a right conferred by Community law. While, as *Houtwipper*[18] has demonstrated, there are limits to the possibilities of mutual recognition of goods, the general tenor of the obligation is clear.

Durand's final element (the duty of sincere cooperation with the Member States imposed on the Community Institutions) is of particular importance not merely in the relationship between the Commission and national courts in investigation of irregularities,[19] it is also the key to the proper functioning of the relationship between the Commission and national courts in the fields of competition[20] and state aids.[21]

---

14. See the case-law cited by Kaptcyn & Ver Loren van Themaat, *op. cit.* 639.
15. *E.g.* Case C-295/90 *European Parliament v. Council* [1992] ECR I-4193 at 4236-4237.
16. See in particular Cases C-46 & 48/93 *Brasserie de Pêcheur SA et al. v. Germany et al.* [1996] ECR I-1029 at 1146-1148.
17. Case 235/87, [1988] ECR 5589 at 5611-5612.
18. Case C-292/93, [1994] ECR I-4249, see Gormley (1996) 21 ELRev. 59.
19. *E.g.* Case 2/88 Imm. *Zwartveld et al.* [1990] ECR I-3367 at 3372.
20. O.J. 1993 C 39/6.
21. O.J. 1995 C 312/7.

What points might be drawn from this analysis of Article 10? First, as regards general principles, it may be observed that Article 10 seeks to set out general principles of conduct affecting the Member States but those principles apply equally to the Community Institutions themselves. Secondly, Article 10 is somewhat hybrid in nature. At the same time as setting out key general principles, it is the more concrete expression of general principles of law: not merely *pacta sunt servanda* but also mutual cooperation and effectiveness. It becomes thus an instrument of integration without any logical limitation, save, it seems, the need to be linked to the infringement of or guaranteeing of a concrete right or obligation founded in the Treaty. It is submitted that it would as yet be going too far to make Article 10 found an action for non-cooperation in the achievement of the objectives of the Treaty *simpliciter*, a concrete duty is needed. Temple Lang has rightly noted that the Court's use of Article 10 has been statesmanlike, although its failure always to base some of its more creative reasoning expressly on Article 10 does indeed lay it open to the charge of judicial legislation. But judges do in fact legislate in practice if not in name all the time. They effectively, as Pescatore put it face the Community legislator – and indeed the national legislatures – with the consequences of their actions.[22] Article 10 has in fact proved a most effective vehicle for ensuring that individuals have some degree of assurance that the Community created for their benefit will work to their benefit, that the rights called into being will not be mere illusions. From the point of view of citizens and others, Article 10 has become a central weapon against abuse.

John Temple Lang – in language reminiscent of Gladstone's famous declaration that the sanctity of life in the hill villages of Afghanistan can be as sacred in the eyes of Almighty God as is your own[23] – put it in these words: 'the farmer in Crete and the farmer in Tuscany have the same rights, under the same legislation, ultimately interpreted by the same Court of Justice, as the farmer in Connemara and the farmer in the Shetlands. Even more important, the Community's citizens are everywhere protected, in their local courts, by the same rules of fundamental rights, both as against the Community institutions and, to an extent still to be fully defined, against national authorities in the Community law sphere.' He has also observed that '[t]he development of general principles of law is the result of a symbiosis between national courts and Community law, in which each can enrich and reinforce the other. The development of common standards of justice in the application of Community law will give rise to a sense of a common tradition, not based merely on common economic interests, and shared across differences of language and of national legal traditions. It is a wholly new, non-economic creation, with enormous psychological and political potential for contributing to European history.'[24]

22. In Lüke *et al.* (eds.), *Rechtsvergleichung, Europarecht und Staatenintegration (*Gedächtnisschrift for Constantinesco) (Cologne, 1983) 559.

23. See Magnus, *Gladstone* (London, pbk. 1963) 262.

24. Temple Lang in Gormley (ed.), *op. cit.* (see note 5, *supra*) 41 at 50.

3.3 General Constitutional Principles of Community Law

Ola Wiklund and *Joxerramon Bengoetxea*

3.3.1 Introduction

The purpose of this article is to examine the role of principles of a constitutional nature in the legal system of the European Communities. This is no easy task since the very concept of principles, all too often taken for granted, is not clear. The concept of general principles and the different meaning of the expression "general principles of law" is dealt with in Part 2 of this article. If we are looking for those general principles of law that are of a constitutional nature, we shall also need a conception of constitutionalism. And if this specifically constitutional aspect of some legal principles is to be applied to the law of the European Communities, we need to develop some basic theory as to what the European Communities constitution may be like. Things get rather complicated, but these steps analysed in Part 3 are essential if the article is meaningfully to advance at all. Part 4 will then be in a proper methodological position to detect which are the constitutional principles of the European Constitution (the EC Treaty and the EU Treaty). Finally Part 5 will analyse what role these principles play in the constitutional setting or process – especially systematicity, coherence and integration – and what challenges they may pose to the rational and democratic legitimation of the European Constitution.

3.3.2 Jurisprudential Queries

It is essential to understand what is meant by general principles of law and why this expression may be relevant when approaching the law of the European Communities.

3.3.2.1 General principles of law and the character of EC law

The goal-orientated character of the Treaty establishing the European Community (hereafter EC Treaty) is a central feature of European Community law (hereafter EC law). Thus, (i) the Treaty formulates the goals to be achieved by legislation, administration and the adjudication of law; (ii) the Preamble and Part One lay down general political, economic and social goals and there is no doubt that these provisions constitute an integral part of EC law since their pivotal role is being constantly emphasised by the Court of Justice of the European Communities (hereafter, the ECJ, or simply the Court) when adopting an interpretative technique based on coherence and teleology.

Ulf Bernitz and Joakim Nergelius (eds.), General Principles of European Community Law, 119–142

The very normative structure of EC law is also framed by other characteristics that reveal the interdependence and proximity between law, politics and morality. Thus, (iii) the ECJ's interpretative strategy is subject to on-going clashes between law and politics since the Community consists of a number of more or less sovereign states with different and sometimes conflicting views on the means and ends of the very enterprise of integration; (iv) the division of legislative and judicial competences is still fuzzy partly because of the lack of supra-national direct means of enforcing EC law in the Member States and partly because development of the law through judicial interpretation based on principle and goal is inherent to the system or the *économie* of the Treaty (the cases on Member State liability for breaches of Community law are an illustration of these factors).

These characteristics imply that the EC legal system is far from being composed solely of written rules. In the European legal tradition, rules are completed by general principles of law accepted by the judiciary. As a result, legal principles are introduced into the legal order and become normative and concrete through legal decision-making by courts and other authorities. In the EC context too, the ECJ has been faced with interpreting a framework Treaty which leaves the interpreter a considerable margin of discretion. The ECJ has, out of this instrument, developped the fundamental principles which provide the foundation for building the Community. These principles of the Community Economic Constitution serve as the theme or *leitmotiv* of an extensive case-law concerned both with the achievement of the free movement of goods and persons and with implementing common policies based on material principles such as equality, freedom, solidarity, unity, and on structural principles of interpretation such as *effet utile* or effectiveness.[1]

Maybe EC law has greater need of recourse to general principles for its completion – its systemic nature and its normative development – than is the case with some national legal orders. It is often contended in the literature that this is due to its lack of maturity and open normative structure.[2] Jean-Victor Louis claims that: "The role of these principles arises from the necessarily incomplete character of the Community legal order as determined by the objectives and substantive rules of the Treaties and by the common traditions of the Member States."[3] While suggesting a contextual approach to the study of EC law, Cappelletti contends that: "Studying Community law merely on the basis of Treaty provisions, regulations, and directives and European Court decisions is like believing the iceberg to be limited to its tip... "[4] In a theoretical piece on the nature of EC law, Dowrick writes: "To leave them [legal principles] out of an analysis of EC law into its elements would be like leaving oxygen out of an analysis of air."[5]

1. See J.V. Louis, *The Community Legal Order*, 1980, p. 30; and P. Pescatore, *Introduction à la Science du Droit*, 1960, p. 120.
2. See *e.g.* Schermers and Waelbroeck, *Judicial Protection in the European Communities*, 5th ed. Kluwer 1992, § 42.
3. Louis 1980, p. 68.
4. Cappelletti, *The Judicial Process in Comparative Perspective*, Oxford 1989, p. 388.

The function of general principles of law in the process of shaping the European polity gives rise to a number of jurisprudential queries. How can the requirements of legality (predictability, coherence) and legitimacy be reconciled when interpreting and applying indeterminate legal principles? What significance does the moral and political context of legal principles have for the "objectivity" of law? In spite of their great importance, we leave these general questions aside to concentrate on the status and anatomy of EC legal principles. Thus, this contribution is not intended as a treatise on legal principles and therefore certain theoretical problems have to be bypassed.

3.3.2.2 Provisions and norms

Let us begin with an essential distinction between provisions and norms, or between normative language, physical or canonical norm, *the instrument*, on the one hand, and *the meaning* of those texts, on the other hand. The first can be called provisions and the second can be called norms. Provisions and norms do not exhaust the juridical universe. In many occasions the provision and the norm will coincide, but sometimes they do not; either because the provision is susceptible of different meanings (different norms may be derived from the same provision) or because the provision is silent on certain aspects and a norm has to be constructed from material that transcends the provision (gaps) or because the provision may clash with another provision and a norm may have to be constructed to solve the conflict. The end result, the norm, may have different forms.

3.3.2.3 Rules and principles

For the purposes of this work an essential distinction will be drawn between rules and principles.[6] One may ask what is a legal principle and is it possible to distinguish it from a specific rule? The standard definition of the term 'principle' states that it is "a fundamental...proposition on which others depend; a general statement or tenet forming the basis of a system of belief...a primary assumption forming the basis of a chain of reasoning".[7] Traditional definitions seem to view principles as substantive justifications of rules. A principle of law underlies a rule and explains the reasons for its existence.[8]

A rule could be seen as a norm of a binary structure, having a *protasis* and an *apodosis* whereas a principle does not have the structure of antecedent and consequence but rather postulates that a given value or state of affairs is desirable. It is often

5. Dowrick, A Model of the European Communities' Legal System, *YEL* 1984 p. 219.
6. See Alexander and Kress, Against Legal Principles (in *Law and Interpretation*, Marmor ed.., Clarendon 1995), pp. 208 on this distinction and other distinctions *e.g.* rules-standards, rules-policies.
7. *The Shorter Oxford Dictionary* (edn., 1993)
8. Sir Gerald Fitzmaurice, The General principles of International Law, 1957 92 *Collected Courses of the Hague Academy of International Law*, p. 7.

said that a principle is a rule with a very high level of generality, but rules can be very general and some principles are quite specific. How does one distinguish a principle with a low degree of generality from a rule of a high degree of generality? The different structure of rules (*if p then q*) and principles (*q is good*) may give a clue. Rules are detailed, principles are not. The structure of the EC and EU Treaties is thus rather principled; they employ a large number of undefined rules and concepts and contain only a relatively small number of precise rules of law. They prescribe objectives, guidelines, aims, and establish principles, they design a programme for integration but relatively few detailed rules to solve specific problems. Judicial interpretation will compensate for the deficit in precise rules

Sometimes the norms of the legal system are not found with a direct physical correspondence in the written language of the law, the provisions. Many principles are of this type, although some principles are indeed written down and directly stated *e.g.* the polluter pays principle (Article 174(2) TEC) or the principle of subsidiarity (Article 5 TEC or Article 2,2 TEU). Other principles may be stated in one language but not in another, *e.g.* the *principe d'ouverture* is stated in the French version of Article 1 TEU whereas the English version only states that decisions must be taken as openly as possible. Still other principles are not stated, but they can be implied from the legal provisions, *e.g.* the principle of the independence of the members of the Commission in the exercise of their function (Article 213(2) TEC). Yet others are the result of abstract theoretical constructions *e.g.* the principle of attributed powers, the principle of institutional autonomy of the Member States, or the principle of procedural autonomy combined with effective remedies. Some of these constructions are the work of the Court of Justice itself and others are coined by doctrine, and since Members of the Court read some of the literature and academics read some judgments, there is a feedback between these professions reinforced in academic gatherings such as FIDE conferences which often leads to the consolidation of the principle in spite of its not having a physical correspondence in the Treaties. That was arguably the case with the principle of direct effect, a principle which is not stated anywhere in the EC Treaty but which can be seen as a result of a feedback between doctrine and case-law[9].

3.3.2.4 Classifying principles

One may attempt to classify principles acording to different criteria. According to the *substance*, one talks about (general) principles of law, constitutional principles, procedural principles, administrative principles, private law principles, etc. Some principles can be seen as *ideological* – *e.g.* the principle of an open market economy in Article 98 of the TEC or those related to the rule of law – whereas others are thought to be more *formal* or procedural – *e.g.* proportionality, non-discrimination or even subsidiarity – but the moment they start applying they will have to fill with substance. For

9. David Edward, Direct Effect, "the Separation of Powers and the Judicial Enforcement of Obligations", in *Scritti in onore di Giuseppe Federico Mancini*, Milano 1998, p. 423-443.

instance the principle of non-discrimination will operate in different ways depending on the subject which is being analysed, sex, nationality, residence, etc. Particular difficulties will arise when considering particular cases. Take discrimination on grounds of sex. The difficulties with the principle may be purely formal – *e.g.* whether affirmative action in favour of one of the sexes in cases of underrepresentation constitutes discrimination – or substantial – does the prohibition of discrimination on grounds of sex extend to discrimination on grounds of sexual orientation?

Another possible distinction is that between principles as a specific *source* of EC law in a given area – *e.g.* non contractual liability – and principles common to the laws of the Member States as an aid to *interpretation.* In the Human Rights cases it could be argued that the approach has followed closely the source method: the European Convention and the constitutional traditions of the Member States become a source of the EC legal order, taking the form of general principles; and the Court has opted for its own interpretation of these principles in the obvious light of an integrationist agenda[10]. Many principles of administrative law have been readjusted from the French and German administrative law traditions. Many procedural principles have followed the common law. In these cases the approach seems to be comparative: what the Member States' laws have in common in certain areas may become general principles as a source of law. On other occasions, principles are used to support certain interpretations: the principle of equality between the sexes has supported a given interpretation of Article 119 (now Article 141) as prohibiting non-discrimination in a wide interpretation of "equal pay", or the principle of the comprehensiveness of the system of judicial protection has reinforced the interpretation in favour of recognising the European Parliament's right of action to defend its own prerogatives[11].

A question which will be addressed in Part Two is whether one adopts the same (comparative) method and looks for constitutional principles of the Member States as adapted to the EU or whether the constitutional principles of the EU or the EC are autonomous. It is in the very legal system of Community law – its written and unwritten norms, its case-law and its wider sources which include the legal traditions of the Member States – that the general constitutional principles of EC law are to be found, but are these general principles predating EC law and *common* to the laws of the Member States, *a priori* and *from below*, and somehow passed on to the new system? Can they be common principles *a posteriori*, by virtue of their being instrumental for the directly effective, uniform and supreme character of the uniform legal system which is EC law and thus common to all the Member States *from above*, because of their higher normative status instead of being distilled from the internal laws of the Member States as a source? Some of those constitutional principles of the

10. See the debate between Weiler-Lockhart and Jason Coppel and Aidan O'Neill in the *Common Market Law Review.* Coppel and O'Neill, The European Court of Justice: Taking Rights Seriously, (1995) 29 *CML Rev* 669; Weiler and Lockhart, "'Taking Rights Seriously' Seriously: The European Court and its Fundamental Rights Jurisprudence", (1995) 32 *CML Rev* 51.
11. See Case C-70/88 *Tchernobyl* [1990] ECR I-2041.

EC may even be principles valid or operating in only one or a few Member States and then they can be exported to the rest through EC law. The (nordic) principles of openness, public access to official documents and transparency may be of such nature. Something similar may be happening with the principles of interim relief and Member State liability for damages. They have become part of the constitutional system of the EC but they were not really common to all the laws of the Member States.

3.3.2.5 "Meanings of principle"

As a provisional classification of the different meanings of the term "legal principles" and with a view to recapitulating some of the ideas expressed so far, the following senses of the expression "legal principles" can be identified:

- Norms or provisions with a high degree of **generality** (that is why they are often referred to as *general* principles): principles of the legal order are more general than say principles of labour law or private law, or administrative law;
- Norms or provisions that are vague or have a high degree of **vagueness** (*e.g.* proportionality, reasonableness, unjust enrichment);
- Norms of a **programmatic** nature addressed to the law maker or administrative authority which impose a given aim or postulate a value (normally these norms are also rather vague *e.g.* the open market, free competition);
- Norms that rank high in the **hierarchy** of sources (*e.g.* constitutional principles); indeed at some stages the Constitution has been thought to be non-justiciable since it contained no rules in the strict sense but rather principles;
- Norms of a fundamental **importance**, i.e. keystones, in the legal or political system or in some area of law such that the system or the area of law would be essentially different if these principles were absent (*e.g.* the rule of law);
- **Meta-norms** or secondary rules addressed to the organs of application to guide them in their job (meta-norms *e.g.* the principle of conform interpretation);
- Norms of a supra-systemic nature obtained by induction from the **comparison** of different legal systems (*e.g.* non contractual liability).

Any of these can be expressly formulated in a provision of law (in the legal language of the Constitutional texts or even in the key rulings of the higher Courts) or they can be implied or inferred from a set of provisions (or from legislative language) as will be seen in Part Four. At any rate their incomplete formal structure (principles lack a clear normative consequence and simply postulate a given value or state of affairs as being desirable), their vagueness and/or ambiguity, their programmatic nature and their higher normative rank call for a specific process of reasoning, or a special methodology of weighing and balancing which is not so clearly applicable to rules in the strict sense.

3.3.3 Specificity of general *constitutional* principles of EC law

We have already warned about some of the difficulties involved in the quest for general legal principles of a constitutional nature. In a certain sense it is easier to identify the principles of the law of nations (e.g. the UN Charter), procedural principles or administrative principles or even private law principles, or amongst those general principles that could be termed constitutional it may be easier to identify fundamental rights. What is specifically constitutional about some general legal principles? This question very much depends on the meaning of constitutionalism.

3.3.3.1 The meaning of Constitutionalism

This paper cannot delve into a full treatment of the notion of constitutionalism, a matter which has largely occupied public lawyers and political scientists. Inevitably over-simplification is in order in this section if the argument of the paper is to get to its climax.

The standard view, adopted in this paper, is more or less the following:

> The constitution deals with (1) the control of power in society and the protection of the individual *vis-à-vis* public power, the elimination of absolute power because of the rule of law (everybody is bound by the law and its procedures) and of fundamental rights which cannot be breached, (2) the federal dynamics, the relations between the different component entities and the territorial organisation of the polis (distribution of competences between different levels of administration), (3) the mechanisms for ensuring and encouraging the participation of citizens (and to some degree aliens) in the public domain either directly or through representatives and procedures for electing those representatives and those who hold public office (parties, unions, NGOs, lobbies, etc.), (4) the hierarchy and structure between the sources of law and (5) the organisation of a decision-making process, the relations between the institutions (separation and balance of powers); this all being the result or the reconstruction of a social contract which makes social life in the polity possible.

A more **empirical** and comparative approach to "constitution" would ask how political power is organised and look for the basic features of the legal-political-social order. This approach, as compared to the value-laden conception expressed above, would not require any particular value to be incorporated in the conception of "constitution".

A **historicist** approach would perceive the constitution as the culmination or crystallisation of a power process, a chain of events that shape a given conception of the constitution through time, adding on, reinterpreting or altering fundamental aspects in different epochs, even if this is not always translated into a single document.

There is also a more **canonical** or formalistic approach that looks at the documents or instruments that contain such basic features. The constitution will then include anything that is incorporated into a text called "Constitution".

A **subjective** approach would rather look for the nature of the *constituting process*, the social dynamics and movements that lead to a body of thought containing some or all of the elements (1 to 5) described above. This approach emphasizes the ideals that moved the actors or catalysors involved in the process, the motos they used, the phantoms they were reacting against, or the interests, social movements and lobbies behind them, *e.g.* the Federalist in the USA, the drafters of the Constitution such as Robert Marjolin or Jean Monnet; the key judges that have made sense of the Constitution such as Robert Lecourt or Federico Mancini, the key theoreticians that have reworked it such as Eric Stein, Emile Noel or Hans Schermers, or even the key documents that inspired the process *e.g.* the Schuman Declaration calling for submitting the production of Franco-German coal and steel under the control of a High Authority, etc. In this view of things, the constitution or constitutionalising process brings about a body of thought which contains the elements described above and can be termed constitutionalism and eventually contributes to the creation of new *demos* based on civic or constitutional identity.

Constitutionalism could thus refer to a bunch of ideas, one of which fundamentally insists that the interactions that take place in social setting are to be governed by a set of authoritative rules. In modern legal systems, these rules both constitute the formal institutions of governance, and specify how all other public acts are to be produced, applied, and interpreted. The constitutional law deserves the attention it gets because of its capacity to organise social structure into a system of hierarchically-ordered rules. The most important feature of constitutionalism is the existence of a mechanism to interpret and defend the constitution as higher law. A system with open-ended higher law rules with an active constitutional interpreter is subject to volatility and constant change. A constitutional system tends to constitute and reconstitute itself through rule-making by way of judicial interpretations. It is therefore hardly workable from a theoretical and methodological perspective to speak about "valid constitutional law" as a snapshot-reflection of the state of affairs in a polity. [12]Alec Stone rightly points out that "...constitutionalism can have no fixed social meaning, except in the most abstract (and, therefore, least social) sense. When we look closely, it shows us 'many faces'".[13]

3.3.3.2 The European Constitution

Not only are there difficulties in defining what is specifically constitutional about some general principles *of law*, but even more so when trying to capture specifically *constitutional* principles amongst the general principles of *European Community law.*

12. Alec Stone Sweet, and James A. Caporaso, "From Free Trade to Supranational Polity: The European Court and Integration," in Wayne Sandholtz and Alec Stone Sweet, eds., *European Integration and Supranational Governance* (Oxford, UK: Oxford University Press, 1998): 92-133.
13. Ibid.

The constitutional culture of the EC or the EU is itself in question. One would have to take into account the special manner in which the EC was brought about as an economic enterprise, the very difficult tension between the Member States and the Common Institutions, the important and influential currents of thought at the time: neo-functionalism, instrumentalism, and the value-laden nature of the enterprise. The new system had to be autonomous from the rest of the laws, but this could not mean ideology-free. In an attempt to sort out particular aspects of the European supra-Constitution one would have to deal with the notion of the single and common market, with federalism and variable geometry, with an Institutional framework and decision-making process that tries to find a balance between intergovernmentalism and supranationality, with the place of the Union in the international order (Art. 11 of TEU), with Subsidiarity and institutional autonomy and with Citizenship and Human Rights (Art. 6 TEU and Art. 17 TEC).

The creation of the European Communities, the constitutionalising process which started with the Treaty of Paris and continued with the Treaties of Rome, Maastricht and Amsterdam and with the Intergovernmental Conferences, constitutional conventions such as the Luxembourg agreement, and the key judgments of the Court, has given rise to a special form of European Constitutionalism, which is very dynamic but quite independent from the constitutionalising process of the Member States.[14] The end result is not important for the meaning of European constitutionalism. It is the process itself that matters and the key to the process is the fact that, in certain strategically important areas, the constitutive Member States have relinquished their sovereign powers for a common enterprise and have undertaken to treat nationals of other Member States as their own, removing any unjustified obstacle to free movement and refraining from any public intervention to favour their own nationals and place them in a more competitive position. This project is to be accomplished by an autonomous system of law, Community law, which has its own logic and which will develop its own formal and material legal principles. Enquiring about the end result and trying to categorise it into neat legal families such as "state", "confederation", "international organisation", etc. simply misses the point that it is the constitutionalising process that matters and that maybe there is no end result. It is therefore suggested that one rids oneself of the conceptual categories of state constitutions, and approaches the issue of the European Constitution with a fresh frame of mind.

Indeed the ideology or political values which inspired the very creation of the European Economic Community – liberal democracy, open market economy with free competition – against the background of totalitarian regimes and planned economies,

14. On the process on the constitutionalisation of the treaties, see: Federico G. Mancini, "The Making of a Constitution for Europe.," in *The New European Community*, eds. Robert O. Keohane and Stanley Hoffmann (Boulder, CO: West View, 1991); For an account of the relation of legal and political integration see Alec Stone Sweet and Thomas L. Brunell, "Constructing a Supranational Constitution: Dispute Resolution and Governance in the European Community," *American Political Science Review* 92 (1998): 63-81; and Joseph H. H. Weiler, "The Transformation of Europe," *Yale Law Journal* 100 (1991): 2403-83.

and the creation of the European Union, where the socio-economic and ideological divisions between East and West, the establishment of a single currency and the new economy have given way to a single market vision (*marché unique*) which seems to correspond with a *pensée unique* in politics and macro-economics (liberal Welfare democracy), are to become guiding principles that feed on to the development of the system and allow to incorporate a certain dimension of political morality into the seemingly pure system of autonomous law. In any analysis of constitutional principles, one must not neglect the ideological points of departure of the constitutuional enterprise. After all the term "principle" refers to the starting point, the origin, the primary cause, (this is very clear in Spanish: *el principio*).

3.3.3.3 Principles as substance and principles as process

It is therefore important to bear in mind the ideological background of the project of European integration, because the constitutional principles inspiring this process will be resorted to in order to develop the legal system or to give it (political-ideological) integrity and coherence and in order to interpret it and solve new problems. The very need to develop the process of integration will originate constitutional principles specific to European integration. Some of the principles will be already mentioned in the Treaties, and others will have to be constructed.

Some principles (i) define the nature of the whole project – open market economy, democracy and fundamental rights including social rights, an area of freedom, security and justice – others will (ii) strive to enhance the legitimacy of the project of integration – ensure economic and social progress, regional cohesion, improving the living and working conditions, preserve and strengthen peace and liberty, incorporation of socio-economic actors into the law-making process – or to (iii) enhance the legitimacy of the legal system devised for integration – the rule of law, procedural guarantees, European citizenship, fundamental rights, transparency – other principles will (iv) ensure its autonomous nature – interpretation in conformity with EC law, *acte clair*, direct effect, autonomous community meaning, external competences, completeness of remedies – others will (v) articulate the relations between the system and those of the Member States – supranationality and primacy, attributed powers, institutional and procedural autonomy, subsidiarity, community loyalty, the construction of a European identity but respect for the history, culture and traditions of the peoples of Europe – others will (vi) ensure the effectiveness of the project – uniformity, direct effect, effective remedies, Member State liability, single administration, multi-speed integration or variable geometry – and yet others will (vii) indicate how to handle new social issues – subsidiarity, openness, proportionality, sustainable development, data protection, social progress, environmental protection, and agreement between social partners. As can be seen, some principles may perform different functions or be inspired by different processes. Thus the principle of non-contractual liability for damages caused to individuals in breach of EC law responds to different rationales: dissuading possible applicants from bringing actions against the institutions or completing the mechanism of sanctions against a Member State that does not comply with EC law.

As the preceding paragraph shows, the General Constitutional Principles of EC law can be seen in two different ways. They can be seen in isolation if one looks at each of the principles inside the hyphens, trying to define their content, their normative impact and implications, their contours and their systemic relations with other principles, their difficulties of application and interpretation or their place in the system of law, the provisions that sustain them or their theoretical construction from other sources. But they can also be analysed according to the function they perform or even the process by which they are brought about. Thus, Nos. i to vii of the previous paragraph look at the functions these principles perform and Part Five will analyse the process by which they are introduced and the interests behind those who allege them and incorporate them into the decision-making process and ultimately into the legal system. This second approach to principles as processes, which will be developed in Part Five, is as important as the first, more conventional analysis of principles as norms.

3.3.4 A provisional classification of the general principles of Community law of a constitutional character

This part looks at principles as norms rather than processes. There are two major levels of analysis: the language used by the Treaties itself and the theoretical language which has reconstructed a theory of principles from the Treaties and from other theoretical material.

The first, superficial or elementary level looks at the very Treaties and sorts out the provisions where the term principle or principles is **used by legal language itself**. The following is a rushed list of instances where the English version of the Treaties (TEC and TEU) use the term "principle". The list, which has been tested by a word processing program, does not claim to be complete but it will at least give an indication of the degree of precision achieved by the drafters when using the term "principle". The expression "in principle", as used in *e.g.* Article 18(2) TEU, is omitted form the list.

*In the **Treaty establishing the European Community**:*

The Preamble of the Treaty contains principles, as Article 182 explicitly recognises, and therefore all the elements of the preamble could be considered principles, but the term is used explicitly only once in order to refer to "the principles of the Charter of the United Nations".

- Part One is entitled "Principles" and therefore all the provisions contained therein (Articles 1 to 16) are to be classified as principles in the legal language of the Treaty. Inside Part One, Article 4(3) is particularly interesting in that it requires the Member States to comply with the following economic "guiding principles": stable prices, sound public finances and monetary conditions and a sustainable balance of payments.
- Article 5 contains "the principle of subsidiarity"

- Finally, Article 16 uses the term in an odd way: the Community and the Member States "shall take care that [public] services of general economic interest operate on the basis of principles and conditions which enable them to fulfil their missions". Here "principles" seems to be synonymous with *conditions* or with *rules*.
- Article 31(2) imposes a standstill clause on Member States by referring to a principle allegedly stated in the preceding paragraph: all monopolies of a commercial character shall be adjusted so that no discrimination obtains between nationals of Member States regarding the conditions under which goods are procured and marketed. The principle in question is non-discrimination.
- Article 44(2)(e) refers to "the principles laid down in Article 33(2)" which, in turn, does not use the term "principle" but talks about the objectives of the Common Agricultural Policy. Here "principle" is synonymous with goals or *objectives*.
- Article 47(2) has another odd use of the term: the Council shall decide on directives the implementation of which involves in at least one Member State amendment of the existing principles laid down by law governing the professions with respect to training and conditions of access for natural persons". Here "principles" seems to refer to rather *specific rules*. These rules do not seem to be particularly fundamental or crucial.
- Article 71(2) speaks of the provisions concerning the principles of the regulatory system for transport, which are probably those contained in letters (a) to (d) of paragraph 1. Here "principles" gathers in its reference a whole area or sector of the law, a *legal sub-system* encompassing common rules, conditions, measures and any other provisions. Let it be said, in passing, that paragraph 2 is very poorly drafted in English (the French version is much clearer).
- Articles 83(1) and 85 refers to the rules on competition laid down in Articles 81 and 82 as "principles" and imply that principles can be infringed, but Article 86(1) refers to them, more accurately, as rules. True, the rules on competition are the keystone of the Treaty. Here, principles and *important rules* are synonyms.
- Article 98 requires the Community and the Member States to act "in accordance with the principle of an open market economy with free competition, favouring an efficient allocation of resources, and in compliance with the principles set out in Article 4."
- Article 105(1) uses identical terms to impose the same obligation on the European System of Central Banks, ESCB,
- Article 108 talks about a principle which is nowhere stated: "the Community institutions and bodies and the governments of the Member States undertake to respect this principle...". Only the initiates will know it refers to the principle of independence of the ECB, the national central banks or their members from any institution, government or body. Indeed the preceding sentence forbids those banks from taking any instructions from such institutions and governments.
- Article 133(1) states that "the common commercial policy shall be based on uniform principles", probably referring to *common rules* regarding "changes in tariff rates, the conclusion of tariff and trade agreements, the achievement of

uniformity in measures of liberalisation, export policy and measures to protect trade such as those to be taken in the event of dumping or subsidies". The term principle does not seem proper in this context.

- Article 141 requires each Member state to "ensure that the principle of equal pay for male and female workers for equal work or work of equal value is applied". Paragraph 3 refers to the "principle of equal opportunities and equal treatment of men and women in matters of employment and occupation, including the principle of equal pay. Here the Treaty seems to distinguish between different levels of generality between principles since the principle of equal opportunities and equal treatment includes the principle of equal pay. Paragraph 4 also refers to the principle of equal treatment as a general rule which allows for a more specific provision for affirmative action.
- Article 174(2) dictates, in not very elegant English, that the Community policy on the environment "shall be based on the precautionary principle and on the principles that preventive action should be taken, that environmental damage should, as a priority, be rectified at source and that the polluter should pay",
- Article 175(5) refers to "the principle that the polluter should pay" as a general rule that may have exceptions if it involves costs deemed disproportionate.
- Article 182, paragraph 3 refers to "the principles set out in the Preamble to this Treaty" as a framework for the association of the overseas countries and territories. Here "principles" refers to *values, ideals*, etc.
- Article 187 refers to the principles set out in the Treaty, which shall be taken into account in order to adopt the detailed rules and procedure for the overseas countries and territories. Here the principles seems to refer to the fundamental norms of the Treaty.
- Article 190(4) requires the European Parliament to "draw up a proposal for elections by direct universal suffrage in accordance with a uniform procedure in all Member States or in accordance with principles *common* in all Member States". Here the use of principles seems to require a *comparative analysis* of parliamentary election laws of the Member States and seems to assume that there are common principles to be found, but allows an alternative solution which is to agree on a uniform procedure should those common principles not really exist.
- Article 202 provides that in case of delegation to the Commission of normative powers to ensure the implementation of Council acts, the delegation procedures "must be consonant with principles and rules to be laid in advance by the Council ...". Here "principles" is synonymous with rules and seems an unnecessary reverberation.
- Article 213(2) is similar to Article 108, but as regards the Members of the Commission. The greater detail of this provision makes it clearer that the principle in question is that of *independence in the performance of their duties*.
- Article 255(2) provides that the Council shall determine "*general principles* and limits on grounds of public or private interest governing [the] right of access to documents". General principles are to be seen here as *rules*.
- Article 274, paragraph 1, requires the Commission to "implement the budget ...

having regard to the principles of sound financial management", and requires the Member States to "cooperate with the Commission to ensure that the appropriations are used with the principles of sound financial management". Here principles refer to the particular guidelines or *rules of the trade*.

- Article 288, paragraph 2 (ex Article 215), is the only reference to the *general principles common to the laws of the Member States*, which shall be resorted to in the case of non-contractual liability of the Community.
- Finally, Article 309(2) provides for sanctions in case of a serious and persistent breach by a Member State of principles mentioned in Article 6(1) of the Treaty on European Union.

*In the **Treaty on European Union**:*

The **Preamble** confirms the attachment of the Member States "to the principles of liberty, democracy and respect for human rights and fundamental freedoms and of the rule of law" , it further states that "the principle of sustainable development" must be taken into account, and it finally declares that decisions are to be "taken as closely as possible to the citizen in accordance with the principle of subsidiarity".

- Article 1 refers to a principle in the French version, but not in the English version. The French text requires respect for the principe d'ouverture, a principle which is ommited in the English version and which means that decisions are taken as openly as possible
- Article 2, paragraph two, requires respect for the principle of subsidiarity as defined in Article 5 EC
- Article 6(1) founds the Union "on the "principles of liberty, democracy, respect for human rights and fundamental freedoms, and the rule of law" identically to the preamble, and states that these principles are "common to the Member States" and Article 7(1) implies that these principles could be seriously and persistently breached by a Member State, in which case a procedure may be opened that could lead to sanctions being imposed.
- Article 6(2) raises fundamental rights – as guaranteed by the ECHR and as they result from the constitutional traditions common to the Member States – to the status of "general principles of Community law" and requires the Union to respect them.
- Article 11(1) imposes on the Union the objectives of safeguarding "the common values, fundamental interests, independence and integrity of the Union in conformity with the principles of the United Nations Charter" and of preserving peace and strengthening "international security in accordance with the principles of the UN Charter, as well as the principles of the Helsinki Fina Act...". More generally Article 11(2), paragraph 3, raises all the objectives and values mentioned in the whole Article to the level of principles that must be complied with: loyalty and mutual solidarity.
- Article 12 provides that the Union will define "the principles and general guidelines for the common foreign and security policy", a task which Article 13(1)

explicitly confers on the European Council. The two terms are synonyms.

- Article 14(2) allows the Council to "review the principles and objectives" of a joint action it has adopted. Here "principles" can be synonymous with terms.
- Article 43(1)(b) states that a closer cooperation decided between some Member States must respect "the principles of the said Treaties"(EC and EU). Here "principles" can mean anything. This is the vaguest reference to principles in the whole system. The norm, as it stands, allows for an extreme margin of appreciation.
- Finally, Article 49, paragraph 1, recognises a right of any European State which respects the principles set out in Article 6(1) to apply to become a member of the Union.

The analysis of the use of the term " principle" by the Treaties has indicated a variety of meanings, and a lack of consistency of usage which makes it extremely difficult to elaborate a theory based exclusively on the normative language.

A second level of analysis would operate with a theoretical notion of principle and identify a given provision or a group of provisions found in the Treaties, or at least norms implied by these which constitute instances of the **theoretical notion of principle**. This second level requires a theory of general constitutional principles of law as sketched in Parts 1 and 2 of this paper. The following is a re-elaboration of the classification which was put forward in Bengoetxea: 1993 (LRECJ:1993):

Constitutional principles which define the legal structure of the Community and the scope of EC law within the Member States: autonomy, direct effect, direct applicability, primacy, supremacy, uniformity, single administration, attributed competences, subsidiarity and respect for national identities, multilingualism, conform interpretation, loyalty to the Community, institutional autonomy, Member State liability (from the point of view of the efficiency of the system of remedies), Multiple speed integration or variable geometry in certain areas... This supralegality is drawn from the system by the ECJ and also in many cases from express provisions of the Treaty: *e.g.* subsidiarity or derived by implication from such express provisions *e.g.* Community loyalty or attributions of competences,

Fundamental principles which assure the protection of the citizens from public authorities and thus legitimise the system: these are related to the very legitimacy of law: rule of law, democracy (transparency, openness, and public access), fundamental rights, non-discrimination, effectiveness of judicial protection or access to justice, procedural autonomy but effective protection, Member State liability (from the point of view of the individual); these are drawn mainly from the constitutional traditions of the MS, from international instruments to which they adhere (esp. the ECHR) and also from the system of the Treaty. These traditions and instruments thus become sources of EC law principles derived from the legal systems of the MS as General principles of Law which only have an indirectly constitutional nature, by virtue of their being devised to protect the individual; many principles of administrative law fit here (retroactive removal of unlawful acts, proportionality, non-payment in days of strike, *force majeure e.g.* in customs law, collegiality) as do principles of legal procedure (*non bis in idem*, equality of arms, confidentiality), arguably also the principle of consumer protection or the principle of sustainability or of environmental protection, socio-economic rights could perhaps also fit here since all Member States have, for instance, a Social Security system,

Special standing of certain provisions of a fundamental nature: non-discrimination, national treatment, the basic freedoms, the open market economy, free competition and perhaps in this sense one can talk about the economic constitution (the European model: single market, open market economy, free competition and limited public intervention in the economy, control of inflation as the new Grundnorm, reduction of public debt?)

Applying these theoretical notions of general principles of Community law and relying on the notion of European constitutionality sketched in Part 2 of this paper, the following is a provisional classification of the constitutional principles of Community law (and the European Union) into basic political premises and constitutional principles:

3.3.4.1 Very general Constitutional Principles or basic political premises

- Regional integration and cohesion
- Divided power system
- Member States as Masters of the Treaty
- Integrity of the EU
- The rule of law (one can be doubtful as regards EU)
- Democracy (or a specific version of it for the Union, but a more conventional view as regards criteria of accession to the EC)

Constitutional principles of Community law:

- A single institutional framework
- The separation of powers
- Limited powers
- Implied powers
- Attributed competences or powers
- Institutional balance
- Institutional autonomy
- Duty of loyalty to the Community
- Cooperation between institutions
- Cooperation between Community institutions and Member State institutions
- Cooperation between the different Member States
- Supremacy
- Direct effect
- Pre-emption
- Subsidiarity
- Non-discrimination
- Respect for fundamental rights

- Respect for national identities
- Respect for diversity (social progress)
- Respect of general principles of law
- Non-retroactivity
- Certainty
- Legitimate expectations

3.3.5 The process of reasoning with principles

3.3.5.1 The study of outcomes and processes

In the foreword of Takis Tridimas'*The General Principles of EC Law* Advocate General Jacobs claims that "...the role of general principles cannot be assessed in the abstract but only by reference to results reached in concrete cases: to be of any use, the study of such principles has to be the study of outcomes."[15] This proposition reflects a traditional pragmatic approach applied by legal scholarship. We do not deny that one can learn something about general principles of EC law merely by studying court cases and their outcomes or results, but this paper intends to suggest a broader approach. In order to enhance knowledge about how European society develops and transforms through juridical discourse, one must try to assess legal principles with regard to their "normative quality". This necessarily requires a theoretical approach. If one for example wants to understand current phenomena like "the judicialization of politics" or "the politization of law" a theoretical study of legal principles is in order.

If one looks at the processes of law making with principles rather than at the outcomes (the substantive principles themselves) the following proposition about how European society constitutes itself and evolves can be made by reference to Alec Stone Sweet and James Caporaso. They make four interesting propositions in relation to the law making process.

They suggest that trade between the Member States (transnational exchange) generates social demands for dispute resolution, and that higher levels of crossnational activity will produce more conflicts between Member State law and EC law, and therefore more preliminary references and greater harmonisation through interpretation. Secondly, higher levels of transnational activity will push for supranational rules to replace local rules. Third, the law making of a well functioning legislative and judicial branch will then feed back on European integration and on an emerging European society (*ubi ius ibi societas).* Thirdly, the consolidation and expansion of European governance will fuel more transnational activity, and provide the normative context for more references for preliminary rulings, in an increasing number of domains. Fourthly, to the extent that the above propositions hold, transnational activity, transnational dispute resolution, and the production of European legislation will develop interdependently, and this interdependence will drive European integration in predictable ways. They then underline that these

15. Tridimas, The General Principles of EC Law, Oxford 1999, p. x.

propositions depend critically on the constitutional principles of supremacy and direct effect.[16]

This process implies that rule making in courts basically depends and develops through policy inputs made by the litigants. Courts only adapt the rules to the interests of the litigants. In this process, the litigants advance interests by reference to legal principles, the courts react and adapt the principles and feed them back onto society. Our point is that the open-ended anatomy of legal principles make them perfectly suitable for the advancement of interests. They form and operate outside the narrow frame of the traditional sources of law used in legal scholarship. They operate on different levels and in different contexts of the law-making process. The role of principles in the law making process has to be assessed as normative entities in courts, in the legislative process, at the level of social interaction between people and traders and in the context of litigation. By applying a broader account of the role of legal principles in the law making process we hopefully will learn more about how morals and politics are incorporated in the legal system.

Although we to some extent draw on the findings of Stone and Caporoso (and others) who argue that the integration process is driven by a connection forged between transnational activity, the responses of the institutions to that activity and the enactment and construction of supranational rules and principles, we recognize that judges do not simply or only respond to demands generated by litigants; they authoritatively interpret abstract legal rules to the concrete requirements of the legal system. We would like to shift focus to some jurisprudential problems linked to the normativity of legal principles in the process of judicial interpretation and justification.

3.3.5.2 The interdependence between outcomes and process

3.3.5.2.1 Legal principles and adjudication

Let us turn back to the courts. As implied above we think that there exists an important link between legal principles as normative outcomes, shaped with regard to internal exigencies of the legal system like legal certainty and coherence, and the surrounding socio-political claims of justice and legitimacy. Thus, legal principles as outcomes are construed in close relation to interests expressed in the process of law making.

We still find it catchy to proceed from a starting-point where we assume that the judicial interpretations of the ECJ are subject to constraints posed by the normative structure of EC law and the judicial and legislative division of competences between the EU and the Member States. Lord Denning put this neatly in *Bulmer v. Bollinger*:

> "The Treaty is quite unlike any of the enactments to which we have been accustomed...It lays down general principles. It expresses its aim and purposes. All in sentences of moderate length and commendable style. But it lacks precision. It uses words and phrases without defining what they mean. An English lawyer

16. Stone Sweet and Caporaso 1998.

> would look for an interpretation clause, but he would look in vain. There is none. All the way through the Treaty there are gaps and lacunae. These have to be filled in by the judges, or by regulations or directives. It is the European way...Seeing these differences, what are the English courts to do when they are faced with a problem of interpretation? They must follow the European pattern. No longer must they argue about the precise grammatical sense. They must look to the purpose and intent...They must divine the spirit of the Treaty and gain inspiration from it. If they find a gap, they must fill it in as best they can...These are the principles, as I understand it, on which the European Court acts."[17]

The link between interpretation and the principled normative structure is reflected in the justifications of the judge-made constitutional principles governing the relationship between EC law and national law. In *Francovich* the ECJ stated that the principle of non-contractual liability of the Member States has to be viewed "...in the light of the general system of the Treaty and its fundamental principles."[18] In *CILFIT* the ECJ stated that

> "...every provision of Community law must be placed in its context and interpreted in the light of the provisions of Community law as a whole, regard being had to the objectives thereof and to its state of evolution at the date on which the provision in question is to be applied."[19]

The ECJ's interpretative strategy seems to be based on the idea of EC law as a system where *lacunae* exist. Thus, many situations are not governed by a rule of law. In such cases the ECJ will resolve the case by deducing from the existing rules a rule or principle which is in conformity with underlying substantive as well as structural premises on which the legal system is based. The conventional picture implies that *lacunae* are more likely to arise in EC law since it is a new legal order in constant flux.. In this context the ECJ (and legal scholarship) emphasises the ideal of coherence. The existence of *lacunae* and the quest for coherence seem to be the primary justification for the authority of the ECJ exercising extensive judicial discretion.

In the context of the gap-filling function of general principles of law the question of judicial law-making arises. The significance of general principles of law is two-fold in judicial law-making: they are relied upon in gap-filling and they bear a determinative influence on the interpretation of written rules.

The function of general principles of law in adjudication raises the theoretical questions which stem from the continuum between strict rule application and judicial legislation. A middle term found here could be labelled "the method of coherence". This is a method through which judges can make new rules of law without consulting their own legislative preferences. Coherence rule making is more or less distinct from

---

17. *Bulmer v. Bollinger* [1974] 2 All E R 1226 s 1237.
18. Joined Cases C-6/90 and C-9/90, *Francovich* [1991] ECR I-5357 p. 30.
19. Case 283/81 *CILFIT* [1982] ECR 3415 p. 20.

the method of developing the definitions of the words in legal rules as an aid to applying them. The method focuses on the choice among different rules proposed to solve a gap, conflict or ambiguity of a legal system seen as an ensemble of rules.[20] The coherence method is elaborated by Dworkin who defines judicial interpretation as follows: "...constructive interpretation is a matter of imposing purpose on an object or practice in order to make of it the best possible example of the form or genre to which it is taken to belong."[21]

We accept that the Community judge is making law by treating the whole corpus of rules as a product of an ideology of integration. By employing the method of coherence or integrity with recourse to general principles of law as gap-fillers or interpretative influence the Community judge can do ideological work when he or she furthers a particular regime by developing it in the face of a gap, conflict or ambiguity. Integration thus becomes the leitmotiv of integrity or coherence.[22]

3.3.5.2.2 Legal principles and judicial discretion

We have claimed that constitutional principles found institutions and place a normative frame on the law making process. Another important strand of constitutionalism is the interpretative mechanism of the constitutional norms, in our case the European Court of Justice cooperating with the national courts under the system of preliminary rulings.

The courts perform their functions in a world of more or less indeterminate norms. While adjudicating, their decisions have to simultaneously fulfil requirements of legal certainty and coherence on the one hand and legitimacy and justice on the other hand. These requirements create theoretical tensions closely linked to the problem of determining the limits of the judicial discretion of the ECJ.

Let us try to define judicial discretion as the authority vested in the judge to make a choice between two or more conceivable alternatives. The legal element of the concept appears in the form of a requirement that the choice must be found within the realm of law. The choice has to be based on a valid legal norm. This definition, which safely rests within the boundaries of legal positivism, is of limited use if we try to establish any significant limitations on judicial discretion by reference to general principles of law. Some attempts have been made but they seem to result in very general propositions. One of the main reasons are stated by Iris Canor: "...despite this consistent development of general principles, often one can find conflicting principles in the same legal order."[23]

One example can be drawn from the theoretical consequenses of the ECJ's structuring of EC law and its supremacy doctrine. In the judiciaries of the Member States

20. Kennedy, *A Critique of Adjudication*, Harvard 1997, p. 33.
21. Dworkin, *Law's Empire*, Cambridge Mass. 1986, p. 52.
22. Bengoetxea, MacCormick and Moral, forthcoming
23. Canor, *The Limits of Judicial Discretion in the European Court of Justice*, Nomos 1998, p. 148.

doubts have been expressed about the ECJ's doctrine of absolute supremacy of EC law as possessing the prerequisites to constitute the basis of a common European constitution. It has been pointed out that the question as to what extent the Member States have transferred powers to the EC/EU both theoretically and practically is an issue for the constitutional law of the Member States. The interest of uniform application of EC law must be set against the interest of Member States asserting their constitutional integrity. A legal positivist might say that this state of affairs creates a problem of coherence. If it is the case that the ECJ's doctrine of supremacy aims to change the validity of the EC legal system, it cannot itself be exposed to a test of validity and cannot thereby be considered legally valid. From the legal positivists' point of view the ECJ's doctrine of "a new legal system" is in this respect self-destructive. As it constitutes an alteration of the legal system's grundnorm it cannot be legally binding for the courts in the Member States.

But how shall we deal with the principal question of competing principles? How shall we reconcile the concept of sovereignty and competing sources of principles with the requirement of coherence in the legal system. We claim that we have to avoid the "all or nothing" choice, and seek to describe the relationship between competing legal principles from the starting point where several applicable principles co-exist and overlap each other. The main point is that classical legal positivism cannot serve as a starting-point for proposals to solve conflicts of principles. The problematic interdependence between law and politics as the foundation for legal principles forces legal positivism to refer conflicts of principles to the political arena. Thus, legal positivism fails to determine any significant limits on the judicial discretion of the ECJ.

The normative hierarchy of national constitutional rights *vis à vis* European law, international and European conventions of human rights and national statutory rights has become confused and ambiguous. Normative statements in judgments or other legal decisions aiming to resolve legal disputes are no longer to be regarded as logical conclusions derived from formulation of legal norms presupposed to be valid taken together with statements of fact which are assumed to be proven or true. Thus, the link between indeterminate principles of constitutional law and legal interpretation unfolds what can be described as a crisis of formal reasoning. This description could be sustained by a number of reasons: the vagueness of legal language, the possibility of conflict between norms, the fact that there are cases requiring a legal statement which do not fall under an existing valid legal norm, and the possibility of a decision which is contrary to the wording of the statute.[24]

As Neil MacCormick has suggested, this takes us from the issue of judicial activism when dealing with gaps, contradictions, interpretation in hard cases, to the broader sphere of practical (rational?) argumentation where the values and principles appropriate to the institutions of the societies, the states and the supranational and international communities are taken into account: the meaning of constitutionalism, Rechtsstaatlichkeit, democracy and the rule of law, separation of powers, distribution

24. Robert Alexy, *A Theory of Legal Argumentation*, Oxford Clarendon Press 1989, p. 1 (footnotes omitted).

of competences, procedural justice, protection of individual rights, citizenship, equality before the law, integrity of public office.[25]

Principles could thus be seen as a shorthand for political morality, but it would be acceptable shorthand; reasoning from principles professes a claim to validity and legitimacy in the legal community. Principles dosify political interferences in legal discourse, they filter them and they hide or disguise them; invoking a principle may be a way of introducing a new norm in a surreptitious manner. But the open debate on the political principle is not allowed because it does not fit into the judicial system: it is not standard practice to discuss political or moral values in the courts, they have to be distilled into legal spirit and principles are just fine distillers. A complex question of political morality may thus be simplified by its incorporation into the judicial process; the social problem is simplified and the judicial process acquires political undertones. If the norm belongs to a normative system which is not legal, but political or moral, then characterising the norm as a general legal principle can be seen as an attempt to give that norm an added value, or a greater legal credibility, or at least the necessary legal pedigree. When a court, *e.g.* the ECJ, refers to General Legal Principles, it is widening its powers: where the surrounding legal-political system does not adopt certain norms that appear to be necessary at the stage of application, then the Courts, the ECJ, may find it acceptable to resort to General Principles of Law. Thus, it could be argued, in Tchernobyl, by relying on the principle of institutional balance, the ECJ expands the Treaty.

As such, legal principles may perform a double function of (i) opening the system to important shared values constitutive of political morality and thus of legitimising the law and (ii) improving the system by adding to its overall coherence and integrity and they may further the cause of integration as a dynamic expression or leitmotiv of integrity or coherence. Given the increasing complexities of the Social Welfare State with a wealth of detailed rules that control discretionary power, resorting to general legal principles may help the interpreter see the light. It is in this context that, in its recent judgments, the ECJ can be seen as becoming more didactic, i.e. more principled.

But if their use is not coherent or if the judgments relying on them are not sufficiently justified, then the abuse of General Legal Principles may also hinder the process of integration and the legitimacy of Community law. This would happen if General Legal Principles were relied upon in order to extend competences or powers in favour of the Community or to shift the constitutional balance in the distribution of competences in favour of the Member State. The excessive self-restraint the Court has shown as regards the protection of fundamental rights when controlling Community acts or the judicial review of Council Regulations are messages sent in the wrong direction.

Thus human rights are principles of EC law, but there is no written catalogue of these. They can be used as a source or as a negative control of validity, but they do not give any active empowerment or competence to adopt norms in the field.[26] The

25. "Argumentation and Interpretation in Law", No. 9 *Argumentation*, 1995, p. 479.

26. As was made clear in the Opinion of the European Court on the Accession to the Convention, Opinion 2/94 [1996] ECR I-1759.

present situation is such that the ECJ can rely on these principles with a wide margin of discretion, and yet relying on general principles – *e.g.* Human Rights – will present the result of ample discretion as a standard judicial decision.

3.3.5.3 Strategies for research

One of the great dichotomies of legal and political theory is that between adjudication and legislation. The dichotomy is closely related to the distinction between a court and a legislature, between making and applying law, between law and politics and between objective and subjective questions.

Even though the ideological element in adjudication is denied or downplayed by many prominent scholars we recognise that courts both perform political functions (upholding the law and adjusting the law to new challenges) and give moral or political justifications for their decisions. By this recognition we do not mean that judges make rules merely on the basis of their personal preferences. The elements of a judge's ideological orientation are far more subtle. They consist of adherence to texts and to widely accepted societal values and *intelligentsia* rather than of clear-cut political ideologies like liberalism and socialism. Thus, when we say politics we do not mean party-politics or when we say morals we do not mean that groups or lobbies can freely influence judges.

We assume that the judge only to some extent makes law as a response to the interests of the litigants. Law making with reference to the interests of the parties could be conceptulized as responses to "external" requirements of justice, fairness or effectiveness. To elaborate on this point we need to engage in empirical investigations trying to establish relations between court practice and responses from the surrounding socio-political environment. Even if descriptively orientated studies certainly enhance our understanding of EC law they tend to distance themselves from normative evaluations. We believe that although it is difficult to find a sound theoretical basis to evaluate the ECJ's justificatory practices from a normative point of view, the most interesting enterprise is to analyse legal principles from a normative or "internal" perspective.

The most interesting and complex theoretical problems arise from the influences and constraints that are "internal" to the legal system. We believe that a major task for the judge is to adapt his or her decision to requirements of legal certainty and coherence. In the making of law the judge creates and interprets more or less indeterminate rules and principles by reference to legal ideals that stem from a Rule of Law-doctrine.

By putting emphasis on the way principles open up the legal normative structure to morals and politics we make an effort to explain the connection between the legal and political strands of integration. An attempt to formulate a normative theory of interpretation of EC legal principles which recognises the political/moral character of judicial interpretation needs to establish a link to external values of some kind. One might say that if a normative theory of interpretation is to be taken seriously it needs a connection with a comprehensive theory of legitimacy for the whole constitutional and institutional system in the broader sphere of practical reason. Such a theory has to consist of values and political ideas. Otherwise it won't bite. In our case, such values and political ideas are those put forward in point 4.2. of this contribution, and above all we find the programme for an ever closer union between the peoples of Europe.

3.4 Institutional Principles: A Special Category of General Principles of EC Law

*Bruno de Witte**

3.4.1 Institutional Principles as "General Principles"

The "general principles of EC law" play a central role in the case-law of the European Court of Justice and its Court of First Instance, and they are now a distinct and rather well-defined third major category of sources of Community law, alongside the EC Treaties and secondary law. They can be defined, for the purpose of this paper, as *unwritten principles, recognised by the European Court of Justice, that have a status of higher law by the fact that they may be invoked as a standard for the review of Community acts.* They are an important instrument for the protection of "individuals" (often, in fact, business firms!) against policies and administrative measures of the European Community and its member states, and are analysed at length in other contributions to this volume. These principles do not form the object of the present contribution. Rather, I sought to assemble some of the dispersed evidence of the existence of another category of unwritten and judge-made principles, namely the *general principles of institutional law.* They do not serve to protect the position of the individual, but rather to regulate the *relations between institutions.* Given the nature of the European Union, such institutional relations take place both at the horizontal level, between the institutions of the European Union, and in a vertical perspective, between these EU institutions and the Member States institutions, so that one can make a further distinction between *horizontal institutional principles* (like the principle of institutional balance) and *vertical institutional principles* (like the principle of subsidiarity or the principle of sincere cooperation).

These institutional principles have been studied *separately,* but hardly at all as a *category.* The reason may well be that, whereas the Court of Justice did make reference once to "the general principles on which the institutional system of the Community is based and which govern the relations between the Community and the Member States",[1] it has never developed this statement into a consistent doctrine of institutional principles. Few of the numerous books and articles devoted to general

---

* Professor of European Law, University of Maastricht. This contribution is a revised version of a paper published in F. Snyder (ed), *The Europeanisation of Law* (Oxford: Hart Publishing, 2000)

1. Joined Cases 205 to 215/82, *Deutsche Milchkontor v. Germany,* [1983] ECR 2633, paragraph 17.

Ulf Bernitz and Joakim Nergelius (eds.), General Principles of European Community Law, 143–159

principles of EC law deal with institutional principles.[2] One could consider this as a simple oversight and think that the concept of general principles of EC law is broad enough to include also the institutional principles.[3] Or one could, alternatively, consider that institutional principles form a distinct reality, and that the use of the common word "principles" hides a profound difference with the "general principles of EC law". The latter approach, then, leaves open the question of how this distinct reality fits within the overall picture of the system of sources of EC law and EU law.

An answer to the foregoing questions presupposes a more precise definition of the concept of "general principles of institutional law". By the word "general", I intend to refer to those institutional principles that apply to horizontal or vertical institutional relations in general, and thereby exclude the institutional principles which are (i) limited to specific subject areas of European Union policy (like, for instance, monetary policy[4] or environmental policy),[5] (ii) limited to the functioning of one particular institution (like, for instance, the Commission),[6] and (iii) limited to

2. Reference can be made to two recently published books which, while offering a full analysis of the general principles of EC law, do not deal with institutional principles: J.A. Usher, *General Principles of EC Law* (London: Longman, 1998), and T. Tridimas, *The General Principles of EC Law* (Oxford: OUP, 1999). Similarly limited to "traditional" general principles are the following essays: A. Adinolfi, "I principi generali nella giurisprudenza comunitaria e la loro influenza sugli ordinamenti degli Stati membri", *Rivista italiana di diritto pubblico comunitario* (1994) 521; A. Massera, "I principi generali", in M.P. Chiti and G. Greco, *Trattato di diritto amministrativo europeo – Parte generale* (Milano: Giuffrè, 1997) 431; G. Nolte, "General Principles of German and European Administrative Law – A Comparison in Historical Perspective", *The Modern Law Review* (1994) 191. A few institutional principles are covered, but only very briefly, by R.-E. Papadopoulou, *Principes généraux du droit et droit communautaire* (Bruxelles: Bruylant, 1996).
3. This is the view proposed, but not elaborated, by D. Simon, "Y a-t-il des principes généraux du droit communautaire?", *Droits* n.14 (1991) 73, p.79 (who calls them "*principes généraux de droit de type constitutionnel"*); the same view is repeated in D. Simon, *Le système juridique communautaire* (Paris: PUF, 1997), p. 231.
4. Article 4 EC Treaty (ex Article 3a) states that economic and monetary policy shall be conducted "in accordance with the principle of an open market economy" and, in its section 3, that the activities of the EC and its Member States in these fields "shall entail compliance with the following guiding principles: stable prices, sound public finances and monetary conditions and a sustainable balance of payments."
5. Article 174 EC (ex Article 130r) stipulates that environmental policy "shall be based on the precautionary principle and on the principles that preventive ation should be taken, that environmental damage should as a priority be rectified at source and that the polluter should pay."
6. The principle of *collegiality*, which governs the functioning of the European Commission, has played a role in several recent Court cases, such as: Case C-137/92P, *Commission v. BASF and others*, [1994] ECR I-2555, paragraph 63; Case C-191/95, *Commission v. Germany*, judgment of 29 September 1998 (not yet reported), paragraphs 33 to 51; Case T-266/97, *Vlaamse Televisie Maatschappij v. Commission*, judgment of 8 July 1999 (not yet reported), paragraph 49.

specific institutional contexts or niches (like, for instance, budgetary matters).[7] By the term "principles of law", I want to refer essentially to the institutional principles that form an independent source of legal obligations. This is by no means the only sense in which the term "principle" is used in the case-law of the ECJ or in the legal literature. Sometimes, the term is used to emphasise the particular political importance of a particular Treaty norm or set of norms, or as a synthetic description for a set of Treaty norms, but without adding any legal value to these norms. Indeed, the ECJ regularly uses the term "principle" where it does not have an independent legal content. An example in the institutional sphere is Opinion 2/94 on Accession to the European Convention of Human Rights. The reference, in that Opinion, to the "principle of conferred powers" does not seem to add anything to the written rule of (what was then) Article 3b, first sentence, EC. One could argue that the deliberate use of this principle, at the start of the Court's reasoning, announces the Court's restrictive interpretation of the (then) Article 235 EC in a later paragraph of the Opinion,[8] but the Court itself does not connect the two statements with each other, so that it would be wrong to see this Opinion as the making of the "principle of conferred powers" a true general principle of interpretation requiring a restrictive approach to the delimitation of the EC's competences.[9] On other occasions, the term "principle" is indeed used by the Court for identifying a guideline, or approach, to be taken into account for the interpretation of written norms of EU law. Such principles of interpretation do have legal value, as they may affect the outcome of cases, including disputes in the institutional sphere. One may offer, as an example, the notorious *Titanium Dioxyde* Case, in which the Court of Justice relied on the principle of democracy in deciding that the consultation procedure and the cooperation procedure could not be combined for the adoption of one and the same Community legislative act.[10]

I will try to identify, in the following pages, those institutional principles which can be considered as "principles of law" in the strong sense indicated above, namely as independent judge-made sources of law. The perspective of the analysis is therefore very much that of the European Courts, and, more particularly, that of the use made by these Courts of institutional principles as tools for the construction of the

7. See, for instance, Case C-284/90, *Council v. Parliament*, [1992] ECR I-2227, paragraph 26.
8. Opinion 2/94, [1996] ECR I-1759, paragraphs 24 and 30.
9. Such use of the "principle of conferred powers" as a principle of interpretation has been recommended by some authors (see, for instance, H.-P. Kraußer, *Das Prinzip begrenzter Ermächtigung im Gemeinschaftsrecht als Strukturprinzip des EWG-Vertrages* (Berlin: Duncker & Humblot, 1991), but the European Court has not, so far, followed that line.
10. Case C-300/89, *Commission v. Council*, [1991] ECR I-2867, paragraphs 18-21.

European Union legal order.[11] This focus on the role of the Courts should, however, not be read as denying the importance of the notion of "general principles" for a study of inter-institutional relations which focuses more on the attitudes and expectations of the political actors of the EU system. Thus, the principle of subsidiarity may, so far, have played only a minor role in the case-law of the European Court of Justice, but it has certainly affected the attitudes and behaviour of the political institutions of the Union.

3.4.2 VERTICAL INSTITUTIONAL PRINCIPLES

3.4.2.1 The Principle of Sincere Cooperation

The duty of sincere cooperation or, as it is more frequently called, the "principle of Community loyalty" has a written basis in Article 10 EC (ex Article 5). The European Court of Justice has, in an impressive string of cases, spelled out the duties which, beyond the text of individual treaty provisions and in recognition of the "communal will", fall upon the Member States of the European Union.[12] But the Court of Justice has done more than adopting a broad interpretation of the Member State obligations as they are enacted in Article 10 EC. It has also reversed the perspective and connected to Article 10 a corresponding duty for the *Community* institutions which is *not* based on the wording of the Treaty. This is where the "duty" of sincere cooperation becomes a true principle of law containing additional legal obligations beyond those to be found in the Treaty. The reciprocal nature of the duty of cooperation was affirmed for the first time in the case *Luxembourg v. European Parliament*, where the Court held that "when the governments of the Member States make provisional decisions [about the seat of the European Parliament] they must in accordance with the rule imposing on Member States and the Community institutions *mutual duties of sincere cooperation*, as embodied in particular in Article 5 of the EEC Treaty, have regard to the power of the Parliament to determine its internal organisation."[13] In *Luxembourg v. Parliament*, this statement was made *obiter*, because the Court was directly concerned, in the quoted passage, with spelling out a duty of the Member States and not a duty of the Parliament. But on

11. As indicated also by the title of this contribution, I take the *European Union* as my overall legal framework. This accords with the view, which is not shared by all authors, that the European Union is the overall organisation within which the European Community has been incorporated as a sub-organisation with distinct rules (arguments for this view can be found in D. Curtin and I. Dekker, "The EU as a 'Layered' International Organization: Institutional Unity in Disguise", in P. Craig and G. de Búrca (eds.), *The Evolution of EU Law* (Oxford: OUP, 1999), 83. To the extent that the EU has a "single institutional framework" (Article 3 EU Treaty), general principles governing vertical and horizontal relations may be considered as EU principles, rather than just EC principles. Yet, in view of the paper's focus on the role of the judiciary, it will deal primarily with European Community law.
12. See the contrubution by L. Gormley in this volume.
13. Case 230/81, [1983] ECR 255, paragraph 37 (emphasis added).

several subsequent occasions, the same approach was adopted in order to impose concrete duties on Community institutions.[14] In one of the most spectacular of these cases, the Zwartveld case of 1990, the Court held that the Commission may not refuse to give information and assistance to a national judge investigating a possible breach of Community law (*in casu*, suspected fraud against the EC fish marketing regulations), because in a Community subject to the rule of law "relations between the Member States and the Community institutions are governed, *according to Article 5* of the EEC Treaty, by a principle of sincere cooperation."[15] The express mention that this is in accordance with Article 5 (now Article 10) is rather odd, as the text of that article certainly does not provide for a *mutual* duty of cooperation, but is addressed to the Member States alone. The better approach seems to be the one adopted in *Luxembourg v. Parliament*, and repeated in several other cases, namely that the duty of sincere cooperation is an overarching, unwritten, principle of which Article 10 is only one manifestation.[16]

3.4.2.2 The "Principle" of the Primacy of Community Law

In the Amsterdam Protocol on Subsidiarity and Proportionality, the Member States specified that "[t]he application of the principles of subsidiarity and proportionality ... shall not affect the *principles* developed by the Court of Justice regarding the relationship between national and Community law." The Court-made principles, to which the Member States approvingly refer in this phrase, can be no other than the principle of primacy, and the related principles of direct effect and effectiveness of Community law. Although these principles directly influence the position of *individuals*, they can, at the same time, be considered as *institutional* principles, as they determine the legal duties of national courts and national political authorities. Indeed, the duty to apply Community law and to set aside conflicting rules of national law has been presented by the ECJ as an "application of the principle of cooperation laid

14. For a survey of the Court's case-law on the "reverse" side of the duty of cooperation, see K. Mortelmans, "The Principle of Loyalty to the Community (Article 5 EC) and the Obligations of the Community Institutions", *Maastricht Journal of European and Comparative Law* (1998) 67.
15. Case C-2/88 Imm., *J.J. Zwartveld and others*, [1990] ECR I-3365, paragraph 17 (emphasis added).
16. In *Luxembourg v. Parliament*, as cited before, the Court invoked "the rule imposing on Member States and the Community institutions mutual duties of sincere cooperation as embodied *in particular* in Article 5 of the EEC Treaty" (emphasis added). See the comment by Kapteyn, VerLoren van Themaat and Gormley: "While the mutual nature of these obligations ... are not immediately apparent from the wording of Article 5 itself (which, after all, is addressed to the Member States), the case-law of the Court becomes logical if Article 5 is itself seen as a specific expression of a more general duty." (P.J.G. Kapteyn and P. VerLoren van Themaat, *Introduction to the Law of the European Communities,* third edition, by L.W. Gormley (London: Kluwer Law International, 1998), p.159).

down in Article 5 of the EEC Treaty",[17] and one could thus consider the principles of primacy and direct effect as elements of the principle of sincere cooperation, rather than as separate institutional principles.

Yet, primacy, and the related concepts, are very peculiar "principles" indeed. In the literature, the epithet "principle" is used to describe them alongside other epithets like "rules", "doctrines", "notions" or "concepts". The Court of Justice itself rarely uses the term principle in this connection: it did not use it in the founding judgments *Costa v. ENEL* and *Van Gend en Loos*, but it did refer to a "principle of precedence" in the *Simmenthal* Case.[18] Usually, the Court simply refers to the concrete obligations that lay on national courts or administrative authorities, namely to apply EC rules, to set aside incompatible national rules, etc. In a recent elaborate restatement of its primacy doctrine, the Court did not once use the term principle.[19]

This terminological restraint seems justified, because primacy (or direct effect) may to some extent be considered as *principles of interpretation,*[20] but they are not *principles of law* in the same way as the "general principles of EC law". Unlike these general principles, primacy is not a separate norm alongside the Treaties and secondary law, but rather a *distinctive legal quality* possessed by all norms of Community law, including the Treaties, secondary law and, indeed, the general principles of law. In conclusion: there is nothing against including primacy and direct effect among the institutional principles of the EC, but such a qualification does not adequately convey their very special status of meta-norms which help to define the overall nature of the Community legal order,[21] much in the same way as the *pacta sunt servanda* rule, from which primacy derives, is a meta-norm defining the nature of public international law.

3.4.2.3 The Principles of Subsidiarity and (Institutional) Proportionality

The most famous of all institutional principles is, probably, the principle of subsidiarity. Yet, it is a *written* principle which was put in the EC and EU Treaty by the

17. Case C-213/89, *The Queen v. Secretary of State for Transport, ex parte: Factortame Ltd and Others*, [1990] ECR I-2433, paragraph 19.
18. Case 106/77, *Amministrazione delle Finanze dello Stato v. Simmenthal*, [1978] ECR 629, paragraph 17 (the French expression is "principe de primauté").
19. Joined Cases C-10/97 to C-22/97, *Ministero delle Finanze v. IN.CO.GE.'90 and others*, judgment of 22 October 1998 (not yet reported), paragraphs 18 to 21.
20. Indeed, primacy and direct effect were developed in the framework of preliminary rulings on the *interpretation* of Community law. However, this involves a very special kind of interpretation, which does not deal with the meaning of particular substantive provisions of EC law, but with the (unwritten) obligations of national courts in respect of these provisions.
21. As to the extent to which these principles make EC law legally different from international law, see B. de Witte, "Direct Effect, Supremacy and the Nature of the Legal Order", in P. Craig and G. de Búrca (eds), *The Evolution of EU Law* (Oxford: OUP, 1999) 177, p. 208.

Member States without having been "discovered" first by the ECJ. Article 5 EC (ex Article 3b) prescribes a particular course of action for the Community institutions,[22] which is described as being "in accordance with the principle of subsidiarity". Do the words "in accordance with" mean that the *principle* of subsidiarity has a legal currency of its own, and embodies more than the particular rules of institutional behaviour contained in Article 5 and (now also) in the Amsterdam Protocol on Subsidiarity and Proportionality? The view that the principle of subsidiarity has a wider scope of application and should, for instance, be seen as a principle to be observed by the Court of Justice, as well, in the exercise of its own competences of Treaty interpretation, has been proposed by several legal authors.[23] The Court itself has, so far, given no indications in this sense: in its view, the legal effect of the concept of subsidiarity seems to be exhausted by the written rules of the Treaty.

The principle of *proportionality* is usually mentioned in the same breath as the principle of subsidiarity. However, for present purposes, the principle of proportionality is rather different, because of its dual nature: it governs institutional relations as well as relations with individuals, depending on the circumstances; there is, one could say, both a substantive and an institutional application of this principle in the EC legal order.[24] There is no doubt that proportionality was originally conceived by the ECJ, along the model provided by some national legal systems, as a principle of administrative law designed to protect the individual. It is often invoked when Community measures impose a burden on particular categories of individuals or firms, as frequently happens, for instance, in the framework of the common agricultural policy. Yet, proportionality is now inscribed in the Amsterdam Protocol on Subsidiarity and Proportionality as a distinctly institutional principle; in that Protocol, the Member States define proportionality as a principle requiring that "any action by the Community shall not go beyond what is necessary to achieve the objectives of the Treaty." In point 7 of the Protocol, they add, presumably with reference to proportionality again: "Community measures should leave as much scope for national decision as possible... While respecting Community law, care should be taken to respect well established national arrangements and the organisation and working of Member States' legal systems." Reference is made, here, to the interest of preserving the *autonomy of the Member States,* whereas abstraction is made of the consequences of the measures for particular categories of individuals or firms. In

22. Namely, that they should take action "only if and insofar as the objectives of the proposed action cannot be sufficiently achieved by the Member States and can therefore, by reason of the scale or effects of the proposed action, be better achieved by the Community."
23. A clear proponent of this view is T. Schilling, "A New Dimension of Subsidiarity: Subsidiarity as a Rule and a Principle", *Yearbook of European Law* 14 (1994) 203. See also, more tentatively, G. de Búrca, "The Principle of Subsidiarity and the Court of Justice as an Institutional Actor", *Journal of Common Market Studies* (1998) 214.
24. One may find a parallel here with *national* administrative law where the principle of proportionality similarly serves for the protection either of *individual interests* or of the *general interest in good administration;* see G. de Búrca, "The Principle of Proportionality and its Application in EC Law", *Yearbook of European Law* 13 (1993) 105, p.106.

fact, this institutional reading of the principle of proportionality could already be found in the last sentence of Article 3b EC (now Article 5), as adopted in Maastricht, although the term "proportionality" itself was not used then. In several recent cases, the ECJ adopted the "new" view and reviewed the proportionality of policy limitations imposed by the Community on national legislative or administrative authorities. The Court examines whether the means employed by the Community legislator "are suitable for the purpose of achieving the desired objective and whether they do not go beyond what is necessary to achieve it".[25] In applying this test, the Court may explore the balance of advantages which result for specific categories of individuals or firms (the "normal" proportionality review) but the concern for the protection of individuals is not always central to the Court's investigation. Proportionality clearly serves for the protection of the autonomy of Member State authorities, in addition to protecting the freedom of individuals. Even though the European Court leaves a large measure of discretion to the Community legislator, the application of the proportionality test in the context of the relations between the Community and the Member States seems, to me, an unhappy development, for which there are no precedents in other federal-type constitutional systems. Even in the German legal system, from which the European Court originally borrowed the principle of proportionality, the Constitutional Court has refused to use this principle as a standard for deciding conflicts of competence between the federation and the Member States.[26]

3.4.3 Horizontal Institutional Principles

3.4.3.1 The Principle of Institutional Balance

In respect of the horizontal relations between the EU institutions, the text of the founding Treaties gives much more detailed guidance than in respect of the vertical relations between the EU and its Member States, so that there would seem to be comparatively less scope for judge-made principles regulating these relations. Occasionally, though, the European Court has actively intervened in the inter-institutional relations by making a creative use of the unwritten principles of *institutional balance* and *inter-institutional cooperation*.

---

25. Case C-84/94, *United Kingdom v. Council,* [1996] ECR I-5755, paragraph 57 (review of validity of working time directive); Case C-233/94, *Germany v. Parliament and Council,* [1997] ECR I-2405, paragraph 54 (review of validity of directive on deposit-guarantee schemes for credit institutions). See already Case C-359/92, *Germany v. Council,* [1994] ECR I-3681, at 3713 (review of Commission's power to adopt a decision requiring Member States to take specific safety measures with respect to a particular consumer product).
26. Judgment of 22 May 1990, *Entscheidungen des Bundesverfassungsgerichts* 81, 310, p. 338.

The concept of *institutional balance* (or *équilibre institutionnel*) was used by the European Court of Justice already during the 1950s, in the context of the Coal and Steel Treaty,[27] and can be found rather regularly in its case-law. Yet, in contrast with many legal writers,[28] the Court has never actually called it a "principle"; it simply refers to "the institutional balance", without qualifying the legal nature of this concept. In fact, the Court mostly refers to the institutional balance as a convenient shorthand for the set of Treaty rules which happen to apply to the particular institutional dispute under consideration. In several cases, the ECJ has firmly rejected arguments that the Treaty rules on the division of powers between the institutions should, if necessary, be disregarded in view of an unwritten higher principle of institutional balance. It did so most clearly in an action for annulment brought by several states against a Commission directive on the transparency of financial relations between the Member States and their public undertakings. It was argued on behalf of the applicants that the Commission's power to adopt directives, under the (then) Article 90(3) EEC Treaty, should not be interpreted as giving this institution an original law-making power, as that would be contrary to the general principles of the division of powers between the institutions. The Court of Justice replied that "the limits of the powers conferred on the Commission by a specific provision of the Treaty are to be inferred not from a general principle, but from an interpretation of the provision in question, in this case Article 90, analysed in the light of its purpose and its place in the scheme of the Treaty." [29] As the Court observed in another of these cases, "the powers of the institutions ... are not always based on consistent criteria",[30] and the Court refuses to use general principles in order to bring consistency where the drafters of the EC Treaty chose not to be consistent.

To the extent that the reference to the institutional balance does not modify the legal position of the institutions, the Court rightly refrains from using the term "principle" as such use would give the impression that the institutional balance is a legal norm with an independent content. There is one major exception to this approach, and that is the case-law dealing with the procedural rights of the European Parliament under Article 173 EC (now Article 230), particularly the *Chernobyl*

---

27. Case 9/56, *Meroni*, [1957-58] ECR 133.
28. G. Guillermin, "Le principe de l'équilibre institutionnel dans la jurisprudence de la Cour de justice des Communautés européennes", *Journal du droit international* (1992) 319; D. Simon, *Le système juridique communautaire* (Paris: PUF, 1997) p. 231; J. Gerkrath, *L'émergence d'un droit constitutionnel pour l'Europe* (Bruxelles: Bruylant, 1997), p. 390.
29. Joined Cases 188 to 190/80, *France, Italy and UK v. Commission*, [1982] ECR 2545, paragraph 6. See also Case C-58/94, *Netherlands v. Council*, [1996] ECR I-2169, paragraphs 32 and 41.
30. Case 242/87, *Commission v. Council*, [1989] ECR 1425, paragraph 13.

judgment of 1990.[31] It is well known that the text of Article 173 EEC Treaty, prior to Maastricht, did not mention the European Parliament, either as an applicant or as a defendant in actions for annulment. After having established in *Les Verts* that, despite the text of Article 173, Parliament could be sued under Article 173 whenever acts of the Parliament had legal effects for third parties, the Court was soon confronted with the reverse question of whether Parliament itself could bring actions for the annulment of acts adopted by other institutions. In the Comitology case, the Court adopted the orthodox view that the Parliament did not have *locus standi* under Article 173. It held, somewhat reluctantly, that "the applicable provisions, as they stand at present, do not enable the Court to recognise the capacity of the European Parliament to bring an action for annulment."[32] Only two years later, in the Chernobyl case, the "applicable provisions" (Article 173 EEC and its mirror provision Article 146 of the Euratom Treaty) did not "stand" any different as they did in Comitology, but this did not prevent the Court from recognising, this time, the European Parliament's right to bring an action for annulment of a Council regulation. This overruling, though not complete, was rather spectacular. In Chernobyl, the text of Article 173 was discarded in the name of the institutional balance, whose importance is emphasised by the Court in several paragraphs of the judgments. The Court concluded that "the absence in the Treaties of any provisions giving the Parliament the right to bring an action for annulment may constitute a procedural gap, but it cannot prevail over the fundamental interest in the maintenance and observance of the institutional balance laid down in the Treaties establishing the European Communities."[33]Although, even then, the Court refrained from calling the institutional balance a "principle", this was a case where the use of that term would have been entirely appropriate, as the concept of institutional balance was used as the source of a specific legal norm which could not be found in the text of the EC Treaty or in any other written legal document.

3.4.3.2 The Principle of Sincere Co-operation between the Institutions

The institutional balance is "counterbalanced" by another Court-made principle, that of *sincere cooperation between the institutions*, which was first formulated in a case opposing Greece and the Council about the Community budget. Upon Greece's request to judge whether certain Community expenditure for the benefit of Turkey was to be considered as compulsory expenditure (and could therefore be approved by

31. Case C-70/88, *Parliament v. Council*, [1990] ECR I-2041 (known as the *Chernobyl* case). See, for a general analysis of the case-law on the institutional balance (in addition to the many annotations of the *Chernobyl* judgment specifically): S. Prechal, "Institutional Balance: A Fragile Principle with Uncertain Contents", in T. Heukels, N. Blokker, M. Brus (eds), *The European Union after Amsterdam – A Legal Analysis* (The Hague: Kluwer Law International, 1998) 273; G. Guilermin, "Le principe de l'équilibre institutionnel dans la jurisprudence de la Cour de justice des Communautés européennes", *Journal du droit international* (1992) 319.
32. Case 302/87, *Parliament v. Council*, [1988] ECR 5615, paragraph 28.
33. Case C-70/88, *Parliament v. Council*, [1990] ECR I-2041, paragraph 26.

the Council) or non-compulsory expenditure (which could only be decided with the agreement of the European Parliament), the Court refused to take sides and opted, instead of drawing a clear dividing line between the powers of Council and Parliament, for the "soft" language of the inter-institutional dialogue. It held that "the operation of the budgetary procedure, as it is laid down in the financial provisions of the Treaty, is based essentially on inter-institutional dialogue. That dialogue is subject to the same mutual duties of sincere cooperation which, as the Court has held, govern relations between the Member States and the Community institutions."[34] Thus, rather than looking for a textual basis in the Treaty provisions dealing with the budgetary procedure, the Court preferred to draw an analogy with the law governing the relations between the Community and its Member States, considering in effect that mutual cooperation is a necessary (but unwritten!) ingredient of *both horizontal and vertical inter-institutional relations.*

The duty of sincere cooperation which, in *Greece v. Council,* had been applied by the Court to a dispute in budgetary matters, was extended to the ordinary legislative process in the judgment of 30 March 1995 in one of the many cases brought by the Parliament under its right of action recognised in *Chernobyl.*[35] The dispute arose from the adoption, by the Council, of a Regulation extending for a further year (albeit with some changes) the existing Community regime of generalised tariff preferences for developing countries. The Council had adopted the Regulation without waiting for the opinion of the European Parliament, with the argument that the adoption was an urgent matter (the existing regime would have lapsed on 1 January 1993) and that the Parliament had failed to show due diligence in dealing with the Council's request for an opinion. In his submissions to the Court, Advocate-General Tesauro came down in favour of the European Parliament, by insisting strongly on the fact that consultation of the Parliament, as the Court had decided in the *Roquette* case in 1980,[36] was part of the institutional balance, and that the balance itself was an essential element of the constitutional system. The Court should not, in his view, allow for exceptions to the right of consultation in the name of urgency (even if such urgency could adequately be demonstrated by the Council) because that would "permit an alteration in the institutional balance outside the procedures and forms laid down for revision of the constitutional charter"; that was "a matter for the constitutional legislator alone".[37]

The Court of Justice took a very different approach from that proposed by its Advocate General. While repeating its standard formula that the participation of Parliament in the legislative procedure "represents an essential factor in the institutional balance intended by the Treaty", it counterbalanced this concept by insisting on the duty of sincere cooperation (which the Advocate-General had not even mentioned). It repeated the formula, coined in *Greece v. Council,* that the "inter-insti-

34. Case 204/86, *Greece v. Council*, [1988] ECR 5323, paragraph 16.
35. Case C-65/93, *Parliament v. Council*, [1995] ECR I-643.
36. Case 138/79, *Roquette Frères v. Council*, [1980] ECR 3333.
37. Case C-65/93, cit., Opinion of Advocate-General Tesauro, paragraph 20.

tutional dialogue ... is subject to the same mutual duties of sincere cooperation as those which govern relations between Member States and the Community institutions" and decided, after a consideration of the facts of the case, that the Parliament had "failed to discharge its obligation to cooperate sincerely with the Council". As "[t]he essential procedural requirement of parliamentary consultation was not complied with because of the Parliament's failure to discharge its obligation to cooperate sincerely with the Council", the action for annulment of the Council Regulation was rejected.[38] One could say that, like in *Chernobyl*, the Court of Justice had overruled the clear wording of the Treaty ("the Parliament must be consulted") in the name of an unwritten, but superior, principle of the Court's own finding: that of interinstitutional cooperation.[39] It would seem that, as a result of the Court's case-law, the relations between the Community institutions are now dominated by the twin values of autonomy and cooperation;[40] the principle of institutional balance serves to ensure respect for the separate powers of each institution whereas the duty of sincere cooperation expresses the countervailing value that the institutions should cooperate beyond the formal rules of procedure laid down in the Treaty. Both principles are unwritten; both were developed by the European Court of Justice; both have served, at least occasionally, for reaching a result that departs from the ordinary grammatical meaning of the EC Treaty. But the two principles often point, as the judgment of 30 March 1995 shows, in a different direction. The choice which of the two principles should prevail is then left to the Court of Justice itself.

3.4.3.3 The Principle of Democracy

The new Article 6, paragraph 1, EU Treaty, as amended by the Treaty of Amsterdam, states that "the Union is founded on the principles of liberty, democracy, respect for human rights and fundamental freedoms, and the rule of law, principles which are common to the Member States." Of these lofty principles, the principle of democracy deserves special consideration here, as it might appear to be the institutional principle *par excellence*. It is difficult, at this early stage, to evaluate the legal importance of this express reference to the principle of democracy in the text of the EU

38. Case C-65/93, *Parliament v. Council*, [1995] ECR I-643, paragraph 28.
39. The Court may have been inspired by the Opinion delivered, a few weeks earlier, by another Advocate-General in another case opposing the European Parliament and the Council. There, Advocate-General Léger had referred to the "constitutional principle of cooperation in good faith between institutions" which is based, according to him, on the fact that the institutions "are united in the attainment of the common objectives set by the Treaty and interlinked in the decision-making process" (Case C-417/93, *Parliament v. Council*, [1995] ECR I-1185, paragraphs 63 and 67 of the Opinion. In paragraph 31, the same principle is referred to as a *general*, rather than a *constitutional*, principle.
40. This development was anticipated to some extent by R. Bieber in an article written in 1984: "The Settlement of Institutional Conflicts on the Basis of Article 4 of the EEC Treaty", *Common Market Law Review* (1984) 505.

Treaty.[41] Although Article 6, paragraph 1, is not one of the provisions which the European Court of Justice is allowed to enforce, the Court could feel encouraged to recognise the principle of democracy as an unwritten principle of law. On one occasion at least, the principle of democracy was used by the Court of Justice as a *principle of interpretation*,[42] and the Court of First Instance has, in its recent UEAPME judgment, used the principle of democracy as a free-standing unwritten norm to be respected by the Community institutions. In an action for annulment brought by the European association of small businesses against a Council Directive adopted on the basis of a European collective agreement, the CFI went out of its way to state that the Council, when it is called to turn a European collective agreement into a directive, must act in accordance with the principle of democracy and check the truly representative character of the agreement's signatories.[43] Despite a veiled reference to the new Amsterdam provision, the nature of the principle of democracy, as used in this judgment, is that of an unwritten principle of higher law against which the legitimacy of Community acts may be reviewed. If this view were confirmed by the European Court of Justice, it would open a wholly new field for judicial intervention in institutional matters.

3.4.4 THE QUESTION OF JUDICIAL ENFORCEABILITY

The *object* of the institutional principles of EU law is obviously different from the object of the "general principles of EC law", in that the former govern the relations between institutions, whereas the latter cover relations between the individual and the European or national authorities. So, even where institutional principles are "genuine" principles containing autonomous legal obligations (and, as shown in the previous sections, this is not always the case), their legal regime could be affected by their different object. More particularly, one could wonder whether even the "genuine" institutional principles are judicially enforceable exactly in the same way as the "general principles of EC law".

At first, this might well seem to be the case. Institutional principles mentioned and defined in the EC Treaty itself (like subsidiarity and "institutional" proportionality), principles only indirectly referred to in the EC Treaty (like the principle of sincere

---

41. See, for some first thoughts about the implications for the EU *Member States*, A. Verhoe-ven, "How Democratic Need European Union Members Be? Some Thoughts after Amsterdam", *European Law Review* (1998) 217.
42. See the reference to the *Titanium Dioxyde* case in the Introduction to this article.
43. Case T-135/96, *UEAPME v. Council*, [1998] ECR II-2335, paragraph 89: "the principle of democracy on which the Union is founded requires – in the absence of the participation of the European Parliament in the legislative process – that the participation of the people be otherwise assured, in this instance through the parties representative of management and labour who concluded the agreement which is endowed by the Council ... with a legislative foundation at Community level. In order to make sure that that requirement is complied with, the Commission and the Council are under a duty to verify that the signatories to the agreement are truly representative."

cooperation of the Member States towards the Community), and entirely unwritten judge-made principles (like the principle of cooperation at the horizontal level) all have the status of "higher law". They would therefore seem to qualify as grounds for the annulment of Community acts[44] under Article 230 EC (ex Article 173), exactly like the "traditional" general principles such as non-discrimination, legitimate expectations or "substantive" proportionality. Furthermore, the *vertical principles* regulating the action of national authorities (mainly the duty of sincere cooperation) would seem to be enforceable against the Member States in the usual two ways, namely through a Commission infringement action under Article 226 EC (ex Article 169) or through a legal action brought by individuals before a national court.

On a closer look, though, there is some uncertainty as to the *invocability* of institutional principles by *individuals*, either before the European Courts or before the national courts. The case-law on this matter is unsystematic and rather confusing. Strong indications in favour of the invocability of institutional principles come from the judgment of the European Court of First Instance in *UEAPME*. The CFI held, somewhat adventurously, that a breach of the principle of democracy should be considered as a possible ground for the annulment of a directive, in an action brought by a private party.[45] The *Opel Austria* case, decided one year earlier by the Court of First Instance, could be read as further authority for the same view, but on a closer look, this judgment involved the use of an institutional principle as a principle of interpretation rather than as a free-standing norm. The Court of First Instance held that the Council, by adopting a regulation conflicting with an international treaty (the EEA Agreement) which was going to enter into force for the EC within days of the adoption of the regulation, had acted in breach of the (international law) principle of good faith. By doing so, it had at the same time violated the, non-institutional, principle of protection of legitimate expectations, which an individual party, Opel Austria, could rely on to oppose application of the regulation.[46] So, in the end, this judgment does nothing but confirm the established view that individuals may rely, before the courts, on the principle of legitimate expectations.[47]

44. Things are obviously different for acts of the European Union institutions adopted outside the framework of the EC Treaty, namely under the "second" and "third" pillars of the Union. Although most of the institutional principles would seem to apply to the EU as a whole, in view of the Union's single institutional framework, the conditions for their judicial enforcement are obviously rather different outside the EC pillar. On the jurisdiction of the ECJ after Amsterdam, see P.J.G. Kapteyn, "The Court of Justice after Amsterdam: Taking Stock", in T. Heukels, N. Blokker, M. Brus (eds), *The European Union after Amsterdam – A Legal Analysis* (The Hague: Kluwer, 1998) 139.
45. Case T-135/96, *UEAPME v. Council*, [1998] ECR II-2335, paragraph 89. One may note, though, that the applicant had invoked, among other grounds, a breach of the principles of subsidiarity and proportionality, but *not* of the principle of democracy (paragraph 23 of the judgment).
46. Case T-115/94, *Opel Austria GmbH v. Council*, [1997] ECR II-39, paragraphs 89-95.
47. P.J. Kuyper, "The Court and the Tribunal of the EC and the Vienna Convention on the Law of Treaties 1969", *Legal Issues of European Integration* (1998-1) 1, p. 16.

In contrast with the Court of First Instance's approach in *UEAPME*, reliance by individuals on institutional principles was rejected in a number of judgments of the European Court of Justice. In *Hurd*, the ECJ held that a private person could not rely on the (then) Article 5 of the EEC Treaty in domestic proceedings against the state, because the substance of the obligation deriving, for the United Kingdom, from its general duty of sincere cooperation with the Community, was not sufficiently precise to have direct effect.[48] This formulation left open the possibility that, in other factual circumstances, the implications of Article 5 *could* be clear enough to have direct effect. In *Vreugdenhil*, a case decided some years later, the Court was confronted with the argument that the Commission had acted in breach of the division of powers between the institutions. The Court held that "the aim of the system of the division of powers between the various Community institutions is to ensure that the balance between the institutions provided for in the Treaty is maintained, and not to protect individuals" and that, consequently, "a failure to observe the balance between the institutions cannot be sufficient on its own to engage the Community's liability towards the traders concerned."[49] It is unclear, though, whether this restrictive attitude is limited to liability cases, where the Court requires the violation of a rule of law for the protection of individuals,[50] or whether it also extends to actions for annulment, where the violation of any higher norm of Community law can be invoked.[51] Yet, an even stronger denial of the invocability of institutional principles came in the recent judgment in *Bettati v. Safety Hi-Tech*. In the course of a preliminary ruling on the validity of a Council Regulation on the protection of the ozone layer, the ECJ rejected an argument based on Article 5 EC Treaty (now Article 10) by stating that this provision imposed mutual duties of sincere cooperation on Member States and the Community institutions and that, consequently, it "cannot relate to a measure adopted by the Community legislature ... which might possibly entail advantages or disadvantages for certain undertakings."[52] The language used in this phrase is fairly general. To the extent that all institutional principles impose, by definition, obligations only on the (EU and State) institutions, one would have to conclude from the statement in *Bettati* that they can never be invoked by individuals. But one should probably not draw such a radical conclusion from this one case. At any rate, there

48. Case 44/84, *Hurd v. Jones (Her Majesty's Inspector of Taxes)*, [1986] ECR 29, paragraphs 46-49.
49. Case C-282/90, *Industrie- en Handelsonderneming Vreugdenhil v. Commission*, [1992] ECR I-1937, paragraphs 20 and 21.
50. P.J.G. Kapteyn and P. VerLoren van Themaat, *Introduction to the Law of the European Communities,* third edition, by L.W. Gormley (London: Kluwer Law International, 1998), p. 497.
51. For discussion of this question, see S. Prechal, "Institutional Balance: A Fragile Principle with Uncertain Contents", in T. Heukels, N. Blokker, M. Brus (eds.), *The European Union after Amsterdam – A Legal Analysis* (The Hague: Kluwer Law International, 1998) 273, pp. 281-283.
52. Case C-341/94, *Gianni Bettati v. Safety Hi-tech Srl*, judgment of 14 July 1998 (not yet reported), paragraph 77 (emphasis added).

have been judgments in which the ECJ recognised, without any discussion, the possibility for individuals to invoke written institutional norms in support of actions for annulment of EC measures.[53] To the extent that institutional principles are laid down in the text of the EC Treaty (as in the case of subsidiarity and "institutional" proportionality), they would seem to be available to individuals as a ground for requesting the annulment or invalidation of EC acts, either in an Article 230-action or in an Article 234-validity reference.

3.4.5 Conclusion: The Development of Institutional Principles and the Role of the Court of Justice

The recognition of general principles of EC law has been a central contribution of the ECJ to the constitutionalisation of the EC legal order. In contrast with the rudimentary distinction between primary law (the Treaties) and secondary law (all the rest) which formed the initial framework, the Community legal order now has, due to the Court's contribution, a rather sophisticated system of sources of law which corresponds to the elaborate hierarchies of sources which one finds in some continental constitutional systems. In an article published in 1992, Pierre Pescatore emphasised "the absolutely fundamental character of what we are used to call the 'doctrine of the sources of law'. Indeed, he who is the master of the sources of law is in truth the master of the criteria of legitimacy of the system, the guardian of the temple as it were."[54] The author of these words may have been inspired by his long experience as a judge at the European Court of Justice. With respect to fundamental rights, the Court's decision to tap a new source of higher law was justified by the glaring *lacuna*, in this respect, in the EC Treaty, and the Member States have subsequently vindicated the Court's active role. With respect to the relations between the Community institutions, such an active attitude would have been less justified, as these matters are dealt with in quite some detail in the Treaties. The Treaty rules may be confusing, or lack consistency, but they are not so rudimentary as to require the European Court to actively fill the gaps. Indeed, the ECJ has respected, by and large, the division of powers as it is established by the wording of the Treaty. The one major exception, namely the use of the principle of institutional balance as the basis for the Parliament's standing to bring actions for annulment, was not seen by the Member States as an undue interference with their prerogatives, as they decided to codify the Chernobyl ruling in the new text of Article 173 enacted by the Treaty of Maastricht. As to the discovery of the additional dimensions of the principle of sincere cooperation, beyond the wording of Article 10 EC, this can, again, hardly be considered as a subversive move, but rather as a useful means for reinforcing, rather than redrawing, the general pattern of horizontal and vertical institutional relations in the European Union legal system. The European Court has, thereby, contributed to the "harmonious functioning of the institutional

53. A famous example is Case 138/79, *Roquette Frères v. Council*, [1980] ECR 3333.
54. P. Pescatore, "La constitution, son contenu, son utilité", *Revue de droit suisse* (1992-I) 41, p. 44.

system"[55] and discouraged the institutions and the Member States from upsetting the existing division of powers and duties.

Therefore, leaving aside the "pseudo-principles" of supremacy and direct effect, institutional principles of EU law have not played a really major role in the development of the EU legal order. However, the recent multiplication of express references to such institutional principles, in the text of both the EC and EU Treaty, may encourage the European Courts to use them more actively in the years to come. One may also hope for a more systematic approach from the side of the ECJ. Indeed, as has become clear from the preceding pages, the reconstruction of the case-law on institutional principles is made difficult by the absence of clear guidance given by the Court on the significance which it attaches to the legal concepts it uses. One may recall, here, the comments of Hartley: "It should not ... be thought that the Court always makes express reference to general principles whenever it propounds new rules of law. Sometimes it simply states a rule without any indication of its source; or it may give a justification based on policy or the general requirements of the Community legal system. However, if a formal source for such rules were required, it could always be found either on the basis of a wide interpretation of a written text or on the basis of the general principles."[56] In contrast with the case-law on the general principles of EC law for the protection of the individual, in which the term "general principles" has become a term of art with a well-defined meaning, the term "principles" or "general principles" is, in the field of institutional relations, used in the erratic way described by Hartley. Sometimes, the term is not used where it would seem to be appropriate, namely where the Court discovers and applies an independent and unwritten source of law (as with the duty of cooperation of the Community towards the Member States, and of the institutions towards each other); on other occasions, the term principle is used where it does not have a distinctive legal meaning and its significance is merely rhetorical. Yet, what is probably more important than terminological consistency, is clarity about the legal status of institutional principles and, more particularly, their invocability by individuals before the European and national courts. These are questions to which, in the years to come, the European judiciary will have to give further thought.

---

55. This expression is borrowed from Jacqué, who concludes his analysis of the institutional principles by stating that these principles "trouvent leur source dans la nécessité de permettre un fonctionnement harmonieux de l'ensemble institutionnel créé par les traités" (J.P. Jacqué, "Charte constitutionnelle et structure institutionnelle de la Communauté", in J.D. Mouton and T. Stein (eds), *Towards a New Constitution for the European Union? The Intergovernmental Conference 1996* (Bonn: Bundesanzeiger, 1997) 73, p. 85).
56. T.C. Hartley, *The Foundations of European Community Law*, 4th ed. (Oxford: OUP, 1998), p. 132.

4. Some Individual Principles and Legal Systems

4.1 Legal Certainty and Legitimate Expectations as General Principles of Law

*John Temple Lang**

There are two kinds of "general principles of law" which the Court of Justice has said are part of Community law: principles of fundamental human rights, and what are essentially administrative law principles. These two categories are descriptive, and not mutually exclusive. The principle of legal certainty has consequences which fall into both categories.

Each of these general principles has two kinds of legal effects:

- it is a rule of interpretation of the Community Treaties and of Community legislation and other acts; and
- it is an overriding rule of law, which invalidates actions taken in the sphere of Community law, which are contrary to the principle.

So, general principles of law need to be kept in mind both when interpreting Community measures and when deciding whether a given act, in the sphere of Community law, is valid. They are part of the intellectual tools of all Community law lawyers.

All these general principles apply, first, to all acts, legislative, executive and administrative, of the Community institutions. Second, they apply to all acts of national and regional authorities of Member States within the sphere of Community law.

The "sphere of Community law", for this purpose, has not yet been comprehensively defined by the Court. It includes the situations in which a national authority is implementing or applying Community law, when it is acting on behalf of the Community, and when it is regulating or restricting any right given or protected by Community law.[1]

This means that in all Member States there must be judicial review by the appropriate courts (usually in practice administrative law courts) of all acts of public

* A Director in the Directorate General for Competition, European Commission ; Professor, Trinity College, Dublin; Senior Visiting Research Fellow, University of Oxford; Barrister. All opinions expressed are purely personal.

1. Temple Lang, The sphere in which Member States are obliged to comply with the general principles of law and Community fundamental rights principles, 1991, Legal Issues of European Integration, 23.
   Case 5/88, Wachauf [1989] ECR-2609: Case C-2/92, Bostock [1994] ECR I-955: Case C-299/95, Kremzow [1997] ECR I 2629.

Ulf Bernitz and Joakim Nergelius (eds.), General Principles of European Community Law, 163–184

authorities in the Community law sphere, to ensure that they are compatible with these general principles of law. The failure to provide sufficient judicial review for this purpose would be a breach of Community law.

All the general principles of law are directly applicable in national courts, except perhaps in the specific cases where they merely involve the duty of Member States to give information to the Commission.

Although the general principles of law appear vague and general when stated in a comprehensive way, the Court has deduced some very practical results from them.

All these principles are *general*, in the sense that they apply in *all* areas of Community law. They are not limited to the common agricultural policy, so *all* Community lawyers need to understand them. However, many of the cases involving *e.g.* legitimate expectations and retroactive measures concern the active regulation and management, which are features of the Community's agricultural policy.

This paper is primarily concerned with the principle of legal certainty[2] as it is shown by the caselaw of the Community Courts. Many examples of the principle can also be found in Community legislation, and indeed in the Treaty itself. For example, since 1990 all directives contain a clause requiring national measures implementing them to contain or to be accompanied by a reference to the directive. Since this makes clear that the measure is to be interpreted so as to be consistent with the directive, it is an example of the principle that the legal situation should always be made clear, which is one consequence of the legal certainty principle.

This paper is also limited in another way. It does not attempt to cover the case-law of national courts on the effects of the principle of legal certainty, even in the Community law sphere.[3] That would be a large, though no doubt fascinating, subject, and an important one, since the general principles of Community law apply to all national authorities' actions in the Community law sphere.

4.1.1 THE GENERAL PRINCIPLE OF "LEGAL CERTAINTY"

The general principle called "legal certainty" is the most complex and difficult of the general principles of law. This is because, unlike, say, the principle of proportionality, it is in fact a group of several principles, distinct but not entirely separate from one another. Sometimes these have been referred to by more precise names, and sometimes merely under the general name of "legal certainty". For clarity in this paper, the phrase "legal certainty" is used only for the broad "umbrella" principle, and not for

---

2. On the principle of legal certainty, see:
Pescatore, rapport Communautaire, Les principes généraux du droit en tant que source du droit communautaire, 12th Fide Congress (Paris, 1986), 17-54: Schwarze, European Administrative Law; Schermers and Waelbroeck, Judicial Protection in the European Communities (1992), pp. 52-69: Cardwell, General Principles of Community Law and Milk Quotas, 29 Common Market Law Review (1992), 723-747.
3. See for example in the UK, *R. v. Inland Revenue Commissioners, Ex parte* MFK Underwriting Agents Ltd. (1990) 1 WLR 1545, at p. 1569 where Lord Justice Bingham referred to the "valuable developing doctrine of legitimate expectation".

the more specific principles. Probably no absolute or clear cut classification of the cases in which the specific principles were applied is necessary, or indeed possible.

Some degree of clarity is necessary for a legal rule to be justiciable. If it is not justiciable, it cannot be applied by a court, but can only be implemented by an authority with powers to lay down policy and make supplementary legal rules.

In a democracy subject to the rule of law, all citizens should, as far as possible, be able to find out their legal rights and duties,[4] and to do so with the minimum cost and inconvenience. This desirable objective has some practical consequences, of which the principal ones may be classified as follows:

- the legal position under Community law should be made clear;
- the principle of "legitimate expectations";
- retroactive legislation is permitted only in exceptional circumstances, for specific reasons, duly explained, and respecting legitimate expectations;

and some narrower rules:

- in some cases, the Court will limit the retroactive effects of its own judgment;
- if a measure is annulled on procedural grounds, the Court may order that some of its effects should remain in force;
- when time limits exist for beginning proceedings under EC law, legal certainty requires that the same issues cannot be raised later in another way by a party who could have raised them directly;
- "provisional validity" of certain restrictive agreements;
- Community institutions may alter measures which they have adopted, which affect the legal and factual situation of persons, only in accordance with the same rules on competence and procedure.[5] Therefore, if a policy has been stated and agreed, it must be followed until it is amended in the same way;
- before the adoption of a rule of Community law imposing a time limit for imposing fines (similar to a period of limitation or prescription), legal certainty prevented the Community institutions from delaying too long the exercise of their power.[6] Time limits for taking legal action are examples of the principle of legal certainty (*e.g.* Article 230 (ex-173)).

---

4. The principle of legal certainty, which requires that legal rules be clear and precise, and aims to ensure that situations and legal relationships governed by Community law remain foreseeable": Case C-63/93, *Duff v. Minister for Agriculture* [1996] ECR I-569 at p. 607, paras. 19-20; Case T-105/96, *Pharos* [1998] ECR II-285, para. 63.
5. Case 81/72, *Commission v. Council* [1973] ECR 575; Case T-229/94, Deutsche Bahn [1997] ECR II-1689, para. 113-116 (The Commission cannot tie its hands in a competition procedure by a reply to a question in Parliament).
6. Case 48/69, *Imperial Chemical Industries* [1972] ECR 619, p. 653. A time limit was later imposed by Regulation 2988/74 in the case of competition fines.

The first three principles apply in a variety of situations. The other principles concern specific situations arising in cases before the Community Courts. Provisional validity is relevant to cases before national courts, but is a narrow rule applicable only in a special type of situation.

There are some indirect effects of the principle of legal certainty, *e.g.* the fact that a directive cannot be relied on, even in litigation against the State, if it is imprecise.

The principle of legal certainty, to enable citizens to find out their legal rights and duties, is the reason why Community law gives a right to obtain legal advice in confidence from an appropriately qualified lawyer without running the risk of creating evidence against oneself.[7] The citizens' right is to find out their legal rights and duties: there is no necessary or general right to have an administrative authority say what they are. Citizens, and their lawyers, have to take their own responsibilities. The right to legal certainty does not mean a right to obtain bureaucratic approval for every action: it is a right to be free from any unnecessary uncertainty in the law, since unnecessary uncertainty inhibits personal freedom to do what one is entitled to do, and causes unnecessary expense and controversy over legal issues, especially undesirable for poorer people.

However, there are strong arguments for saying that, in some circumstances at least, private parties should have a right to go to a national court to get a declaration of their legal rights under Community law against other private parties. They should not be compelled to run the risk of infringing a national law and having themselves brought before a court in order to get an opportunity to argue that a national law is contrary to Community law. The principle of legal certainty may give a right to get a court ruling clarifying the legal position: anything else would discourage private parties from claiming their Community law rights.

Legal certainty is linked in practice to the principle of equality. Legal certainty would be impossible unless similar cases were treated similarly, and if the law is unclear some private parties will act on an interpretation of the law which is less favourable to them, and others, more determined, better advised, or with more money for litigation, will act on an interpretation more favourable to them.

Another aspect of the principle of legal certainty is the rule by which, if a law is unclear or ambiguous, it must be interpreted in favour of the citizen. So, for example, when legislation imposed a time limit on claims against the State, the time limit began to run only when the citizen could first have known with confidence that there was a right to make a claim.[8]

7. Case 155/79, *AM&S v. Commission* [1982] ECR 1575.
8. Case 78/77, *Lührs* [1978] ECR 169, at pp. 179-181: Case C-208/90, *Emmott v. Minister for Social Welfare* [1991] ECR I-4269: Case C-94/95, Bonifaci [1997] ECR I-3969. Prescription periods are examples of the principle of legal certainty: Case C-188/95, *Fantask* [1997] ECR I- 6783, at p. 6838, para. 48.

4.1.2 THE PRINCIPLE THAT THE LEGAL POSITION SHOULD BE MADE CLEAR

This principle applies in several different kinds of situations, which it is useful to distinguish:

- Community regulations must be certain and their application foreseeable, especially if they have financial consequences;
- Community directives must be implemented in such a way that the rights and duties of individuals and companies under Community law are clear;
- conflicts between Community law and national laws must be avoided[9] and if they arise they must be resolved so that there is no doubt that the legal position is as Community law requires it to be in all respects;
- when a Member State is introducing a new State aid which has been notified to the Commission and not opposed within two months, legal certainty requires that the Member State gives notice to the Commission before putting it into effect;[10]
- a Community measure does not, except when retroactive effects are permissible, come into force before it is published.[11]

In a series of cases the Court has repeated that directly applicable Community measures must be clear and their application foreseeable, especially if they have financial consequences (taxes, fees or fines):

> "legal certainty is a fundamental principle of Community law which requires in particular that rules imposing charges on a taxpayer be clear and precise so that he can ascertain unequivocally what his rights and obligations are, and act accordingly".[12]

---

9. Case C-234/89, *Delimitis*, 1991 ECR I 935, para. 47: Case 14/68, *Walt Wilhelm*, 1969 ECR I.
10. Case 120/73, *Lorenz v. Germany* [1973] ECR 1471 at p. 1481.
11. Case 98/78, *Racke* [1979] ECR 69, p. 84.
12. Case 169/80, *Gondrand* [1981] ECR 1931; Case 325/85, *Ireland v. Commission* [1987] ECR 5041; Case 70/83, *Kloppenberg* [1984] ECR 1075; Case 92/87, *Commission v. France* [1989] ECR 405, para. 22; Case C-143/93, *Van Es Douane Agenten* [1986] ECR I-431, para. 27; Case C-236/95, *Commission v. Greece* [1996] ECR I-4459, para. 13 and Advocate-General at p. 4465; Case C-177/96, *Banque Indo Suez* [1997] ECR I-5659, at para. 27 and Advocate General Jacobs, at pp. 5669-5672: cp. *The Sunday Times* case, European Court of Human Rights, April 26 [1979] (No. 30) 2 EHRR 245; see also Case C-137/92P *BASF and Others*, 1994, ECR I 2555 at para. 75; joined Cases T-305/94 and others, *Limburgse Vinyl*, April 20, 1999, paras. 294-304, 409. It may be enough that the legal position can easily be found out: Case C-161/97P, *Kernkraftwerke Lippe-Ems*, 22 April 1999. There must be no doubt about the text of an act adopted by the Commission: Case C-137/92P, *Commission v. BASF*, 1994 ECR I 2555 para. 76: Joined Cases T-305/94 and others, *Limburgse Vinyl*, 20 April 1999 paras. 183-193, 299-304.
    This principle does not oblige the Community institutions to include in every attackable act a statement of the way in which it can be challenged and the time limits for doing so: Cases C-153/98P and C-154/98P, *Guérin Automobiles v. Commission*, 5 March 1999.

If this principle is infringed, the result is that the rule in question is invalid *pro tanto* as against the taxpayer.

The principle requires the legal rule in question to be reasonably clear. There can be no guarantee that a legal rule can be applied to every set of facts easily and with confidence: there may be many situations in which crucial facts are unclear or are on a borderline between what is legal and what is prohibited.

It follows *e.g.* that when the Commission requires disclosure of documents for competition law purposes, its request should be as clear as it can be expected to make it *without* knowing what documents exist.

4.1.3 CONSEQUENCES

The consequences of a violation of this principle depend on the circumstances.

If a Community measure, or the legal position in the light of such a measure, is not sufficiently clear, the usual consequence is that the measure may not be relied on against anyone whose position was not clear,[13] to the extent of the ambiguity or uncertainty. The party concerned may be either a company or a Member State.

If a directive is not properly implemented, or if a national law has not been duly repealed, the State is in breach of its obligations under Article 249 (ex-189), and may be obliged to pay compensation in the circumstances described in the Francovich judgment.[14]

In some circumstances (apparently, when it is sufficient for the protection of the private party), the Court has simply said that the interpretation of the law which is more favourable to the private party must be adopted.[15]

4.1.4 IMPLEMENTING DIRECTIVES

Defective implementation of directives has been the subject of many judgments of the Court. The whole subject of the effects of directives was discussed fully at the FIDE conference in Stockholm in 1998, and need not be analysed again here.[16] Of course, not all defects in the implementation of directives involve the principle of legal certainty, and it is not always possible or useful to try to decide if the principle on which the Court is acting should be thought of as the legal certainty principle if the Court does not use the phrase.

The rules relating to directives, insofar as they relate to legal certainty, can be summarized as follows:

---

13. Case 169/80, Gondrand [1981] ECR 1931: joined Cases 92 and 93/87, *Commission v. France and UK* [1989] ECR 405, at pp. 443-444: Case C-143/93, *Van Es Douane Agenten* [1996] ECR I-431.
14. Joined Cases C-6/90 and C-9/90, *Francovich* [1991] ECR I- 5357.
15. Case 78/77, *Lührs* [1978] ECR 161 at pp. 179-181 (based on "natural justice" rather than legal certainty): Case C-208/90, *Emmott* [1991] ECR I-4269 at para. 23.
16. Federation International pour le Droit Européen, XVIII Congrès, (Stockholm, 1998), Volume I.

- implementing measures must fully satisfy the requirement of clarity and certainty,[17] so that individuals know the full extent of their rights and can rely on them in national courts, and the measures must be legally binding;[18]
- Member States must clearly and precisely inform the Commission of the measures taken to implement each directive.[19]

4.1.5 CONFLICTING LEGAL MEASURES MUST BE REPEALED

The principle that conflicts between national law and Community law must be resolved, by amending or repealing the national law, applies even if the relevant rule of Community law is directly applicable and so prevails in case of conflict: the principle of legal certainty requires that the legal position must be made clear. The repeal must have the same legal force or status in the hierarchy of national legal norms as the rule to be repealed. The national law must not create any doubt about either the substantive legal position or the procedural position, so that a national law in terms identical to a Community regulation was contrary to Community law, partly because it would give the impression that Article 234 (ex-177) was not applicable to its interpretation.[20]

17. Case 300/81, *Commission v. Italy* [1983] ECR 449, para. 10. Case 363/85, *Commission v. Italy* [1987] ECR 1733, para. 7; Case C-59/89, *Commission v. Germany* [1991] ECR I-2607, para. 18; Case C-208/90, *Emmott* [1991] ECR I-4269, paras. 19, 21-22; Case C-95/92, *Commission v. Italy* [1993] ECR I-3119; Case C-197/96, *Commission v. France* [1997] ECR I-1489, para. 15; Case C-236/95, *Commission v. Greece* [1996] ECR I-4459, paras. 13-14; Case C-360/87, *Commission v. Italy* [1991] ECR I-791.
18. Case 102/79, *Commission v. Belgium* [1980] ECR 1473 at p. 11.
19. Case 96/81, *Commission v. Netherlands* [1982] ECR 1791.
20. Case 93/71, *Leonesio* [1972] ECR 287; Case 112/77, *Töpfer*, 1978 ECR 1019, para. 19: Case C-90/95 P, *de Compte v. Parliament*, 1997 ECR I 1999 paras. 39-40: Case 173/83, *Commission v. France* [1985] ECR 491; Case 269/80, *R. v. Tymen* [1981] ECR 3079; Case 168/85, *Commission v. Italy* [1986] ECR 2945; Case 247/85, *Commission v. Belgium* [1987] ECR 3029; Case 262/85, *Commission v. Italy* [1987] ECR 3073; Case 157/89, *Commission v. Italy* [1991] ECR 85, para. 17; Case C-80/92, *Commission v. Belgium* [1994] ECR I-1019; Case C-151/94, *Commission v. Luxembourg* [1995] ECR I-3685; Case C-236/95, *Commission v. Greece* [1996] ECR I-4459, para. 13. In Case C-151/94, *Commission v. Luxembourg* [1995] ECR I-3685, Advocate-General Jacobs (at p. 3691) said ".... the general rule that the rights of individuals under Community law must be clearly laid down in binding legal provisions .... accordingly, where a Member State's legislation is incompatible with Community law, it must enact a clear amendment to that legislation in order to remedy the incompatibility". He also cited Case 102/79, *Commission v. Belgium* [1980] ECR 1473; Cases 96/81 and 97/81, *Commission v. Netherlands* [1982] ECR 1791 and 1819; Case 300/81, *Commission v. Italy* [1983] ECR 449; Case 38/87, *Commission v. Greece* [1988] ECR 4415.

4.1.6 LEGITIMATE EXPECTATIONS

The principle of legitimate expectations[21] is a superior rule of law for the protection of individuals and companies. Breach of this principle by a Community institution can create liability to pay compensation under Article 288 (formerly 215).

Two distinctions must be made. The principle of legitimate expectations is not necessarily the same in its application to relations between Member States and the Community institutions as it is in relations between private parties and those institutions.[22] Second, it is necessary to distinguish between legitimate expectations said to have been created by specific assurances given in individual cases, and those said to have been created by regulations or other general measures.

The principle of legitimate expectations is a general one: any economic operator to whom an institution has given justified hopes may rely on the principle.[23] The principle can be invoked only to the extent that the Community itself has created a situation, which can give rise to legitimate expectation.[24]

There is a considerable volume of case law on the principle of legitimate expectations, although it has not been successfully relied on very often.

The Court of First Instance has recently summarised the law as follows:[25]

> "It follows from the case-law of the Court of Justice that there is a breach of the principle of the protection of legitimate expectations if, in the absence of an overriding matter of public interest, a Community institution abolishes with immediate effect and without warning a specific advantage, worthy of protection, for the undertakings concerned without adopting appropriate transitional measures... As is also clear from the caselaw, the scope of the principle of the protection of legitimate expectations cannot be extended to the point of generally preventing new rules from applying to the future effects of situations which arose under the earlier rules, especially in a field such as the common organization of the markets, whose very purpose involves constant adjustments to the variations in the economic situation (see the judgment of the Court of Justice in Case 203/86 *Spain v. Council* [1998] ECR 4563)."

---

21. On the principle of legitimate expectations see Sharpston, European Community law and the Doctrine of Legitimate Expectations: how legitimate, and for whom? 11 Northwestern Journal of International Law and Business (1990), 87-103.
22. Case 262/87, *Netherlands v. Commission*, 1989, ECR 225.
23. Case 289/81, *Mavridis* [1983] ECR 1731; Case T-466/93, *O'Dwyer* [1995] ECR II-2071; Case T-81/95, *Interhotel* [1997] ECR II-1265 (a detailed judgment); Case T-105/96. *Pharos* [1998] ECR I; Case T-336/94, *Efisol* [1996] ECR I-1343.
24. Case C-177/90, *Kühn* [1992] ECR I-35, para. 14; Case C-63/93, *Duff* [1996] ECR I-569, at p. 608; Case T-465/93, *Murgia Messapica* [1994] ECR II-361 (specific assurances needed); Case T-493/93. *Hansa-Fisch* [1995] ECR II-575, at paras. 48-50; Case T-113/96, *Dubois* [1998] ECR II-125, at para. 68 ("precise assurances").
25. Case T-472/93, *Campo Ebro* [1995] ECR II-421 at para. 52. The reference is to Case 74/74 CNTA [1975] ECR at paras. 42-46.

In another recent case, the Court of First Instance added:

> " .... It is important to determine whether a product trader could have guarded against the risks ...traders must bear the economic risks inherent in their activities, taking account of the circumstances of each case ... with a tendering procedure, those economic risks include, inter alia, the costs connected with the preparation of the bid ... on the other hand, if, before the contract ... is awarded to the successful tenderer, a tenderer is encouraged by the contracting institution to make irreversible investments in advance and thereby to go beyond the risks inherent in the business under consideration. ...non-contractual liability may be incurred ... the Parliament induced in its intending co-contracting party the certainty of winning a contract and in addition encouraged that party to make irreversible investments".[26]

Where the principle of legitimate expectations applies, it may provide protection only for a transitional period, or only for goods already in transit, or may give a right only to a reasonable transitional period.[27] It does not give permanent exemption from new legislation applicable in the future. It is not a guarantee that the status quo will be permanent. It is therefore rather confusing to use the phrases "acquired rights" or "vested rights" in this context, and in one case[28] the Court of First Instance distinguished expressly between the two principles.

Legitimate expectations can arise in several ways:

- as a result of a precise and specific assurance, given by a public authority in an individual case;[29]
- as a result of a clear indication in a regulation or other general measure;[30]

26. Case T-203/96, *Embassy Limousines v. Parliament* [1998] ECR II (17 December 1998), paras. 75-76 and 80 citing *inter alia* joined cases 83/76 and others, *HNL v. Council* [1978] ECR 1209, para. 7 and Case 267/82, *Dévelloppement and Clemessy v. Commission* [1986] ECR 1907, para. 33 (the alleged principle of strict liability).
27. Case 127/80, *Grogan* [1982] ECR 869.
28. Case T-113/96, *Dubois* [1998] ECR II-125, para. 63-71.
29. Case 268/80, *Gugliemi* [1981] ECR 2295, Advocate General Capotorti at p. 2307 ("The expectation must be based on precise assurances given by the administration to the persons concerned"); Case 289/81, *Mavridis* [1983] ECR 1744; Case T-123/89, *Chomel* [1990] ECR II-131, para. 26 (silence is not enough to create a precise assurance which is necessary for legitimate expectations); Case T-20/91, *Holtbecker* [1992] ECR II-2599; Case T-465/93, *Murgia Messapica* [1994] ECR II-361; Case T-521/93, *Atlanta* [1996] ECR II-1707; Case T-195/95, *Guerin Automobiles* [1996] ECR II-171; Case T-336/94, *Efisol* [1996] ECR I-1343; T-571/93, *Lefebvre* [1995] ECR II-2407; Case T-105/96, *Pharos* [1998] ECR II-285; Case T-266/97, *Vlaamse Televisie*, Judgment dated 9 July 1999, paras. 71-78.
30. Case C-152/88, *Sofrimport* [1990] ECR I-2477.

- as a result of a misleading impression created by the authority or institution;[31]
- as a result of a reasonable expectation, created by the action of the Community, based on a clear rationale which is inherent in the situation, especially if the expectation is selective, i.e. if realised would benefit only certain groups.[32]

There is never a right to be exempt from future general, non-selective legislative changes or other general measures. The Court has said in a long series of cases that there cannot be a legitimate expectation that an existing situation capable of being altered by the Community institutions in the exercise of their discretionary powers will be maintained, especially in the Common Agricultural Policy, the purpose of which involves constant adjustment to economic changes.[33]

The principle of legitimate expectations is similar to the principle of estoppel in English law, and the principle *nemo contra factum proprium* (an authority must not repudiate its own promises), or *patere legem quam ipse fecisti* (an authority must respect its own rules).

The principle of legitimate expectations is not applicable:

- if it would defeat the purpose of EC measures, or if there is an overriding general interest, or if the Community institution needs promptly to correct an error or an unexpected result;[34]

---

31. Case T-81/95, *Interhotel* [1997] ECR II-1265.
32. Case C-348/89, *Mecanarte* [1991] ECR I-3277, paras. 23-24; Case C-264/90, *Wehrs* [1992] ECR I-6286; Case 120/98, *Mulder* [1988] ECR 2321; Case C-104/89, *Mulder* [1992] ECR I-3061.
33. Case 84/78, *Tomadini* [1979] ECR 1801; Case 112/80, *Dürback* [1981] ECR 1095, para. 47 ff.; Case 278/84, *Germany v. Commission* [1987] ECR I, para. 36; Case 424/85, *Frico* [1987] ECR 2755, para. 33; Case 120/86, *Mulder* [1988] ECR 2321, para. 23; Case 170/86, *von Deetzen* [1988] ECR 2355; Case 350/88, *Delacre* [1990] ECR I-395 (in which many of the earlier cases are cited); Case C-177/90, *Kühn* [1992] ECR I-35, para. 13; joined Cases C-258/90 and others *Pesquerias de Bermeo* [1992] ECR I-2901; Case C-133/93, *Crispoltoni* [1994] ECR I-4863, para. 57; Case T-466/93, O'Dwyer [1995] ECR II-2071; Case C-63/93, *Duff* [1996] ECR I-569; Case T-243/94, *British Steel* [1997] ECR II-1887; Case C-244/94, *Moskof v. E.O.K.* [1997] ECR I-6441, paras. 68-69; Case T-521/93, *Atlanta* [1996] ECR II-1707; Case C-22/94, *Irish Farmers Association v. Minister for Agriculture* [1997 ECR I-1809; Case C-315/96, *Lopez Export* [1998] ECR I-317, at pp. 342-343.
34. The Court said that it would defeat the purpose of the Community measure if there were legitimate expectations that some enterprises would be exempt from it, in Case 112/80, *Dürbeck* [1981] ECR 1095, para. 47 ff (transitional measures exempting contracts already entered into would have deprived the protective measures of practical effect by allowing a volume of imports likely to jeopardise the market); Case 152/80, *Debayser v. Firs* [1981] ECR 1305 (monetary compensation amounts are a necessary part of the Common Agricultural Policy and must be altered when rates of exchange alter); Case

- if it was foreseeable to prudent and discriminating operators that changes would be likely (because the situation was inherently likely to change, or because warnings had been given);[35]
- if the measures said to create expectations are withdrawn within reasonable time;[36]
- if the conduct said to be promised would be contrary to EC rules, or was a promise not to apply EC law to the extent needed to make it effective;[37]

211/80, *Advernier* [1984] ECR 131, para. 19 (aim of second measure was to end unjustified increases in payments to staff due to the previous measure); Case C-152/88, *Sofrimport* [1990] ECR I-2477, paras. 16, 19; Case 74/74, *CNTA* [1975] ECR 533, para. 44; Case 84/78, *Tomadini* [1979] ECR 1801; Case C-183/95, *Affish* [1997] ECR I-4315 (overriding public interest in public health precluded transitional measures when fish imports were banned for reasons of hygiene); Case C-51/95P, *Unifruit Hellas* [1997] ECR I-727, para. 27; cp. Case C-189/89, *Spagl* [1990] ECR I-4539 (the general interest could have been safeguarded by general, non-selective measures).

35. The Court said that there could be no legitimate expectations because warning had been given or because a prudent and discriminating operator would have foreseen that changes in the law were likely, in Case 78/77, *Luhrs* [1978] ECR 169 (once imports encouraged, measures to discourage exports foreseeable); Case 276/82, *De Beste Boter* [1983] ECR 3331 (previous measure said "special measures" might be adopted, and advance fixing of export refunds had already been suspended several times in one year); Case 265/85, *Van den Bergh* [1987] ECR 1155, para. 44; Case 310/85, Deufil [1987] ECR 901; Case C-350/88, *Delacre* [1990] ECR I-395, para. 37; joined Cases C-13/92 and others, Dreissen [1993] ECR I-4751 (a Commission proposal cannot create legitimate expectations since it may be amended at any time); Case C-22/94, *Irish Farmers Association* [1997] ECR I-1809, para. 25; Case T-466/94, *O'Dwyer* [1995] ECR I-2071 (no legitimate expectations if measures could have been foreseen); Case T-243/94, *British Steel* [1997} ECR II-1887, paras. 77-78 (a prudent and discriminating trader must foresee measures to deal with crises, especially in a cyclical industry); C-24/95, *Rheinland-Pfalz v. Alcan* [1997] ECR I-1591 (a diligent businessman should be able to decide if the procedure for notifying a State aid had been followed); Case T-455/93, *Hedley Lomas* [1997] ECR II-1095, para. 49.
36. Withdrawal of the measures said to create the legitimate expectations, if carried out within a reasonable time, defeats the expectations: Case C-III/63, *Lemmerzwerke* [1965] ECR 677, at p. 690; Case 14/81, *Alpha Steel* [1982] ECR 749, at p. 769 (withdrawal of an unlawful measure is permissible if it is done within a reasonable time and due account is paid to how far the company concerned may have relied on the first measure); Case 15/85, *Consorzio Cooperative d'Abruzzo* [1987] ECR 1005, paras. 12-17; Case T-336/94, *Efisol*, 1996 ECR I 1343.
37. A promise or practice which is contrary to EC law, or a promise not to apply it effectively, cannot create legitimate expectations, Case 1252/79, *Lucchini* [1980] ECR 3753 (laxity by Commission does not excuse infringement); Case 5/82, *Maizena* [1982] ECR 4601; Case 188/82, *Thyssen* [1983] ECR 3721; Case 100/80, Musique Diffusion *Française* [1983] ECR 1815 (fines); Case 228/84, *Pauvert* [1985] ECR 1969; Case C-5/

Contd.

- if the operator did not rely, or could not have relied, on the measure, or does not comply with the conditions required, or has misled the authority;[38]
- if the proper procedure for authorisation was not followed, and the operator could reasonably have found this out.[39]

It will be seen that when the principle of legitimate expectations and the principle of legality conflict, it is the principle of legality, which prevails. Legitimate expectations based on laxity of enforcement cannot make something legal which is not legal.

It will also be seen that the principle of legitimate expectations is a flexible one. However, the case-law now seems to have identified most of the elements one would expect to find in a developed principle.

Contd.

89, *Commission v. Germany* 1990 ECR I 3437; Case T-123/89, *Chomel* [1990] ECR II-131; Case T-83/91, *Tetra Pak* [1994] ECR II-755 (compliance with the Commission's recommendations does not create a legitimate expectation that the Commission will not later impose measures necessary to end an infringement); Case T-20/91, *Holtbacker* [1992] ECR II-2599; Case C-415/93, *Bosman* [1995] ECR I-4921, at para. 136 ("the Commission may not give guarantees concerning the compatibility of specific practices with the Treaty"); Case T-336/94, *Efisol* [1996] ECR I-1343; Case C-325/96, *Fabrica de Queijo* [1997] ECR I-7249, at p. 7268.
This rule is linked to another general principle of law, that a public authority cannot rely on its own unlawful conduct: see *e.g.* Case C-377/89, *Cotter and McDermott* [1991] ECR I-1155, at paras. 21 and 26.

38. If the company claiming legitimate expectations did not in fact rely on the measure in question, or did not fulfil the necessary conditions, or has given misleading information, there is no legitimate expectation:
Case 100/74, *C.A.M. v. Commission* [1975] ECR 1393; Case 133/84, *U.K. v. Commission* [1986] ECR 1259, p. 1277 ff; Case 67/84, *Sideradria* [1985] ECR 3985; Case C-348/89, *Mecanarte* [1991] ECR I-3277, paras. 23-24; Case C-153/94, *Faroe Seafood* [1996] ECR I-2465; Case T-551/93, *Industries Pesqueras Campos* [1996] ECR II-247, para. 76; Case T-331/94, *IPK v. Commission* [1997] ECR II-1665; Case T-455/93, *Hedley Lomas* [1997] ECR II-1095; Case T-73/95, *Oliveira* [1997] ECR II-381, para. 27: Case 366/95, *Steff Houlberg*, 1998 ECR I, 2661.
This means *e.g.* that the legitimate expectations must have arisen *before* the event which is said to infringe the principle: joined cases T-466/93 and others, *O'Dwyer* [1995] ECR II-2071, para. 57.

39. The Court said no legitimate expectations arise if the proper procedure for authorisation (of a State aid) is not followed, and the company concerned could reasonably have found this out:
Case C-5/89, *Commission v. Germany* [1990] ECR I-3437, para. 13-14; Case C-169/95, *Spain v. Commission* [1997] ECR I-135, para. 51; Case C-24/95, *Rheinland Pfalz v. Alcan* [1997] ECR I-1591; Case T-67/94, *Ladbroke Racing* [1998] ECR II 1, at paras. 182-183.
Similarly, an opinion not expressed by an official who was authorised to make a commitment cannot give rise to legitimate expectations: Case 71/74, *Frubo* [1975] ECR 563, para. 20: Case T-141/89, *Trefileurope Sales* [1995] ECR II-791, at para. 116.

As the Court pointed out in one leading case,[40] the principle of legitimate expectations is linked to the principle of equal treatment. If an authority formally agrees its policy, and acts on it in some cases, if it then acts differently in some other cases its later actions are contrary to the principle that similar cases should be treated similarly, as well as to the principle of legitimate expectations. In effect, the authority agreed to treat all cases in the way stated until the measure is repealed or revised by a second measure having at least the same force. This means that although constant practice does not in itself create legitimate expectations, it may also protect a private party from being treated differently because of the principle of equality

One of the most common uses of the principle of legitimate expectations, which has worked satisfactorily and give rise to almost no litigation, is the Commission's practice of dealing with agreements notified under Community competition procedures by administrative letter rather than by formal decision.[41] These letters are not expressly envisaged in the competition regulations. Although the phrase "legitimate expectations" is rarely used in connection with them, the effect of these letters is essentially governed by the principle. The Commission's services say, in effect, that unless the circumstances as the Commission understands them alter significantly, the Commission will, if necessary, confirm in a formal decision the view stated in the letter that Article 81(1) is not applicable or that the conditions of Article 81(3) are fulfilled. The Commission ties its own hands, but could not, of course, bind potential complainants. Each such letter mentions that it may become inapplicable if circumstances alter, and it would not be binding on the Commission if the notifying parties had misled the Commission on some significant point. These letters also illustrate one aspect of the principle of legitimate expectations, which is that it is only the authority which has given rise to the expectations which is bound, and not third parties or, formally, other authorities. As it is not legally binding on them, third parties apparently have no right to challenge such a letter under Article 230 (ex-173).

It is important to distinguish between letters written to individual companies about individual agreements, which create legitimate expectations in accordance with their terms, and general descriptions by the Commission as to how it understands the law or how it will exercise its discretionary judgment in competition and antidumping cases, which are intended to inform but which cannot bind the Commission to act in a specific way in the specific, and not precisely foreseeable, circumstances of an individual case.[42] This is so in particular as these descriptive Notices are deliberately

40. Case 81/72, *Commission v. Council* [1973] ECR 575, at p. 584.
41. Joined Cases 253/78 and 1-3/79, Guerlain [1980] ECR 2327; Case 48/72, *Brasserie de Haecht v. Wilkin* II [1973] ECR 77; Case T-7/93, *Langnese* [1995] ECR II-1533, para. 36.
42. See Case C-119/97P, *Ufex, DHL and CRIE v. Commission* [1999] ECR I, March 4 1999, paras. 79-80.

written so as to preserve the flexibility needed to adapt policy to individual cases, and because there may be overriding needs of Community policy, *e.g.* that fines should deter, which may apply in individual cases. One must also distinguish between Notices on which companies are specifically intended to act, such as that on reduction of fines for companies which cooperate with the Commission,[43] and notices which are intended merely as information.

"Specific assurances" which are enough to create legitimate expectations do not need to be, and usually are not, acts with legal effects which could be challenged under Article 230 (formerly 173). The legal consequences of the principle of legitimate expectations are not enough to make the assurances into decisions with legal effects to which Article 230 would apply.

The Commission's practice also shows that legitimate expectations, even when created, will come to an end if the circumstances giving rise to them alter in some significant respect. No legitimate expectations can be relied on if the company has been warned that changed circumstances may alter the Commission's views. It often is implicit and foreseeable that changed circumstances will lead to new action and a new result.

The Court of Justice has not had to decide how far the principle of legal certainty applies, under Community law, as between private parties. The principle of legitimate expectations, as stated by the Court, does not do so. But the Commission invites private parties to comment on agreements or practices, which have been notified to it, when publishing a summary of the agreement in the Official Journal. In such cases, legal certainty probably deprives companies which could then have commented, and did not, of the right to object later, just as the principle of legal certainty obliges plaintiffs to make their claims within the time limits laid down in limitation or prescription statutes, or lose their right to do so.[44]

4.1.7 CONSEQUENCES OF BREACH

Again, the consequences of a violation of the principle of legitimate expectations depend on the circumstances. If loss has been caused, compensation can be recovered under Article 288 (ex-215).[45] In any case, the later measure cannot be relied on, and

43. O.J. No C-207/4, July 18, 1996.
44. See however Case T-96/92, *CCE de la Société Générale des Grandes Sources* [1995] ECR II-1213, at para. 36 (the Court has never held that the participation of third parties in a Commission procedure is a necessary condition for the Commission's decision to be of direct and individual concern to them).
45. Case C-152/88, *Sofrimport* [1990] ECR I-2477; joined Cases C-104/89 and C-37/90, Mulder [1992] ECR I-3061; joined Cases T-195/94 and T-202/94, *Quiller and Heusmann* [1997] ECR II.

is invalid, insofar as it is inconsistent with the principle.[46] There is no right to compensation if expectations not protected by the principle are disappointed.[47] In *CNTA*,[48] the Court said that there could not be compensation for failure to maintain monetary compensation amounts, but only for loss suffered as a result of their being withdrawn unforeseeably from transactions already entered into.

In *Mulder II*,[49] the Court made it clear that not every breach of the principle of legitimate expectations is a "grave and manifest" breach serious enough to make the Community liable to pay compensation. The amount of compensation should correspond to the damage caused by a serious breach. In *Mulder II* (farmers who had agreed to suspend milk production temporarily had been treated as if they had terminated production permanently), the breach was serious because there was no overriding public interest, and the specific situation of a clearly defined group of producers had not been taken into account, and they had been prevented from resuming sales of milk.

4.1.8 RETROACTIVITY AND LEGISLATIVE CHANGE

It is convenient to distinguish cases involving retroactivity from other cases involving questions of legitimate expectations, in spite of the fact that the two issues are linked.

The general principle is that:

> "although in general the principle of legal certainty precludes a Community measure from taking effect before its publication, it may exceptionally be otherwise where the purpose to be achieved so demands and where the legitimate expectations of those concerned are duly protected, and provided that the decisions include, in the statement of the reasons on which they are based, particulars which justify the retrospective effect".[50]

---

46. Community measures were held invalid in Case 81/72, *Commission v. Council* [1973] ECR 575; Case 127/80, *Grogan* [1982] ECR 869; Case 159/82, *Verli-Wallace* [1983] ECR 2711; Case 232/81, *Agricola Commerciale Olio* [1984] ECR 3881; Case 264/81, *Savma* [1984] ECR 3915; Case 223/85, *Rijn-Schelde-Verolme* [1987] ECR 4617; Case 170/86, *von Deetzen* [1988] ECR 2355; Case 120/86, *Mulder* [1988] ECR 2321; Case C-152/88, *Sofrimport* [1990] ECR I-2477; Case C-189/89 *Spagl* [1990] ECR I-4589; Case C-217/89, *Pastätter* [1990] ECR I-4585; Case C-264/90, *Wehrs* [1992] ECR I-6285.
47. Joined Cases T-466/93 and others, *O'Dwyer* [1995] ECR II-2071, at para. 50.
48. Case 74/74, *CNTA* [1975] ECR 533, at paras. 45-46.
49. Joined Cases C-104/89 and C-37/90, *Mulder* [1992] ECR I-3061, also the conclusions of Advocate-General van Gerven; Case C-189/89, *Spagl* [1990] ECR I-4539.
50. Case 99/78, *Decker* [1979] ECR 101; Case 98/78, *Racke* [1979] ECR 69; Case 212/80, *Salumi* [1981] ECR 2735; Case 276/80, *Padana* [1982] ECR 517, para. 16; Case C-133/93, *Crispoltoni* [1994] ECR I-4863; Case 1/84R, *Ilford* [1984] ECR 423; Case C-260/91, *Diversinte and Iberlacta* [1993] ECR I-1885, para. 9; Case C-337/88, *SAFA* [1990] ECR I-1, para. 17.

If no reason is given for the retroactive effect, the measure can be annulled on that ground alone.[51]

Article 7 of the European Convention on Human Rights deals with retroactive legislation.

Article 7

> "1. No one shall be held guilty of any criminal offence on account of any act or omission which did not constitute a criminal offence under national or international law at the time when it was committed. Nor shall a heavier penalty be imposed than the one that was applicable at the time the criminal offence was committed.
>
> 2. This Article shall not prejudice the trial and punishment of any person for any act or omission which at the time when it was committed, was criminal according to the general principles of law recognised by civilised nations."

In Kolpinghuis Nijmegen,[52] the Court said that "a directive cannot ... [retrospectively] have the effect of determining or aggravating the liability in criminal law of persons who act in contravention of the provisions of that directive".

The principle of legal certainty is directly applicable in the national courts of Member States of the Community. The European Convention on Human Rights is not, unless it has been received in the national legal system by legislation or otherwise.

It is important to understand that it is retroactive *changes* in the law, which may be contrary to the principle of legal certainty. It does not prevent judicial or administrative determination that a given behaviour in the past was contrary to the law as it was at the time when the behaviour occurred: lack of foresight or ignorance of the law, or even genuine uncertainty as to the legal position, is not the same as retroactive effect.

The first consequence of this principle is that a Community measure should not be interpreted as having retroactive effect unless that effect is clear from the text: there is a presumption that Community measures are *not* intended to be retroactive.

Retroactivity is permitted only "where the purpose to be achieved so demands", or if there is an overriding public interest.[53] There was a sufficient justification for retroactive effect if the alternative would have involved recalculating monetary compensation amounts in the previous units of account, which would have involved

51. Case C-260/91, *Diversinte and Iberlacta* [1993] ECR I-1885.
52. Case 80/86 [1987] ECR 3969 at p. 3986; Case 14/86, *Pretore di Salo v. X* [1987] ECR 2545.
53. Case 74/74, *CNTA v. Commission* [1975] ECR 533.

disturbing prices and the agrimonetary system.[54] In another case, the need to stabilise prices necessitated retroactivity.[55]

A private party cannot object to retroactive measures if a warning has been given that such measures are possible, or if adequate transitional measures have been adopted, or if retroactivity was sufficiently clearly foreseeable. These are simply the usual rules about legitimate expectations.

4.1.9 The Court's power to limit the retroactive effect of its judgments (Article 231) EC Treaty

The Court's judgments normally declare or interpret the law, as it was in the past. The fact that a judgment may have adverse financial consequences for a Member State is not a sufficient reason for limiting the effects of the judgment and making it operate only *ex nunc*: to do this would seriously diminish the judicial protection of Community law rights.[56]

But the Court will exceptionally order that a judgment should take effect only from the date on which it is given, and in respect of legal proceedings begun before that date, to provide legal certainty to many arrangements previously made. In effect, the Court decides that the harm done by reopening a very large number of transactions carried out on a mistaken legal basis would be greater than the harm done by denying interested parties rights under Community law which they had never claimed in legal proceedings.[57]

4.1.10 Maintaining the effects of unlawful measures: Article 231

If a Community measure is annulled by the Court on procedural grounds, Article 231 gives the Court power to order that some of its legal effects should remain in force all the same.[58] This may be purely to achieve legal certainty, or it may be because no

54. Case 84/81, *Staple Dairy Products* [1982] ECR 1763.
55. Case 108/81, *Amylum* [1982] ECR 3107.
56. Case C-35/97, *Commission v. France* [1998] ECR I, Sept.
57. Case 43/75, *Defrenne v. Sabena* [1976] ECR 455 at p. 481; Joined Cases 66 and 127/79, *Meridionale Salumi* [1980] ECR 1237, at p. 1261; Case 41/84, *Pinna* [1986] ECR I, p. 26; Case 24/86, *Blaizot* [1988] ECR 379; Case C-163/90, *Legros* [1992] ECR I 4625 – "overriding considerations of legal certainty preclude legal relationships whose effects have been exhausted in the past from being called in question when this would retrospectively upset the system of financing the local authorities...."; Case C-415/93, *Bosman* [1995] ECR-I 4921, at pp. 5078-5081; Case C-106/06, *UK v. Commission* [1998] ECR I, 2729; Case C-212/94, *FMC v. Intervention Board* [1996] ECR-I 389. See also Case C-262/88, *Barber v. Guardian Royal Exchange Assurance Group* [1990] ECR I-1889, at pp. 1955-56 and the Protocol concerning Article 119 of the Treaty ... the second protocol to the Treaty on European Union: Case C-435/93, *Dietz* [1996] ECR I-5223.
58. Case 41/84, *Pinna* [1986] ECR I, p. 26; Case 264/82, *Timex* [1985] ECR 849; Case C-388/92, *Parliament v. Council* [1994] ECR I-2067.

objection to the substantive effects of the measure has been proved, and it is desirable that they should continue without interruption.

4.1.11 AVOIDING TIME LIMITS FOR PROCEEDINGS TO ANNUL COMMUNITY ACTS

Article 230 EC Treaty imposes a time limit of two months within which proceedings must be begun to have an act of a Community institutions annulled. However, it is also possible for parties who have no standing to bring proceedings under Article 230 instead to plead that a regulation was unlawful (Article 241), and this is without any time limit.

The Court has held that at least in some circumstances the principle of legal certainty prevents a party, which *could* have challenged a Community act under Article 230, and does not do so, from contesting its validity later in other proceedings.[59]

4.1.12 PROVISIONAL VALIDITY

The Court has held that some restrictive agreements which are contrary to Article 81(1), and the status of which under Article 81(3) has not yet been decided, should be regarded as "provisionally valid". This is based on the principle of legal certainty.

The problem arose in connection with restrictive agreements, which had been entered into before Article 81 (formerly 85) became applicable to them (before 1958, in the case of the original six Member States: before the date of accession, in the case of other Member States). Such agreements, even if duly notified, might not be dealt with by the Commission before they came before a national court. In the case of such "old" agreements, the Court said:

> "... the general principle of contractual certainty requires, particularly when the agreement has been notified in accordance with the provisions of Regulation No 17, that the court may only declare it to be automatically void after the Commission has taken a decision by virtue of that Regulation."[60]

The reasoning, insofar as it concerns legal certainty, can be summarised as follows. When the validity of an "old" restrictive agreement becomes an issue before a national court which has no power to decide if Article 81(3) applies, if the agreement has been

---

59. Case C-188/92, *TWD Textil Deggendorf* [1994] ECR I-833; Case C-178/55, *Wiljo*, 1997 ECR I 585 at paras. 19-24: Case C-183/91 *Commission v. Greece* 1993 ECR I 3131 paras. 9-10: See the opinion of Advocate General Colomer dated 28 Jan. 1999 in Case C-310/97P, *AssiDomän Kraft* [1999] ECR I Judgment dated 1999.
60. Case 48/72, *Brasserie de Haecht v. Wilkin-Janssen* [1973] ECR 77 at pp. 86-87; see Case 209/84, *Asjes* [1986] ECR 1425, at p. 1469; Case C-39/96, *Free Record Shop* [1997] ECR I-2303.

notified or did not require notification, the uncertainty as to the legal position is not due in any way to negligence or fault of the parties. It would therefore be unfair that they should be prejudiced by uncertainty, and therefore their agreement should be treated as valid until the Commission decides otherwise. The legal order can not immediately end the legal uncertainty, but ensures that it causes no serious inconvenience in the interim.

4.1.13 LEGAL CERTAINTY AND OTHER GENERAL RULES

The principle of legal certainty does not require every rule of Community law to make clear all of its implications when it is read. Community law includes several broad principles which sound vague and the implications of which can be seen only when specific fact situations are analysed. To see the implications of a broad rule such as Article 10 (formerly 5) EC Treaty (the duty of national authorities to help and not to obstruct the Community), one must see what the relevant Community policy is or how the Community system is designed to work in each specific situation. Legal certainty, in other words, is not a self-contained principle, but one which must be applied in specific legal and factual situations. That is why it has been necessary, in this paper, to classify the principal legal situations in which the principle has been applied by the Community Courts.

4.1.14 COMMENTS AND CONCLUSIONS

This paper does not attempt to describe the development of the principle of legal certainty, or its specific rules in Community law, or to trace its sources in the national laws of the original six Member States. It is now a largely independent principle of Community law, and its origins do not now influence its development.

This paper does not consider some questions of more topical interest: does the principle of legal certainty apply differently to directives and to regulations? One would certainly expect that Community measures which are intended to be implemented would be more general and vague in their terms than regulations which apply directly and are not intended or allowed to be re-enacted or implemented. The Court in its case-law on State liability and in its case-law preventing State authorities from pleading in litigation the State's failure to implement directive has distinguished between provisions in directives which are precase enough to be justiciable and those which are not. This is an interesting and potentially important topic, but it is not developed here.

It must be stressed that national authorities are fully bound by the principle of legal certainty, in the Community law sphere.[61] This obligation is not limited to the

61. See *e.g.* Case 32/79, *Commission v. UK (fisheries)* 1980 ECR 2403 at para. 46: Case 196/88, *Cornée* 1989 ECR 2309, at pp. 2348-49: Case 205/82, *Deutsche Milchkontor*, 1983 ECR 2633, paras. 27-33: Case 5/82 *Maizeno*, 1982 ECR 4601: Case 63/83, *R. v. Kirk*, 1984 ECR 2689, p. 2718: Case C-24/95, *Rheinland-Pfalz v. Alcan*, 1997 ECR I 1591, paras. 25, 37, 41, 49: Case C-153/94, *Faroe Seafood*, 1996 ECR I 2465.

implementation of directives, where is it well known. It also means that the legal position under national law must be made clear if Community law applies, so that Community citizens can see what their rights are and make sure that Community law is being complied with.[62]

The more widely the principle of subsidiarity is acted on, the more important will be the application of Community law principles such as legal certainty to national action in the Community law sphere.

How far national courts will use Community law principles of legal certainty where the national law is not clear will depend on various factors. Some national courts will be reluctant to see too big a difference between Community law and national law on such issues, especially if the national law gives less protection than Community law. A ruling that Community law and national law were the same would avoid having to decide the perhaps difficult issue of whether Community law applied at all. The more similar the national and Community rules on a given issue, the more likely it is that national courts will conclude that they are identical, at least in their application in a given case. More extensive judicial review of administrative action will make it more likely that these issues will arise.

The principle that the law should be clear enough to enable citizens to find out what their legal position is, to rely on it, and if necessary to defend it, is essential to the rule of law (Rechtsstaatsprinzip). Since the European Community is based on law,[63] this is one of the fundamental principles of the Community. It is a prerequisite to the right to go to court for judicial protection,[64] since one needs to know in advance whether a court case is worth bringing. Although the principle that the law should be clear has not given rise to as many judgments as the principle of legitimate expectations, it is in fact an even more important principle.

62. In Case 32/79, *Commission v. United Kingdom*, 1980 ECR at p. 2445. The Court said: "In order to safeguard the rights and interests protected by Community law for other Member States and their nationals it was necessary to lay down and publish all the detailed rules for the implementation of the system chosen by the British authorities for the implementation of Regulation No. 1779/77 so as to enable all Member States and all persons concerned, in the same way as the Community authorities, to see whether the system put into operation fulfilled both the United Kingdom's obligations under the relevant regulation, Regulation No. 1799/77, and the general requirements of non-discrimination and equality as regards the conditions of access to the fishing grounds enshrined in Article 2 of Regulation No. 101/76 and Article 7 of the EEC Treaty. This obligation to introduce implementing measures which are effective in law and with which those concerned may readily acquaint themselves is particularly necessary where sea fisheries are concerned, which must be planned and organized in advance; the requirement of legal clarity is indeed imperative in a sector in which any uncertainty may well lead to incidents and the application of particularly serious sanctions."

63. Case 294/83, *Les Verts v. Parliament* [1986] ECR 1339, at para. 23, and conclusions of Advocate-General Mancini, pp. 1349-1352.

64. Case 294/83, *Les Verts*, and Case 222/86, *Heylens* [1987] ECR 4097; Case 222/84, *Johnston v. R.U.C.* [1986] ECR 1651; Case C-120/97, *Upjohn* [1999] ECR I, 21 January 1999: Case C-97/91, *Borelli* 1992 ECR I, 6334.

"Legal certainty" is less a legal principle than a policy and an objective or ideal which influences the Court of Justice (and of course most other courts) and gives rise to legal principles, most notably of course the principle that courts usually follow previous judgments. In essence, this policy is that when faced with a choice between conflicting arguments, one should prefer the alternative, which makes the legal position more clear unless there is a strong reason (*e.g.* the legality principle)[65] to do otherwise.

Although legal certainty is not a "strong" policy (in the sense that it does not always override contrary principles) its importance in a legal system should not be underestimated. Compensation for its breach may be payable, under Article 288 EC Treaty. Economic prosperity is possible only if legal rights and duties are known and understood. Individuals and companies need to be able to rely on assurances given to them by public authorities. Laws must not be so imprecise that public authorities can find any citizen they wish in breach. In short, a legal certainty principle is essential to make a legal order satisfactory and acceptable in a democracy.

General principles of law have procedural as well as substantive consequences. As already mentioned, the principle of legal certainty combined with the duty of national courts to protect effectively rights given by Community law means, in my view, that a national court may have a duty to give a declaratory judgment if that is necessary to protect a Community law right.

This paper does not exhaust the issues in which the legal certainty may be relevant. For example, the European Commission may some day challenge an agreement between companies for the acquisition of shares, and it may be argued that the principle of legal certainty means that even if the agreement is unlawful the Commission cannot challenge the acquisition of shares after enough time has gone by.[66] If the agreement had never been notified, that argument would not seem to be valid (rights can be protected only if the private party has done all it can to safeguard its position)[67] but it might be otherwise if, as the Commission now proposes, notifications will be no longer possible in the future in Article 81 Cases.

Legal certainty was not invented by the Court of Justice: the same principles are found in most if not all European national legal systems. This means that there will remain scope both for comparative legal studies and for cross-fertilisation, that is, importation of Community rules into national law and further importation of national rules into Community law.

65. On the principle of legality see Case 134/85, *Williams* [1985] ECR 2225, para. 14; Case 133/85, *Rau v. Balm* [1987] ECR 2289, para. 29; Case T-227/95, *Assidomän Kraft* [1997] ECR II paras. 70,72; Case T-308/94, *Cascades* [1998] ECR II 14 May, para. 259.
66. See joined Cases 142 and 156/84, *British American Tobacco and Reynolds Industries*, 1987 ECR 4487.
67. Cp Case 48/72, *Brasserie de Haecht v. Wilkin-Janssen*, 1973 ECR 77 at pp. 86-87.

This also means that even outside the sphere of Community law, legal certainty is protected, at least to some extent, by national laws. But legal certainty is such an important principle that it may become important to define more clearly what exactly "the sphere of Community law" is.[68]

68. C-5/88 *Wachauf* 1989 ECR 2609; Case C-2/92 *Bostock* 1994 ECR I 955; Case C-299/95, *Kremzow* 1997 ECR I 2629;
Temple Lang, The Sphere in which Member States are obliged to comply with the general principles of law and Community fundamental rights principles, 1991 Legal Issues of European Integration 23.

4.2 The General Principles of Community Law in the Creation and Development of Due Process Principles in Competition Law Proceedings: From Transocean Marine Paint (1974) to Montecatini (1999)

*Xavier Groussot**

4.2.1 Introduction

The aim of this article is to provide a "framework for understanding" the *modus operandi* of the General Principles of Law (GPL) in the EC competition law proceeding field. More exactly, it will assess if the General Principles constitute effective tools for the development of due process principles. The basic assumption is that the EC Competition Law proceeding is a law in "gestation". Most of the principles protecting the undertaking against the Commission, are unwritten principles. The General Principles are created by the "judicial activism" of the European Court of Justice (ECJ). This implies that the law in this area is not static, it is in constant evolution. What are the scope, limits and future of this development? This article will try to provide an answer in the light of the recent case law and the need of an "extensive codification".

A legal order cannot incorporate only written provisions, in no legal system is it possible for the written law to supply a response to each question that arises before the Court. Therefore, General Principles complement written rules and principles. According to Advocate General (AG) Duteillet de Lamothe these principles form "*the philosophical, political and legal substratum common to the Member States from which, through the case law, an unwritten Community law emerges*".[1] In relation to the Treaty founding the European Community, there was no clear firm reference to the General Principles such as in international law where Article 38 of the International Court of Justice statute provides that the Court shall apply the General Principles of Law recognised by civilised nations. However, they can be deduced from the wording of Article 220 (previous Article 164), which requires a general duty to ensure that the law is observed. Article 288(2) (previous Article 215)

* Doctorate student in European law at the University of Lund. Maîtrise de Droit public, University Jean Moulin, Lyon. Master of Public International Law, Raoul Wallenberg Institute, Lund. Master of European Affairs, Lund.

1. Opinion of the AG in the case 11/70, Internationale Handelgesellschaft, [1970] ECR 1125.

Ulf Bernitz and Joakim Nergelius (eds.), General Principles of European Community Law, 185–204

makes a more explicit reference to General Principles in relation to the tortuous liability of the Community. Finally Article 6(2) of the Treaty on European Union incorporated a direct reference to the General Principles of Community Law by stating that "the Union shall respect fundamental rights, as guaranteed by the European Convention for the Protection of Human Rights and Fundamental Freedoms signed in Rome on 4 November 1950 and as they result from the constitutional traditions common to the Member States, as General Principles of Community Law". This last provision however, refers only to the fundamental rights principles and does not take into consideration administrative or procedural principles.

Following an etiological approach, the operative General Principles can be divided into three main ensembles. The first one is constituted from the administrative principles (such as proportionality and legitimate expectations). The second one is formed of the so-called procedural principles (due process principles). Finally, the last group is composed of the fundamental rights principles *"stricto sensu"(*such as the right to property). It should be stressed that the EC has no comprehensive legislation concerning the procedural rights.[2] The General Principles constitute fundamental tools in the building of procedural requirements. The procedural rights constitute "*hybrid rights*". They enshrine both administrative and constitutional values common to the Member States. They are influenced by national law (not only constitutional law) in their creative process, and interact with the European Convention on Human Rights (ECHR). In competition law proceedings, the notion of due process corresponds to a variety of sub-rights. The right to be heard is the largest notion and is accompanied by so-called "corollary rights" such as the right to access to file and the right to a hearing in a reasonable time. Other principles enter in the definition of due process such as the principles of confidentiality between lawyers and clients, the protection against arbitrary or disproportionate interventions by the Commission, the principle of self-incrimination and the presumption of innocence. These principles are created by the judicial activism of the ECJ, most of them are General Principles of Community Law.

This article will be divided in two chronological parts (with two sub-parts). The first one will deal on a theoretical approach with the creative process (1.1 gap filling and the functional approach of comparative law in the early case-law) and its limits (1.2 The efficiency theory and its implications). The second one will consider the extent of the development of EC competition law proceedings with the help of the General Principles of Law. It will assess the protective scope of the principles through the jurisprudence of the 1990s. Particularly, the most recent developments in the light of Baustahlgewebe (1998) and Montecatini (1999) (2.1 The development of the protective scope). Finally, it will consider the hypothetical evolutions such as the creation of new principles and the need of codification (2.2 Conclusive remarks on the hypothetical developments).

2. Only Article 88(2) (previous 93(2)) concerning state aids requires the Commission to give notice to the parties concerned to submit their comments. However no secondary legislation exists so as to cope with state aid proceedings.

4.2.2 THE CREATION OF DUE PROCESS PRINCIPLES THROUGH THE GPL THEORY

4.2.2.1 Gap fillings and the functional approach of comparative law in the early case law

The role of the principles arises from the necessarily incomplete character of the Community legal order. According to Pescatore, "*legal principles transform the law into a coherent system*".[3] As it has been suggested by Lord Denning in the *Bulmer LTD v. Bollinger S.A case*,[4] the General Principle of Community law because of the "*sui generis*" nature of the EC system are "filling the gap" of Community law. According to Schwarze, "*the Court has to analyse the different national approach, make a synthesis and find a common principle, which can fit in the European legal order.*"[5] AG Lagrange in his Opinion in *Hoogovens*, considered that the case law of the Court, when it comes to invoke national laws does not limit to the "common denominator" between the different national solutions, they choose the solution in relation to the object of the treaties, the most progressive solution.[6]

The General Principles of Law are created generally by influence of national Members States law (but also by influence of International instruments, such as the European Convention on Human Rights).[7] The General Principles created by the inspiration of the law of the Member States, but also inspired by the European Convention on Human Rights, are the results of the comparative search done by the Court of Justice and the Advocates General. However in early competition proceedings cases, the ECJ emphasised that neither the wording of Article 6 of the European Convention on Human Rights nor the decisions of the European Court of Human Rights indicate that it upheld the right not to give evidence against oneself.[8] Similarly, it refuted the application of Article 14 of the International Convention on Civil and Political rights as it relates only to criminal offence.[9] *Hoechst* and *Orkem* referred respectively to Articles 6 and 8 of the European Convention on Human Rights. In both cases, the ECJ ruled that the principles did not fall into the ambit of the articles. In *Hoechst*, Article 8 was said to apply only to man's personal freedoms, whereas in *Orkem*, Article 6 could not be read as implying a right against self-incrimination.

---

3. Pescatore, "Introduction à la Science du Droit", (Luxembourg), 1960, p.120.
4. *Bulmer LTD. v. Bollinger S.A*, (1974) 2 All E.R, 1226 at p.1236.
5. Schwarze, "Tendencies Towards a Common Administrative Law", ELR, 1991. Schwarze, "The Administrative Law of the Community and the Protection of Human Rights", CML Rev, 1986, 415.
6. Case 14/61 *Hoogovens v. HA*, [1962] ECR 253 at pp. 283-284.
7. *Stauder v. Ulm* [1969] ECR 419, Case 4/73 *Nold v. Commission* [1974] ECR 491Case 11/70 Internationale Handelsgesellschaft [1970] ECR 1125, Case 222/84 *Johnston v. Chief Constable of the Royal Ulster Constabulary* [1986] ECR 1651. Ibid Hoechst §13, Dow Benelux §24, Dow Chemical Ibérica §10.
8. Ibid. Orkem § 30 and Otto § 11.
9. Ibid. Orkem § 31 and Otto §11.

In competition law proceedings, the cases represent the richest seed for analysing the comparative law approach. It should be highlighted immediately, that the ECJ rarely made direct reference to comparative methodology in its case law on the General Principles. Nonetheless, in certain instances and especially in the field of competition law proceedings, the ECJ used a direct reference to the various laws of the Member States in order to elaborate a particular principle such as in *AM&S, Hoechst* and *Orkem*. In addition, the explicit mentions of the comparative methodology are generally found in the AG Opinions, which provide an extreme useful basis so as to understand the *modus operandi* of the creative process. AG Warner in Mills considered that "in the search for the General Principles common to the laws of the Member States, it is unhelpful to use terms derived from particular national systems and unknown or bearing different meanings in others. One should look for the reality behind the label, seeks to identify the substance of the legal rights, powers and obligations recognised and enforced in the different systems".[10]

A clear example of the comparative law approach is reflected in the *Transocean Marine Paint* case (17/74).[11] AG Warner undertook a general comparative analysis of the law of the Member States, in relation to the right to a fair hearing. AG Warner analysed the clear existence of the "*audi alteram partem*" principle in the law of England, (being a principle of natural justice), but also in Denmark, Germany, Ireland and Scotland.[12] Then it analysed the situation in France,[13] Belgium and Luxembourg,[14] where the respective "Conseils d'Etat" have developed such "principes généraux du droit de la défense" in administrative law, applicable in the absence of any specific legislative provisions. Finally, it came to the third group, composed of Italy and the Netherlands, where this principle does not exist in the administrative proceeding.[15] Thus the principle was not common to the whole Community. Two Sates were not recognising the existence of this principle in the administrative proceedings. Nonetheless, the Court emphasised the presence of such principle in the Community law order. The approach of the Court can be deemed progressive. An even more progressive approach has been taken in *AM&S*.

In the AM&S case,[16] AG Slynn pinpointed that "the question is not whether legal professional knowledge is identical with the secret professionnel, but whether from various sources a concept of the protection the legal confidence emerges". In the words of Slynn what matters is the overall picture. The Court in ruling on the existence of a principle of confidentiality between lawyers and clients was clearly

10. Case 110/75 *Mills v. Investment Bank* [1976] ECR 955 at p. 975.
11. Case 17/74 *Transocean Marine Paint* [1974] ECR 1063.
12. Ibid. p. 1088.
13. Certain authors in France such as Professor Vedel do not consider the existence of the "*audi alteram partem*" principle in France, but consider it under "les droits de la défense".
14. The case law in Belgium and Luxembourg is deemed to be less hesitant than in France for developing this principle.
15. Ibid. AG Warner Opinion in the *TMP* case, p.1082 at pp 1088-1089.
16. Case 155/79 *AM&S* [1982] ECR 1575.

influenced by the common law, which represented the most advance system in terms of protection. "The Court has to weigh up and evaluate the particular problem and search for the best and most appropriate solution".[17]

In the *Hoechst* case,[18] AG Mischo, considered that the situation was not identical in all the Member States.[19] Certain Member States such as Spain[20] and Germany[21] assimilated the business premises to home. In others such as Belgium, the question had not been definitively settled. Finally, two Member States, Ireland and the Netherlands, expressly defined in their case law and constitutions that the concept of dwelling as only applies to private persons living there.[22] AG Mischo despite the divergences was ready to endorse the existence of a fundamental right protecting the business premises, "Above and beyond those differences a general trend is discernible in the national legal systems...I therefore propose that it should be expressly stated that there is at Community level a fundamental rights to the inviolability of business premises".[23] In addition, the Court considered also that Article 8 of the ECHR did not apply to business premises. In *Hoechst*, the ECJ did not acknowledge the protection of business premises as falling under Article 8, whereas in Noviflora Sweden Aktien-Bolag,[24] the Commission on Human Rights has admitted complains based on Article 8 of the ECHR in case of visits at the business premises. The European Court on Human Rights in the *Niemitz* case of the 12 December 1992 has followed the Commission in its jurisprudence. Whereas three years before, in the *Chappell* case,[25] concerning the application of Article 8 to the seizure of videocassettes and documents from premises used as an office, the Court did not discuss if commercial premises fell within the ambit of the cited article.[26] The Court in *Hoechst*

17. AG Opinion Slynn in *AM&S* p.1649. AG slynn is also making direct references to AG Lagrange in *Hoogovens v. High Authority*.
18. Case 46/87 and 227/88 *Hoechst* [1989] ECR 2859. *Hauer* and *Hoechst* constitute the rare cases where the Court made explicit references to the national laws of the Members States. See also *AM&S* case and *Orkem*.
19. AG Mischo in *Hoechst* at p. 2893.
20. Ibid. 2887, § 64 and 65. Citing a Spanish case law of 1985.
21. Ibid. 2888, under Article 19(3) Basic Law, legal persons enjoy Fundamental Rights and both the case law and legal written provisions are unanimous in considering that the term home covers business premises.
22. Ibid. 2889, § 73 (for Ireland): The case law seems to indicate that the constitutional protection does not apply to legal persons or to business premises, § 83 and §84 (for the Netherlands): Article 12 of the constitution does not apply to natural persons or to places other than the dwelling of natural persons.
23. Ibid. 2893,§ 103.
24. 12 October 1992, req. n14369/88.
25. *Chappell* case of 30 March 1989, series A, Vol. 152.
26. See the opinion of AG Mischo in the *Hoechst* case, using a comparative analysis in connection to the excessiveness of the Investigative powers of the Commission. ECR, 1989, pp. 2884-2894. See Usher, "Principles Derived from Private Law and the ECJ", ERPL, 1993, 109 at p. 131. See also Clapham, "Human Rights and the EC": a critical overview. Nomos, Baden-baden, 1991, 59.

did not establish the existence of General Principles in relation to the protection of the business premises. Following the *AM&S* case law, it is submitted that the Court could have searched for the most progressive solutions. The ECJ has taken a minimalist approach.

Concerning the right against self-incrimination, the scope of this principle was established in *Orkem*[27] and *Solvay*[28] and subsequently enlarged expressly to criminal penalties in *Otto v. Postbank.*[29] Citing and using the "functional method"[30] of AG Slynn in *AM&S,* AG Darmon concluded that such principles existed in criminal law,[31] but not in the administrative proceedings. AG Darmon observed that "an analysis of national laws has indeed shown that there is a common principle enshrining the right not to give evidence against oneself. But it has also shown that that principle, becomes progressively less common as one moves away from the area of what I shall call classical criminal procedure".[32] Lenaerts argued that the ECJ went beyond the application of the ECHR in certain cases.[33] As for example in connection to Article 6, the protection afforded at the Community level is larger than the one afforded by the Strasbourg Court. However, two years after the *Orkem* case, the European Court of Human Rights in the Funke case,[34] indicated that Article 6 did protect the right to remain silent and not to contribute to incriminating oneself. The Principle can be deemed to cover administrative proceedings, such as competition law procedures. The European Court of Human Rights has been clearly influenced by

27. Case 374/87 *Orkem v. Commission* [1989] ECR 3283.
28. Case 27/88 *Solvay v. Commission* [1989] ECR 3255.
29. Case C-60/92 *Otto v. Postbank* [1993] ECR I-5683 §16.
30. Ibid. AG Darmon, p. 3332 § 118: "He took care first to draw attention to the fact that, despite the inevitable differences between the Member States, a principle whereby relations between lawyers and client were confidential could be identified and classifies as a rule of Community law. Then, in a second phase, he endeavored to clarify how that principle applied and the extent to which it applied in the Community law order". Case 155/79 *AM&S* [1982] ECR at p.1654. "To achieve the best and most appropriate solution, not only in the light of the practice of the Member Sates, but the interests of the Community and individuals". See also AG Lagrange in the *Hoogovens* case.
31. Ibid. AG Darmon, p. 3331, §111.
32. AG Darmon in Orkem, p. 3327, § 98.
33. Lenaerts, "Fundamental Rights to be Included in a Community Catalogue", ELR, 1991(16). *Lenaerts, ELR, 1991*(16). See also Lasok, K.P.E, "the Privilege against self-incrimination in Competition Cases", E.C.L.R, 1990. Joshua, "The Powers of the Commission: Efficiency and swiftness in investigative procedures", in Rights of the defense and Rights of the European Commission in EC Competition Law", Association européenne des avocats (ed.), Bruxelles, 1994, 32-36.. Kerse, "Case C-60/92, *Otto BV v. Postbank NV,* Judgment of the Court of Justice of 10 November 1993", CMLRev, 1994. Van Overbreek, "The Right to Remain Silent in Competition Procedures", ECLR 1994. Goffin, "Observations: le Droit au Silence", Cahiers de Droit Européen, 1994. Stessens G, " The Obligation to Produce Documents versus the Privilege against Self-incrimination: Human Rights Protection extended too far? ELRev. Checklist No. 1, 1997.
34. Series A, No. 256A.

the case-law of the ECJ. This constitutes a typical example of interaction between Community Law and Strasbourg Law. The interaction between national law in the AG opinions and the rulings of the Court was obviously visible. Nevertheless, the interaction with the European Convention on Human Rights remained problematic. The ECJ was not ready to follow the Strasbourg case-law in procedural matters. Finally, it can be sustained that the Court in the creation of General Principles in the competition proceedings is clearly using a functional approach. Nevertheless, the functional approach is sometimes conflicting with a certain "EC efficiency interest". This strife leads in particular instances to inconsistencies in the case-law of the Court of Justice.

4.2.2.2 The Efficiency Theory and its implications

The notion of "efficiency of Community law" can be understood as the conceptualisation of the respect of the "overall objectives of the Treaty". The case-law provides here the most relevant source of study. As it has been ruled in the *Internationale Handelsgesellschaft* case,[35] "protection of fundamental rights, whilst inspired by the constitutional traditions must be ensured within the framework of the structures and objectives of the Community". The development of the General Principles is limited into "the framework and objectives of the Treaty". What does it mean? There is in the European Legal order, certain objectives, which might be superior to the judicial protection of the individual or the undertakings. What can be called "EC Efficiency limit" is expressed in the Competition law proceedings by the need for the Commission to preserve the *useful effect* of Regulation 17. *Hoechst* and *Orkem* provide clear examples for this theory in the competition law proceeding. In relation to Regulation 17, it was already expressed in National Panasonic, that the function of Article 14 is to prevent competition from being distorted to the detriment of the objectives, individual, undertakings and consumers.[36] The noticeable thing here is that the Court is placing the public interest before the individual. The notion of efficiency prevails over the protection of the individuals. Moreover, AG Warner in *AM&S* in connection to the scope of Article 11 argued that the inclusion of a rule requiring not to answer incriminating questions might have defeated the very purpose of the article or at least rendered it largely ineffective.[37]

In *Hoechst* the Court's approach was minimalist. If the Court had admitted the protection of business premises it would have undermined the investigatory powers of the Commission. The effectivity of the EC legal order was deemed superior to the protection of the undertakings, the same holds true in relation to self-incrimination. Is that because the Protection existed expressly only in two Member Sates? Of course not, the Court is following the same lines of reasoning as in *Internationale*

35. Ibid. Case 11/70 *Internationale Handelsgesellschaft*.
36. National Panasonic [1980] ECR 2033 at p. 2057.
37. Ibid. Warner in *AM&S* at p.1621. See also Joshua, "The powers of the Commission", in Rights of the Defence and Rights of the EC Commission in EC Competition Law, 1994.

Handelsgesellschaft or *Hoechst*. Indeed, the Court in *Orkem* made explicit reference to the need to preserve the useful effect of Regulation 17. Especially, in the present situation to protect the powers of investigation of the Commission under Article 11 of Regulation 17.[38] Nonetheless in both cases, the ECJ in a difficult exercise tried to balance the protection of the undertakings with the effectivity of the EC legal order. It has been recognised by an abundant jurisprudence that the rights of the defence constitute fundamental principles of community law. These rights are particularly endangered in the preliminary proceedings, particularly in the investigatory powers under Articles 11 and 14.[39] *Hoechst* recognised a General Principle against arbitrary interventions and *Orkem* founded a narrow fundamental principle protecting the undertakings against incriminatory questions under Article 11 of Regulation 17.

As it was stressed in *Hoechst*, the powers of the Commission might be limited to a certain degree, particularly, when the rights of the defence are at stake. The ECJ undertook a comparative analysis of the Member States. It concluded that in all legal systems of the Member States any intervention by the public authorities must have a legal basis. Despite a certain degree of divergences, those systems laid down protection against arbitrary or disproportionate interventions. This protection was held to be elevated to the rank of General Principle.[40] In *Hoechst*, even if the court ruled that the development of man's personal freedom is not extended to business premises. The Court recognised the need of protection of the private sphere of activities considering that the interventions must have a legal basis and justified by law. The individuals have a right to be protected against arbitrary or disproportionate interventions on the part of public authorities in their sphere of competence. The Court in *Hoechst* had chosen the lowest common denominator, considering that the protection of the inviolability does not extend to the business premises. What are the consequences of this choice? In Germany and Spain, where the Commission had acted, business premises are protected constitutionally. According to Nolte, "The Court has deprived the individuals and enterprises of a hard core of rules. They are less protected against the Commission than against their own administration".[41] In the 17 FIDE congress, Lenaerts stressed that the case-law of the ECHR has developed a "harmonizing framework". Indeed in many Member States the right to the inviolability of the home has been extended to the business premises. In Belgium, France and Ireland it has been achieved by the legislation, whereas, in Germany and Spain, the constitution and the case-law already guaranteed it. In practice, if the competent authorities possess a warrant, they can circumvent the prohibition and undertake the search.[42] Citing Lenaerts, "The statement of the ECJ according to which the legal systems of the Member States are considerably different in regard to the protection of

38. Ibid. *Orkem* § 34
39. Ibid. *Hoechst* §15, *Orkem* § 34, *Otto* §12. See also AG Gulmann in *Otto* at p. 5698.
40. Ibid. *Hoechst* § 19, *Dow Benelux* § 30, *Dow Chemical Ibérica* § 16.
41. Nolte, "General principle of German and European Administrative Law – A Comparison in Historical Perspective", Modern Law Review; 1994, 191.
42. FIDE Kongress, "procedures and sanctions in economic administrative law", Berlin 1996

business premises against on-the-spot investigations, cannot readily be confirmed from comparative analysis of the national reports that have been prepared".[43]

Similarly, the Court in *Orkem* even if rejecting the existence of a General Principle protecting self-incrimination in administrative proceedings has in order to safeguard the rights of the defence in the preliminary stage created a principle (the "*Orkem* principle") limiting the powers of the Commission. In *Orkem*, the Court pointed out that respect for the rights of the defence, a fundamental principle of Community legal order, precluded the Commission using its powers under Article 11(5), from compelling an undertaking to provide its answers which might involve an admission on its part of an infringement which it is incumbent upon the Commission to prove.[44] The European Court of Justice in *Otto* extended the scope of the principle to criminal penalties, while not recognising the existence of a General Principle. Similarly, in the decision Société Générale of 1995, the CFI confirmed the "narrow" case-law (in the sense that it applies in relation to Article 11(5)) regarding self-incrimination.

Whereas, in *Orkem*, the principle was not existing in the Strasbourg system, in *Otto* and *Société Générale*,[45] the right to remain silent had been expressly recognised in the meantime by the European Court on Human Rights. The ECJ could have conceived the reality of a General Principle based on the existence of such a principle in the Strasbourg order. Practically, this was impossible for the ECJ to adopt such a view without undermining the effectivity of Regulation 17. AG Darmon in *Orkem* stressed that for one reason or another the Commission was deprived of the right to request information, or to ask for information. It would have to make systematic use of more coercive measures.[46] The principle of self-incrimination in administrative proceedings only existed in Germany and Spain, whereas in France, Luxembourg and Greece, it was categorically excluded. The ECJ by creating this principle has permitted it to impact at national law level. So, in the three national legal orders, the judicial authorities have taken measures in order to comply with the Community Law requirements. For instance in France, in a judgment of 1990 the Court of Appeal in BOCCRF[47] has expressly protected the right against self-incrimination as a right of the defense in national proceedings against the "conseil de la concurrence".

The European Association of Lawyers pinpointed in its "livre blanc" the modifications at the national level. They argued that the position taken in *Orkem* and *Solvay* should be revisited, "The position adopted by the Court in Orkem and Solvay was based on the fact that the right to silence was not sufficiently recognized in the Member States. At the time many Member States did not have any legislation comparable to Articles 85 and 86 of the Treaty. Since 1989, several Member States

43. Ibid. *Lenaerts*, pp. 529-530.
44. Ibid. *Orkem* § 34 and § 35, *Otto* §12.
45. CFI, Case T-34/93, *Société Générale v. Commission*, J.T.D.E., 1995, 137.
46. Ibid. AG Darmon in *Orkem* at p. 3342.
47. Arrêt de la Cour d'Appel (1er ch. Sef. Concur.) 21 May 1990, BOCCRF, n 13 du 1er Juin 1990. See also Pliakos, "La protection des droits de la défense et les pouvoirs de vérifications de la Commission des Communautés européennes: une issue heureuse?", RTDE 1995, p. 449.

including Belgium, Italy and Denmark have adopted legislations heavily inspired by Article 85 and following. One can therefore reasonably expect that in these States the competition authorities and the courts will be confronted with the defense of the right to silence. The comparative analysis of the legal systems on which the Court based its reasoning in the *Orkem* and *Solvay* decisions should be therefore be brought up to date."[48]

Consequently, the principle against self-incrimination sounds like an old advertisement. The *Orkem* principle has the same smell, color and the same taste as a General Principle but it is not a General Principle. What is it? An Ersatz? The *Orkem* principle is clearly part of the Rights of the Defense. According to the rich case-law of the Court, the safeguarding of the rights of the defence is held to be a fundamental principle of Community law. So the need to respect the *Orkem* principle is a fundamental Principle of Community law but is not a General Principle of Community Law.[49] In the light of those developments, the question is to know if the ECJ might reconsider *Hoechst* and *Orkem* and recognise the existence of General Principles in both areas. On a practical point of view, the protection against self-incrimination is a fundamental principle of Community Law, protected as such in the Community law order. In addition, the ECJ in *Hoechst* even if not establishing a General Principle protecting the privacy of business premise, has protected the undertakings against arbitrary interventions. On a theoretical Point of view, it seems that the jurisprudence of the ECJ is inconsistent with the recent developments. The European Court of Justice should reconsider its approach.

4.2.3 THE DEVELOPMENT OF DUE PROCESS PRINCIPLES

4.2.3.1 The development of the protective scope in the nineties

The basic assumption is that the General Principles constitute "open principles" in the wording of AG Mischo in *Maizena v. BALM*.[50] This feature stresses their dynamics, and thus constitutes a stark element for their development. The use of General Principles in the development of competition law proceedings must be understood on a multi-polar basis. First of all, the scope of a particular principle can be modified or extended by the jurisprudence. The examination of the case-law on legal privilege and access to file will provide grounds for this assessment. The basic assumption is that EC competition law proceedings is a law "in gestation". The Court and the Tribunal (CFI) motivated by the protection of the undertakings are enlarging

48. Ibid. "Rights of Defence and Rights of the European Commission in EC Competition Law", at p. 346.
49. We can pinpoint here, that all the rights of the defence do not constitute General Principles of Law. Hoffmann-La Roche §9 and §11, for an illustration of the difficulties involved in the definition of the right of defence.
50. Case 137/85 *Maizena v. BALM* [1987], ECR 4587 at p. 4594.

stone by stone the scope of due process through the use of the General Principles. As it was pinpointed earlier, a fundamental limitation exists to this development, that is to say the "efficiency theory". Secondly, the General Principles can be used by the ECJ in the creation of new principles, which might be extremely useful to ensure a solid protection for the defendants. The concept of presumption of innocence and the right to be heard in a reasonable time will be analysed in the light of the recent case law.

In *Hilti*,[51] the Tribunal extended the scope of the principle of legal privilege to the internal notes of the companies addressed to the members of the company. More precisely, those were notes internal to the undertaking, reporting the content of advice received from independent legal advisers.[52] Despite this, as the advice was not received by way of correspondence, it was held that the principles of legal privilege could not be frustrated on the sole ground that the legal advice was reported in documents internal to the undertaking.[53] Furthermore, the Tribunal appreciated the scope of protection afforded to the documents covered by the legal privilege. In comparison with US case-law,[54] a document can lose its protection if it is distributed outside the undertaking or largely diffused in the firm. In this instance the judge will use the concept of "group control" in order to assess the extent of the protection. In the *Hilti* case, the fact that the document was spread over a large scale between the staff managers in the undertaking did not affect its privileged nature. Maybe the future case-law will provide a certain development in this field.[55]

AM&S and *Hilti* have been criticised by the doctrine. Despite the recognition of a General Principle protecting the legal privilege, its scope remains below the Common law concept. Two main modifications or should I say extension of the principle should be undertaken. First of all, the Court should widen the scope to the in-house lawyers who are under the same rules of professional ethics than the independent one. Secondly, the principle should apply to notes and advice given before the initiation of the proceedings. The dynamic nature of the General Principle Law is offering a perfect framework for any extension of the "legal privilege".

In the *Akzo* case,[56] the ECJ developed the principle of confidentiality to the protection of the business secrets of the defendants *vis-à-vis* the third parties. The Court ruled that the business secrets should be afforded special protection. The Court went on to say, that despite the existence of Articles 19 and 21 in Regulation 17, those provisions must be regarded as the expression of a General Principle which applies

51. T-30/89 *Hilti Aktiengesellschaft v. Commission* [1990], II-163.
52. *Hilti* §16.
53. *Hilti* §18.
54. *Upjohn v. United States*, 449 US 383.
55. Winckler A., "Legal Privilege et Droit Communautaire de la Concurrence", in "Rights of Defence and Rights of the European Commission in EC Competition Law", p. 62. "*AM&S* and *Hilti* are just the commencement of the case law. The comparison with the system of the legal privilege is permitting us to appreciate the essential lines of the future debate" (my translation).
56. *Akzo Chemie v. Commission*, [1986] ECR 1965.

during the course of the administrative procedure.[57] In the SEP case,[58] concerning the protection of the business secrets, the Court applied the principle to the national authorities. The ECJ by referring to Akzo extended the scope of protection, "*where an undertaking has expressly raised before the Commission the confidential nature of a document as against the national authorities, on the grounds that it contains business secrets, and where the argument is not irrelevant, the general principle of the protection of the business secrets, may limit the Commission's obligation under Article 10(1) to transmit the document to the competent national authorities*".[59]

The case-law relating to access to file provides also an interesting example. Access to file is a procedural safeguard intended to protect the rights of the defense. The proper existence of this principle is realised through the need to submit observations on the truth and relevance of the facts, charges, circumstances relied on by the Commission. The reference of access to file as General Principle of Law was recognised quite recently by the CFI in the *Cimenteries* case,[60] the Tribunal ruled that "Observance of the rights of the defense, in all proceedings in which sanctions may be imposed is a fundamental principle of Community law. Due observance of that General Principle requires that the undertakings concerned must have been afforded the opportunity during the administrative procedure to make known their views on the truth and relevance of the facts and circumstances alleged by the Commission".[61] It can be asserted that the ECJ assimilates the rights of access to a General Principle of Law. By using this phrasing, the Court seems to define access to file as a General Principle being a "corollary of the right to be heard".

It should be stressed that the definition given is favourable to the administration in the sense that the Commission is only obliged to give access to the documents it has itself decided to use as objections or evidence. As the Court in various cases such as AEG, Akzo or VBVB ruled, "*there are no provisions which requires the Commission to divulge the contents of its file to the parties concerned*".[62] Nonetheless, being a General Principle and Regulation 99 being silent on the question of disclosure, the right to access is subjected to potential praetorian evolution. Consequently in Hercules,[63] following AG Vesterdorf reasoning, the Tribunal considered that apart of non-communicable Documents, the Commission had an obligation to disclose to the firms, all documents whether incriminatory or exculpatory, which it had obtained in the course of an investigation.

57. Ibid. *Akzo*, §28 p. 1992.
58. Case C-36/92 P, *Samenwerkende Elektriciteits-Produktiebredrivjen NV v. Commission*, [1994] ECR I-1911.
59. Ibid. SEP, §36 and §37 at p. 1942.
60. T-15/92 *Cimenteries CBR and others v. Commission* [1992] ECR II-2667.
61. §39 Cimenteries, §59 Solvay and §69 ICI.
62. Ibid. §25 VBVB, §24 AEG and §16 Akzo. Case 43 and 63/82 *VBVB and VBBB v. Commission* [1984] ECR 19. Case 107/82 *AEG v. Commission* [1983] ECR 3151. Case 62/96 *Akzo v. Commission* [1991] ECR I-3359.
63. Case T-7/89, *Hercules Chemicals v. Commission* [1991] ECR II-1711. §54.

The scope of the right to access was furthermore confirmed and developed in the *Solvay* and *ICI* cases.[64] The main critical problem remaining was the extent of the discretionary powers of the Commission in the determination of the documents as accessible. The Court ruled that it couldn't be for the Commission alone to decide which documents are of use for the defense. The judgment resorted to a General Principle of "equality of arms" in order to justify that the undertaking should have the same knowledge of the file than the Commission. The Court went on to say that " the principle of equality of arms and its corollary in competition cases, namely the principle that the information available to the Commission and the defense should be the same, required that the applicant should be able to assess the probative value of documents of another firm, which the Commission has not annexed to the statement of objections".[65]

In the recent *Hercules* case of July 1999,[66] the Court stated that the General Principles of Community law governing the right of access to the Commission's file are designated to ensure effective exercise of the rights of the defense, including the right to be heard enshrined in Regulations No. 17 and 99.[67] The breach of this principle in the proceeding prior to the adoption of the decision can lead, in the instance of an infringement of the rights of the defense, to the annulment of the decision.[68] However, the Court *in casu*, considered that the refusal to access to the replies of the other producers to the statement of objections do not lead to the annulment of the "polypropylene decision".[69] Indeed, the scope of access to file is limited to the documents collected under the course of the investigatory powers conferred by Articles 11 and 14 of Regulation 17. This case-law is not revolutionary in itself, however it demonstrates the potential of the Court to specify through its jurisprudence the extent of the rights of the defense such as the right to access in competition law proceedings on a case by case analysis.

It has been seen previously that the General Principles are able to permit the development of the rights of the defense in the competition law proceedings by sharpening the meaning and extending the scope of protection of the existing principles. Finally, it can be asserted that the General Principles might create new principles, which could enter in the definition of the rights of the defense and foster the protective scope of the undertakings. Baustahlgewebe[70] and Montecatini[71] provide two precious examples of the activism of the Court in building new procedural principles. Those two cases afford an exemplification of the Court technique in the elaboration of due

64. Case T-30/91 *Solvay v. Commission*, [1995] ECR II-1775. Case T-36/91 *ICI v. Commission* [1995] ECR II-1847.
65. Ibid. *Solvay* §81 and §99 and ICI §91 and §93.
66. Case C-51/92 P *Hercules Chemicals NV* [1999] ECR I-0000.
67. Article 19(1) of Regulation No. 17 and Articles 3, 7 and 9 of Regulation No. 99.
68. Ibid. *Hercules* §76 and §77.
69. Ibid. *Hercules* §82.
70. Case C-185/95 P, *Baustahlgewebe GmbH v. Commission* [1999] ECR I-8417.
71. Case C-235/92 P *Montecatini v. Commission* [1999] ECR I-0000. See the Case on the website www. Europa.eu.int

process principles. On the one hand, Baustahlgewebe specifies the *audi alteram partem* principle by extending the scope of this "umbrella concept". On the other hand, in Montecatini, the Court adds a new principle, the presumption of innocence, to the rights of the defense (a concept wider that the right to be heard).

4.2.3.1.1 Baustahlgewebe and the right to a hearing within a reasonable time

The appellant argued that the time taken by the CFI to give judgment (66 months) was excessive and consequently, Article 6(1) of the ECHR was violated. They pinpoint that the time taken for the proceedings was not due to the circumstances of the case, but should be imputed to the Tribunal. Subsequently, "such a delay constitutes a Prozeβhindernis (a bar to proceedings with the case) justifying the setting aside of the contested judgement, the annulment of the decision, and closure of the proceedings".[72]

AG Léger in its Opinion stressed, that according to a constant jurisprudence, the fundamental rights form an integral part of the General Principles of Law from which the Court ensures the respect.[73] For this purpose, the Court is inspired from the common constitutional traditions of the Member States and the international instruments concerning the protection of human rights. On the one hand, the AG pinpointed the importance of the European Convention on Human Rights, and its use by the Court as source of inspiration to recognise fundamental rights, which lies at the top of the hierarchy in this domain. On the other hand, he pointed out the influence of the common constitutional traditions in the elaboration of the General Principle. In the present situation, the AG indicated clearly that all the Member States and Article 6(1) of the ECHR recognised the right to a hearing within a reasonable time. Finally, he considered that even if the ECJ did not mention it yet, Article 6(1) is applicable to natural persons according to the Stenuit opinion of the European Commission on Human Rights in 1991.

The Court ruled that Article 6(1) of the European Convention on Human Rights provides that in the determination of his civil rights obligations or of any criminal charge against him, everyone is entitled to a fair and public hearing within a reasonable time by an independent and impartial tribunal established by law.[74] The Court highlighted that the General Principle of Community law according to which everyone is entitled to a fair legal process has for source the fundamental rights and is applicable to the proceedings concerning undertakings on which the Commission has issued a decision imposing a fine.[75] The General Principle of Community Law on the right to be heard includes the right to a hearing within a reasonable time. This right appears as a corollary right of the *audi alteram partem* principles, precisely as the right to access to the Commission's file.

72. Ibid. Baustahlgewebe §26.
73. Opinion of AG Léger, IV, A. 1.a) la norme invoquée.
74. Ibid. § 20.
75. Ibid. § 21.

The Court estimated that the duration was extremely important.[76] Nonetheless, the Court stressed, citing expressly the jurisprudence of the European Court of Human Rights such as *Erkner and Hofauer,*[77] *Kemache*[78] or *Phocas v. France,*[79] that in the appraisal of the length of the period, the circumstances specific to the each case and particularly the importance of the case for the person, the complexity and the behaviour of the applicant and of the concerned authorities should be taken into consideration.[80] *In casu*, the Court ruled that despite the complexity of the case, indeed 14 manufacturers of welded steel mesh had infringed Article 85 of the Treaties by a series of agreements or concerted practices,[81] the fine fixed to the sum of 3 million ECU should be revised.[82] However, considering the outcome of the case, the duration of the proceedings had no impact on the judgment. Consequently, the judgment could not be set aside on its entirety.

4.2.3.1.2 Montecatini and the presumption of innocence

In *Dow chemical Ibérica* and more recently in *Solvay* (1995), the defendant invoked a principle of presumption of innocence. The ECJ rejected the submission without examining the existence of such a right in the Community law order.[83] Drawing a parallel with the Strasbourg legal order, such a right is enshrined in Article 6(2) of the European Convention on Human Rights. According to this Article, "*everyone charged with a criminal offence shall be presumed innocent, until proven guilty according to the law*". The scope of this article has been confirmed in the *Öztürk* case in the field of criminal law.

Can we apply such a principle in the EC Competition law order? More precisely can we apply this principle of criminal law to the competition law proceedings? AG Darmon in its opinion in *Orkem* observed that the *Öztürk* judgment should not be seen as being so far-reaching. The concept of "charged with a criminal offence" within the meaning of the Convention should be taken to extend to undertakings that are the object of administrative proceedings. According to Darmon, in the Member States competition law is largely administrative law. Therefore, there is no certainty that the Strasbourg Court would, in competition matters, follow the same reasoning as in the *Öztürk case.*[84] Consequently, in the situation it is clear that no General Principle of presumption of innocence could be sculpted. Nevertheless, it is

76. Ibid. § 29.
77. Cases of the 23 April 1987, Series A No. 117, §66.
78. Case of the 27 November 1991, Series A No. 218 §60.
79. Case of the 23 April 1996, Recueil des arrêts et décisions 1996-II, p. 546 §71. See also *Garyfallou AEBE v. Greece* of the 27 September 1997, Recueil des arrêts et décisions 1997-V, p. 1821, §39.
80. Ibid. *Baustahlgewebe* § 29.
81. Ibid. *Baustahlgewebe* § 35 and § 47.
82. The Court reduced the fine to 2950000 Ecus.
83. Ibid. *Dow Chemical Ibérica,* § 56 at p. 3195.
84. Ibid. *Orkem,* Darmon Opinion at p. 3337.

also clear from the recent case-law of the Strasbourg court such as *Saunders* (1996),[85] that the presumption of innocence is linked to the concept of self-incrimination.

In the recent *Montecatini* case of 8 July 1999, the defendant invoked once again the principle of presumption of innocence against the "polypropylene decision" of the CFI as a "principle common to all the civilized judicial order".[86] The Court finally recognised that the principle of presumption of innocence is part of the fundamental rights protected by the case-law of the Court as reaffirmed in the preamble of the single European Act and Article F (2) of the TEU, and which results notably in Article 6 §2 of the European Convention on Human Rights.[87] The Court also highlighted, citing the *Öztürk* and *Lutz* jurisprudence[88] of the ECHR, that this General Principle applies to all types of proceeding against undertakings, leading to fines or penalties.[89] According to *Montecatini*, the Tribunal had introduced a presumption of culpability in affirming that it did not contest its participation to the meetings and consequently had assumed that the firm had participated to the whole meetings. However, the Court did not consider that the principle of presumption of innocence was infringed, as the conclusion of the CFI was based on the existence of a founded anti-competitive agreement.[90]

4.2.3.2 Conlusive Remarks on the Hypothetical Developments

In the *AM&S* case it can be said that the ECJ has established a high standard of protection. However, this standard remains below the Common law order, as it was not extended to in-house lawyers. In *Hoechst*, the Court having refused to protect business premises as a General Principles has undermined the rights of Spanish and German undertakings, which are constitutionally protected. In *Orkem* even if the Court did not accept the existence of a General Principle, the protection afforded to European undertakings corresponds to a high standard of protection. Indeed in France, Greece and Luxembourg such a protection did not exist. In addition, the jurisprudence of the European Court on Human Rights in *Niemitz* and *Funke* contradicted the judgments of the ECJ. The case-law of the ECJ in this matter is thus inconsistent. Paradoxically, the ECHR has been willing to follow the ECJ jurisprudence. The *Funke* case is a flagrant example of this influence. Nonetheless, in the light of the new case-law, such as *Baustahlgewebe* and *Montecatini*, it would be bad faith not to acknowledge that the Court has made a tremendous effort in incorporating the Strasbourg case-law.

85. Ibid. *Saunders* §68.
86. Ibid. *Montecatini* §135 and §173.
87. Ibid. *Montecatini* § 175.
88. *Östurk* case of 21 February 1984, series A No. 73 and *Lutz* of 25 August 1987, series A No. 123-A.
89. Ibid. *Montecatini* § 176.
90. Ibid. *Montecatini* §180.

The General Principles of Law are clearly playing a strong role in the creation and development of EC competition law proceedings. As it was emphasised by AG Mischo, they constitute "open principles". Due to their praetorian creation and gap filling function, they afford effective tools in the development of competition law proceedings. In most of the cases, the Advocates General have used an extensive comparative methodology in order to deduce the existence of a General Principle of Law. The interaction between national law in the AG Opinions and the rulings of the Court is obviously visible. In its early case-law, the Court has established wide principles such as the right to a fair hearing. The subsequent jurisprudence has specified and extended the scope *rationae materiae* of this vast concept in European law, for instance by referring to access to file and to the right to be heard in a reasonable time.

The EC competition law proceedings is blatantly in *statu nacendi*. Even if the Court has created principles with a reasonable protective scope such as in *AM&S* and *Hoechst*. The level of protection remains below certain European national legal orders. Nonetheless, the ECJ and the CFI are building stone by stone the future shape of competition law proceedings. Those instances are always motivated by the aspiration to afford maximal or I should say natural protection to the undertaking. The other hallmark of the "gestation" in this area is also reflected in the inconsistency of the case-law. In the *Orkem* case, the ECJ has created a principle which is not a General Principles but which sounds like one. In *Solvay* and *ICI*, one the one hand, the CFI is assimilating clearly access to file as a corollary to the right to be heard. The right to be heard according to the case-law is a General Principle. So it can be assumed that access to file constitute a General Principle. On the other hand the Tribunal made explicit reference to a General Principle of "equality of arms". What is the borderline between this principle and the right to access? The General Principle of equality of arms can be seen as an expression of access to file which give the applicant a right to assess the probative value of the Commission's file. Therefore, we can deduce that there is a major problem in the definition of the legal scope of the due process principles. All the due process principles are fundamental principles of Community law. However, being a Fundamental Principle does not lead them automatically to be recognised as General Principles of Community Law. The *Orkem* principles provide a clear example for this assessment. Nonetheless, the recent evolutions at the national level provoked by the influence of the ECHR and ECJ case-law seems to open a new path to developments. The principle against self-incrimination and the protection of the business premises could be assimilated theoretically nowadays to General Principles of Community Law. This lack of clarity justifies the need of a codification.

The crucial question is to foresee the future shape of the rights of the defense. Can we assume that the General Principles of Law constitute the only tools to develop EC competition law proceedings? Perhaps, some deeper reforms needs to be undertaken in order to improve the European system. I mean here the potential reform of Regulations 17 and 99. It might be the time to incorporate clearly the jurisprudential evolutions in the regulations so as to provide a maximum of legal certainty. We can wonder if the simple crystallisation of the case-law in legislation would be enough.

Such a codification should not only be a pale crystallisation of the case-law, but should attempt to embody a comprehensive body of procedural principles. Indeed, even if the case-law of the Court is more and more advanced, the Court can only elaborate and develop its jurisprudence when "a meal is served". As it was pinpointed earlier, lots of rights can and should be developed but the development can only occur through the litigations presented before the Court. Consequently, such a codification will still leave a lot of holes unfilled. The General Principles are here disclosing their limits. In this sense, a hypothetical codification should also lead to legislative development. For instance the clear reference of the legal professional privilege in Regulation 17 might permit the extension of its scope to in-house lawyers under the same rules of professional ethics that the independent ones. The next step seems to be orientated towards a legislative evolution and the incorporation of the General Principles in the regulations. It can be argued that a possible codification of the General Principles will undermine their dynamic and evolutive character, which render them so interesting. Nonetheless, the comparisons with the 5th and 14th Amendments of the US Constitution, where due process principles have been incorporated, permit us to consider that the US Supreme Court was not restricted by such a codification. In the event of a codification, an article similar to Article 27 of the EP Declaration of 1989 on Fundamental Rights should be expressly included. This declaration has listed some General Principles of Law such as the right to access to the Court in Article 19. Article 27 considers the list as non-exhaustive. Consequently, the Court could always elaborate and add certain "forgotten Principles" in order to enhance the protective scope of due process.

The codification should be an "extensive" one, in the sense that the principles not yet developed by the Court should be incorporated. It remains to determine what can be the scope *ratione materiae* of such procedural principles. As was pinpointed by the European Association of Lawyers, the Court in the *Dutch Book* case[91] ruled that Article 7 of Regulation 99 is giving a reasonable margin of appreciation in deciding whether or not to hear a witness.[92] It should be stressed that the right to call witness is in most of the European legal systems a stark component of the rights of the defense. It is submitted that the ECJ should develop such a General Principle, being a corollary right of the *audi alteram partem principle.*[93] Other types of principles could be develop in order to enhance the procedural rights of the parties such as the rights to successful parties or the enlargement of the legal privilege to in-house lawyers. Indeed, concerning the last principle, the legal privilege affords a decent degree of protection to the undertakings concerned. Nonetheless, it remains below the level afforded in Common Law. A large numbers of criticisms have been issued in relation to the scope of protection. Indeed, the principle should be extended to in-house

91. *VBVB and VBBB v. Commission* [1984] ECR 19.
92. Livre Blanc, "Rights of the Defence and Rights of the European Commission in EC Competition Law", p. 352.
93. Other rights could be developed in this sense, such as the right to necessary legal representation during the investigation.

lawyers who are under the same professional rules as the independent lawyers. The rules of professional ethics and discipline as AG Slynn stressed it should be the relevant criteria in order to assess the relationship between lawyers and clients. Moreover the principle does not apply to non-member States lawyers, including the states affording such a protection to Community lawyers, thus creating a discriminatory treatment.

Another interesting example is given by the submission of the party in *Baustahlgewebe* to a General Principle of promptitude *"in line with the codes of civil and criminal procedure in a majority of the Member States which involves an obligation on the part of the CFI to deliberate immediately after the hearing of a case and to deliver its judgments shortly after the hearing"*.[94] This principle should require a prompt determination of judicial proceedings by giving judgment in a reasonable time after the closure of the oral proceeding. AG Léger in its Opinion considered the allegation of the violation of the principle of orality due to the 22 months period between the close of the procedure and the pronunciation of the judgment. First, the AG defined the principle of orality as pertaining to the notion of immediacy in the UK, to "Unmittelbarkeit" in German Law and "inmediación" in Spanish law. The concept established that the judge should be in "direct contact" with the justiciable. For instance a judge who did not participate to the audience cannot participate to the ruling. The AG considered that the allegation of a General Principle of promptitude is a sort of "temporal immediacy" which differs however from the concept of "reasonable time" in its consequence. Indeed, at the difference of the right to a hearing in a reasonable time, the proceeding can be annulled and recommenced when the interests of parties are not irremediably impaired.[95]

The AG finally undertook a comparative analysis of the laws of the Member States so as to discover the hypothetical existence of a "common principle". It appeared from the analysis, that "*une très grande majorité*" of the Member States have an obligation to give their decisions in a determined delay close to the end of the debate (citing Austria, Denmark, Finland, Germany and finally the Netherlands). Certain Member States impose such an obligation (submits to certain exceptions) the same day than the closure of the oral proceedings (such as Belgium, Ireland, Portugal, Sweden, United Kingdom). Léger stressed that those measures are generally found in the procedural civil, penal and administrative texts and not in constitutional documents. Nonetheless, in certain countries, the non-respect of such an obligation does not lead to any sanction (Belgium, Denmark, Ireland and United Kingdom). He concluded that *in casu*, the laws of the Member States do not permit by themselves to characterise a "*common supra-legal tradition justifying the affirmation of a General Principle applicable to their jurisdiction in Community matters*".[96]

94. Ibid. *Baustahlgewebe*, § 50.
95. Ibid. AG Léger, IV B "sur le deuxième moyen tiré de la violation du principe dit "d'oralité".
96. Ibid. Section IV paragraph B.

The Court ruled that the appellant did not establish that the length of the deliberation had an influence on the proceedings and considered the argument of the Commission according to which the principle of promptitude does not exist in Community Law.[97] However, the Court did not use the AG argument. In my opinion, there is a room opened to the elaboration of a General Principle of promptitude, particularly if the duration of the deliberation has an impact on the outcome of the proceedings. *Montecatini* provides an excellent example of praetorian development due to the circumstances, whereas a few years earlier in *Solvay*, the Court did not examine the existence of presumption of innocence.

Finally, the "extensive codification" of the principles in the sense of incorporation of a comprehensive set of principles appears to offer an interesting solution as a palliative to the *lacunae* of the General Principles of Community law. Indeed, as it was stressed previously, the Court can only elaborate new principles through the cases brought before it. Subsequently, a codification will permit a rapid recognition of the most fundamental due process principles avoiding also the pitfall of the "non-commonality"(the principle of promptitude could subsequently be inserted). It can be concluded that the ECJ shows always a profound interest in the establishment of an elevated standard of protection for the undertakings. It is also certain that the Court is not so preoccupied to boost protection when the effectiveness of the EC system is at stake. In the present case, the effectivity of Regulation 17 can be undermined. The Court has to strike a difficult balance between the protection of the undertakings and the objectives of the EC order. This paradox of the competition law proceeding development reflects indeed the whole theory on the General Principles of Community Law.

97. Ibid. *Baustahlgewebe*, § 53.

4.3 General Principles of Community Law: Procedural Guarantees – A Note

C.S. Kerse

4.3.1 Introduction

I had the honour of chairing the Working Group on Procedural Guarantees. In this brief note I endeavour to set out a summary of the discussions of the Working Group. That the Group reached no conclusions may reflect the fact that it had only a limited time, one afternoon, to survey an extensive and growing area of law and that there were quite numerous and divergent views on issues and priorities. Or it may simply indicate poor chairmanship on my part! It was a stimulating and challenging task. In summarising the Group's deliberations, I have taken the liberty to add some personal commentary and views on the matters discussed. I hope that those who participated in the Group will nevertheless be able to recognise some of what follows as a true record of what transpired.

4.3.2 Importance of procedural guarantees

As a starting point the Group recognised the importance of procedural guarantees in both Community law and at national law. As regards Community law in particular, two factors were especially noteworthy. First, there is the decentralised nature of the application of Community law. This is a matter of established fact and, since Maastricht and with the imminent prospect of enlargement, a practical necessity and a political imperative. In very many areas, the application of Community law is committed to the hands of national courts or authorities. The process of decentralisation seems likely to increase. For example, in relation to the application of Community competition rules, the Commission has recently proposed[1] that its monopoly over granting individual exemption for restrictive agreements should be removed and that national competition authorities and national courts should be empowered to apply Article 81 TEC *in toto.* Such an idea is not uncontroversial, in concept or in its detailed implementation. But the idea that the Commission would propose something so radical would have been unthinkable only a few years ago.

Second, the scope of application of European law is rapidly expanding, particularly following the entry into force of the changes to the EC Treaty and the Treaty on European Union made by the Amsterdam Treaty. The establishment of "an area of

1. White Paper on modernisation of the rules implementing Articles 85 and 86 of the EC Treaty. COM (1999) 101 final.

Ulf Bernitz and Joakim Nergelius (eds.), General Principles of European Community Law, 205–211

freedom, security and justice", now established as one of the main objectives of the Union, will mean that European law will increasingly impinge upon areas affecting the individual. The Treaties provide for the taking of "appropriate measures" with respect to external border controls, asylum, immigration and the prevention and combating of crime. Such measures may raise politically sensitive issues, frequently complicated by a conflict of competing interests. There may be a difficult balance to be struck between, for example, the public need for an effective policy on the detection and prosecution of crime and, on the other hand, the rights and protection of the individual. There is a sense that to date many Third Pillar proposals,[2] particularly those relating to police and judicial cooperation, have been "law and order" driven. But the accused also has a place in "an area of freedom, security and justice". That has now, in the Tampere European Council conclusions,[3] been recognised at the highest political level.

4.3.3 Development of procedural guarantees in Community law

The Group noted that procedural guarantees are well-developed in Community law, especially in the context of staff cases and competition cases.[4] Those guarantees are sometimes given statutory expression in Community Regulations such as, in relation to competition cases, Regulation 17/62 and 99/63. But they have been substantially developed and augmented by the Community Courts. In this context it should be recalled that Community law is not constituted solely by the Treaties and regulations etc., made thereunder. In the performance of its duty under Article 220 (formerly 164) of the EC Treaty to ensure that "the law" is observed the Court of Justice may have regard to and apply General Principles of Law. And the Court of Justice has said:

> "it is well settled that fundamental rights form an integral part of the general principles of law whose observance the Court ensures. For that purpose, the Court draws inspiration from the constitutional traditions common to the Member States and from the guidelines supplied by international treaties for the protection of human rights on which the Member States have collaborated or of which they are signatories. In that regard, the [European Convention on Human Rights] has special significance. Respect for human rights is therefore a condition of the lawfulness of Community acts".[5]

2. Proposals brought forward Under Title VI (formerly Article K) of the Treaty on European Union (TEU).
3. Presidency Conclusions. Tampere European Council 15 and 16 October 1999, at para. 40.
4. Their historical significance can be seen by looking at the first edition (1976) of Schermers, *Judicial protection in the European Communities*, pp. 27-39.
5. Accession by the Community to the European Convention on Human Rights: *Opinion 2/94*: [1996] E.C.R. I-1759, at para. 33.

General Principles, including procedural guarantees, may thus be distilled from the laws of the Member States and from international legal instruments.

As to the former, the laws of the Member States have over the years provided a fruitful source of Community law. National law, especially in the area of administrative law, has had a dynamic impact on the application and development of Community law. *Transocean Marine Paint*[6] is a good example. The Court of Justice held that notwithstanding the absence of any express provision in the relevant Community subordinate legislation, Regulation 99/63, an undertaking on whom conditions or obligations are to be imposed in connection with the grant of exemption under Article 81(3) (formerly 85(3)) has a right to be heard on the matter. Advocate General Warner analysed the position in the laws of the different Member States in relation to the rule which in English law is known as *audi alteram partem* and reached the conclusion that whilst not all Member States had such or a similar rule nevertheless the right to be heard should form part of "the law" within the meaning of Article 220 (formerly164). The Court did not repeat such analysis in its judgment but referred simply to "the general rule that a person whose interests are perceptibly affected by a decision taken by a public authority must be given the opportunity to make his point of view known". That general rule has been stated and relied upon by the Community Courts in numerous cases since.[7]

As regards the contribution made by international legal instruments to the development of the general principles of Community law, the European Convention on Human Rights clearly has a special importance. That is acknowledged by the fact that the Convention was recognised in the preamble to the Single European Act[8] and is now expressly referred to in the Treaty on European Union. Article 6(2) states:

> "The Union shall respect fundamental rights, as guaranteed by the European Convention for the Protection of Human Rights and Fundamental Freedoms signed in Rome on 4 November 1950 and as they result from the constitutional traditions common to the Member States, as general principles of Community law".

The Community is not, however, a party to the European Convention and probably cannot be so without Treaty amendment.[9] And the principle of "respecting" fundamental rights is not the same thing as directly applying the European Convention on Human Rights and its jurisprudence. That said, there is no doubt that the Convention has had a significant impact in the development of procedural guarantees in Community law, though the Community Courts have occasionally been criticised in their

6. Case 17/74, [1974] E.C.R. 1063.
7. For a recent example, see Cases T-129/95, 2/96 and 97/96, *Neue Maxhutte Stahlwerke Gmbhand Lech-Stahlweke Gmbh v. Commission* [1999] 3 C.M.L.R. 366, at para. 228.
8. See also the Joint Declaration of 5 April 1977 of the European Parliament, the Council and the Commission: [1977] O.J. C103/1.
9. *Opinion 2/94*, [1996] E.C.R. I-1759. There is room for argument that the position has changed following the amendments made by the Amsterdam Treaty.

"application" of the European Convention.[10] The Convention has nonetheless had a substantial impact on the Luxembourg jurisprudence in this area.

4.3.4 DEFINITION OF PROCEDURAL GUARANTEES

A preliminary question facing the Group was that of definition. What do we mean by the term "procedural guarantees" in this context? Given the limited time available, the Group decided that rather than trying to define "procedural guarantees" in the abstract, it would be more profitable to give examples based on knowledge and experience of the working of the Community institutions and the European Convention. The Group identified the following "procedural guarantees":

- The right to effective judicial review;
- The right to an effective remedy;[11]
- The requirement that proceedings be brought within a reasonable time;
- The right to silence/ the privilege against self-incrimination;
- The right to be heard;
- The right to legal representation/ the protection of the confidentiality of legal advice/ the right to legal aid and assistance;[12]
- The right of access to the file;
- The right to have reasons for decisions;
- Proportionality and the doctrine of limited intervention;
- The language of the proceedings – the right to translation/interpretation;
- Limits on powers of investigation;
- *Nulla poene sine lege*;
- *Non bis in idem*;
- Restriction on use of information;[13]
- The impartiality of the decision-taker.

This list, it must be said, does not purport to be exhaustive, though the Group considered it to be reasonably comprehensive. It was essentially intended to be illustrative

10. The criticism is twofold, firstly, as to the preference of the Community Courts to develop their own version of ECHR procedural guarantees (finding too often for the Commission) and, secondly, as to the failure to have regard to Strasbourg judgments in particular instances. For example, much excitement has been generated by the apparent failure of the Court of Justice in Case 60/92 *Otto v. Postbank* [1993] E.C.R. I-5683, to have regard to the European Court of Human Rights judgment in *Funke v. France* [1993] I C.M.L.R. 897
11. Including interim relief, see *Factortame,* Case C–213/89, [1990] E.C.R. I-2423.
12. And, some members of the Group argued, the right of successful party to reimbursement of its costs.
13. See *Spanish Banks*, Case C-67/91, [1997] ECR I-4785, for the difficulties which may arise when information obtained in one context is pertinent to other proceedings.

of the content of "procedural guarantees" and to provide the basis for the discussion of the main issue described below.

4.3.5 Codification/harmonisation

The Group debated two questions. First, should procedural guarantees codified in Community law and national laws be harmonised? Second, if there is such a need, what form should any codifying/harmonising measure take? Answers to these questions involve an analysis and complex assessment of factual, constitutional, political and cultural considerations. As already mentioned the Group did not reach any definitive conclusions, but two or three issues emerged as particularly significant, at least from a practical legal standpoint.

4.3.6 Relationship with the European Convention on Human Rights

Central to the question whether there should be some form of codification of procedural guarantees under Community Law is the question of the position of the European Convention and what, if any, relationship any Community/Union measure should have with the Convention. A number of procedural guarantees are set out in the Convention, especially in Articles 5, 6, 7 and 8. The Group did not doubt the importance and value of these provisions of the Convention and of their application by Strasbourg Court. But though all Member States are Party to the Convention and the Convention is central to human rights standard setting in the Union, the Convention has intrinsic limitations as an instrument for "harmonising" Community and national laws. Questions can legitimately be raised *inter alia* as to its scope and width of application, as to whether its provisions deal sufficiently with modern practice and problems and whether a separate Community instrument is a necessity. Any answer to the last question, it is suggested, raises not just major legal and constitutional issues, with implications for the judicial architecture of the Union, but also fundamental political and cultural ones after Maastricht and Amsterdam.

4.3.7 A task for the judges or for the legislators?

The Community already has a substantial body of procedural law and remedies. That law is developed but still developing. As was observed elsewhere during the conference, the Court of First Instance has *de facto* begun the work of codification. It is a feature of its judgments in cases where a plea of infringement of the rights of the defence, frequently of the right to be heard, or other procedural guarantee has been that the Court will summarise the "well-established" law in the field. There were those in the Group who preferred to leave it to the Community Courts to continue this work. Others took the view that any codification was properly for the Community legislature, not its courts however well-qualified. Legislators could look at the matter systematically whereas any development of the law by the Community Courts would be dependent upon the "accidents" of litigation. There was also a concern that the courts might confuse remedies and procedures. A further point in favour of any development being undertaken by the Council and the Parliament was that the Court of Justice's "legislative powers" are limited, by reference to existing institutional arrangements.[14]

On the other hand, the Group did not underestimate the difficulties in getting agreement by Governments to any constitutive codifying/harmonising measure. It considered whether it would, or at least at the present time, be preferable to have a "restatement",[15] that is a systematic and comprehensive analysis and statement of the current law. The immediate value of such a document would be twofold. First, it would be a guide for use by national courts in the application of Community law,[16] and, second, to provide Community and Union legislators with a minimum checklist and benchmark against which detailed proposals under Titles IV EC and VI TEU could be measured and tested.

4.3.7.1 The EU Charter of Fundamental Rights

A further point might be added in the light of recent developments. At the time of writing, work is beginning on the establishment of an EU Charter of Fundamental rights. The politicians have set a demanding timetable, agreement by the end of 2000. The recent Tampere European Council settled the composition and method of work of the body responsible for drafting the document. The (earlier) Cologne Council indicated the potential scope of the Charter. It will include:

- universal rights guaranteed by the European Convention of Human Rights;
- rights derived from the constitutional traditions of Member States, recognised in the case-law of the Community Courts as general principles of Community law; and
- rights exclusive to Union citizens under the Treaties.

---

14. This can be seen most clearly from cases such as *AM&S*, Case 155/79, [1982] ECR 1575, where the Court had to devise an adequate arrangement for safeguarding the confidentiality of lawyer/client communications within the existing institutional structure of the Community.
15. The Group had in mind the Restatement of Law produced in the United States of America: "A series of volumes authored by the American Law Institute that tell what the law in a general area is, how it is changing, and what direction the authors (who are leading scholars in each field covered) think this change should take; for example, Restatement of the Law of Contracts; Restatement of the Law of Torts. The various Restatements have been a formidable force in shaping the disciplines of the law covered; they are frequently cited by courts and either followed or distinguished; they represent the fruit of the labour of the best legal minds in the diverse fields of law covered". Black's Law Dictionary (6th edit. 1990).
16. On the nature and extent of the obligations on national courts to apply Community law, including respecting human rights principles, see Temple Lang, *The Duties of National Courts under Community Constitutional Law* (1997) 22 E.L.Rev. 3.

Procedural guarantees may be found in each of these categories and it will be particularly interesting to see how they are identified, clarified and described in the Charter. More important, however, will be the question of the status of the Charter. Whether the Charter will be more than a declaratory measure (a "solemn proclamation") and how it will affect existing rights is unclear. The UK Government has taken the view that the exercise is essentially one of increasing the visibility of existing rights and that the Charter should take the form of a "political statement" rather than a legal text to be incorporated into the Treaties.[17] However the expectations of many outside Government, especially of representatives of civil society, are higher and look to the Charter being a measure of real substance conferring legally enforceable rights.[18]

17. See The Prime Minister, Mr Blair's Written Answer given to the House of Commons on 30 November 1999. Hansard H.C. Vol. 30. No. 10 col.81W.
18. See, for example, the evidence given by interested parties to the House of Lords Select Committee on the European Union, *EU Charter of Fundamental Rights*. 8th Report 1999–2000 HL Paper 67.

4.4 General Principles of Law in Swedish Law

Göran Schäder

I have been asked to speak under the headline General Principles of Law in Swedish Law. This being a conference on community law, I have not understood as to why my subject is a survey of the Swedish legal order and the principles that it is based upon. My subject should rather be the impact of the general principles of community law in Sweden and how those principles are applied by Swedish courts and authorities.

To begin with I must however say a few words about principles in the Swedish legal order. Like with any other legal order it is also when studying the Swedish system possible to detect some tacit precepts that remain unspoken but are reflected in different ways throughout the whole system. In that sense however, the general principles of law could be defined as the sum of the norms actually applied by the judicial instances. They are not general principles of law derived from natural law that a legal system must be built upon to qualify as a system of justice.

Having been gravely abused by the jurisprudence of the 19th century the ideas of natural law fell in disrepute in Sweden at the time of the First World War and they have – even if tendences to a renascence can be seen today – been of small importance since then.

The Swedish legal system is basically built on written law and the bulk of the fundamental principles of our legal order are therefore expressed in our constitution or in other laws. When those principles are applied, this becomes the result of the application of the laws where they are formulated. You could say that the Swedish courts has not very often had to apply the principles as such but rather as they are laid down in the written law. In such a system it is an important task for the legislator, i.e. Parliament, to formulate the general principles.

I have a background as a legal draftsman in the Ministry of Justice and I can assure you that the discussion about principles is very much alive in the work performed there. But it is regarded as bad draftsmanship just to mention a certain principle. The exact meaning and significance of a principle can often be a moot point and a legal technique where the principles are just mentioned can thus in itself lead to disputes. In the interest of legal certainty you should therefore not just refer to the applicable principle but instead state the content of it in the law where it should be applied.

The Swedish Instrument of Government is for example full of principles. The principle of legality appears already in chapter 1 Article 1 where it is said that the public power shall be exercised under the laws. That principle is also reflected in Article 9 of the same chapter where it is said that the courts, public authorities and others performing functions within the public administration shall in their work observe the equality of all persons before the law and shall maintain objectivity and impartiality. And to take another example, in chapter 2 Article 12 it is said that the fundamental

Ulf Bernitz and Joakim Nergelius (eds.), General Principles of European Community Law, 213–216

freedoms and rights listed earlier in that chapter may be restricted only in order to protect important public interests and that the restrictions must never exceed what is nessessary having regard to the purpose for which it is restricted. If that is not the principle of proportionality I don't know what to call it.

There are many other principles expressed in our constitution and this is not the place to make a full list. However, being a swede talking about principles of law I quite naturally have to mention the principle of public access to official documents. This is something much more farreaching than the right of an interested party to have access to a certain file. Public access means the access of anyone, not just the parties. This is not yet a principle of community law but let us see what happens in a few years.

That the principles of law are explicitly stated in the legislation is quite natural in a legal system based on written law where the legislator has an all-comprising competence, as the case is in Sweden.

In a system based on case-law, the basic principles becomes the result of all the cases that together form the legal order and the formulation of the general principles becomes the work of judges and scholars.

In community law there are both kinds of principles. Some of them are laid down in the Treaties and others are developed by the Court of Justice in Luxemburg. This is to some extent the result of the fact that the legislator in the Community has only very limited competence. This is by the way one of the basic principles of community law: The Community shall according to Article 5 of the EC Treaty act within the limits of the power confered upon it by that Treaty.

Many of the principles laid down by the Court of Justice concerns issues where the Member States have not given the Community powers to issue legislation that would be directly applicable in the Member States. But in order to make the community legal order function the court has been obliged to fill in the blanks. What I am thinking about is for example the principle of the supremacy of community law, the principle of direct effect of directives, the right to access to court for a citizen envoking his rights under community law and the principle of state liability for wrongful implementation of community rules.

The formulation of those principles by the court could perhaps be seen as a form of application of the principle of implied powers, which in some cases gives the community legislator powers where the Treaties are silent but where such powers are necessary to obtain the goals laid down in them.

I should perhaps add that the general principles of community law have not been developed by the court out of nowhere. Most of them are found in the national legal orders of the Member States and should therefore not be unfamiliar to the national legal systems of the Member States.

What I have been trying to show is that I think that general principles of law becomes of much greater importance in what I would call an incomplete legal system such as Community law, where the legislator only in a fragmentary way can regulate the social order. In what could then be called a complete legal system, where the legislator has an all-comprising competence, general principles of law will not necessarily play the same role.

When Sweden joined the European Union on 1 January 1995 all aspects of community law became parts of our national legal order and all principles of community law became applicable by Swedish courts and authorities when they apply community law. At the same time the European Convention on Human Rights was incorporated into Swedish law and thus made direcly applicable by Swedish courts and authorities.

My impression is that the Swedish courts and authorities where well prepared to deal with the problems that are inevitable when such a huge amount of new rules as the whole of the *acqui communautaire* is introduced all at once. Everything has of course not been perfect. But as a whole I think we have managed quite well. In the old Member States the development has been gradual. We had it all in one go.

In the court-system it is the administrative courts that most often has to apply community law. From the Supreme Administrative Court, where I spend my days, there is a rich variety of cases where community law is applied, such as cases on free movement of capital, value added tax, social insurance for migrating workers, public procurement and many others. In most of them however, it is a specific article in a regulation or directive and not the general principles of community law that is the issue.

The best example of a case where a general principle was invoked is perhaps the case of *Lassagård*. It concerns the right of access to court.

Lassagård is the name of a Swedish farm that applied for a specific kind of agricultural subsidy. According to the Government ordinance regulating the procedure for those subsidies an application should be tried by the County Government Board. A refusal could be appealed to the National Board of Agriculture, against whose decision there was no appeal. When *Lassagård* applied to the County Government Board the application was rejected because it had been filed to late according to the rules. *Lassagård* appealed to the National Board of Agriculture that refused the application and stated that its decision was final and could not be appealed.

Lassagård was not content with this and went to court. It made a long journey there, but to make a long story short I will not go into all the steps of the procedure. However, the case ended up before the Supreme Administrative Court, that in a ruling in November 1997 (RÅ 1997 ref. 65) stated that the prohibition of appeals against the decisions by the National Board of Agriculture was not compatible with the general principles of community law as those had been expressed by the Court of Justice in Luxembourg in for example the *Borelli* case. Since the community rules have primacy over national rules, the prohibition of appeals should not be applied. In the absence of rules determining which court should try the case, the Supreme Administrative Court by analogism applied a rule otherwise applicable and sent the case to a lower administrative court to be tried in substance.

In a case two years earlier (RÅ 1995 ref. 58) the Supreme Administrative Court had not been convinced that Article 6 of the European Convention on Human Rights made it necessary that agricultural subsidies could be tried by a court. That case had started before Sweden's entry into the European Union and the subsidies in question where purely national. I am however not quite sure that a case like that would be adjudicated the same way today.

It is a well known fact that community law and the general principles of community law are more often invoked by the parties than applied by the courts. At least not applied in the way the parties want it to be. I think it is important to stress that it is not only when national laws are quashed that the courts apply community law. The application may very well result in the finding that the national rule is quite in order and fully compatible with community law.

An example of a case where I think every conceivable objection against the national legislation and the application of the laws was made is the case concerning the closing down of the nuclear plant of Barsebäck.

The Supreme Administrative Court there had to try if the Governments decision to cancel the permit to operate the nuclerar plant was lawful. And in so doing it had to apply many general principles of law such as the principle that laws shall have general application, that restrictions of the use of property should only be allowed if it is done for an important public interest and if the injured party gets remuneration, that favourable administrative decisions normally are irrevocable, that legislation should not be retroactively applicable and that administrative decisions should not be in conflict with legitimite expectations. The court found that the Governments decision did not contradict either of those principles.

The principle most extensively dealt with in the judgment was however the principle of proportionality. That is also the principle in European law that as such has had the greatest impact on the Swedish legal system after the accession to the European Union. In earlier cases the Supreme Administrative Court has quashed administrative decisions because they have been in conflict with this principle (see RÅ 1996 ref. 44 and 56). In this case however, the court did not find reason to do so.

The ruling in the Barsebäck case has given the Supreme Administrative Court the opportunity to deal with a whole variety of legal issues. The question most discussed in the press has not been the courts application of general principles but if the court should have refered the case to the Court of Justice in Luxemburg for a preliminary ruling. That is however a topic for another seminar.

The general principles of community law are now a part of the Swedish legal system and the Swedish courts has had to learn them and has gradually started to apply them. I think this will vitalise the legal life in Sweden and that a greater consciousness of the importance of general principles of law is a good thing.

But when I hear people saying that general principles of law are so useful because they make it possible for the judge to reach an appropriate decision even when the legislation in question leads to another conclusion, I would like to issue a warning against excessive use of general principles. That would be to use the general principles of law as a drunkard uses a lamppost: not to seek light, but to seek support. And that cannot be the task of a judge in a democratic society.

5. Concluding and Summarising Notes

5.1 General Principles of Community Law – Concluding Remarks

*Leif Sevón**

I have been requested to make some concluding remarks on the issues before this conference. The organisers of the conference have asked me not try to summarise the discussions or draw any conclusions from them. I should rather discuss the future role of general principles in Community law. This does not necessarily prevent me from picking upon some of the points made during our discussions.

The task thus identified calls for two remarks. First, in order to be profoundly unfair with the organisers of the conference, one could assume that the subject and the speaker have been chosen in order to find out how the Court of Justice intends to develop the general principles. This could be regarded as a specific application of the theory that the Court has an agenda that it intends to put into operation whenever an opportunity presents itself. If the choice of theme had been based on such an assumption it would presuppose that a Member of the Court could be seduced to present that agenda. However, the reason why I am not in the position to be that indiscreet is found in the fact that there simply is no agenda to reveal. All I can do is to seek any tendencies that could be read out of the case-law of the Court.

Secondly, there is another limitation to my possibilities to predict the future. The future of the general principles depends not only on the development of the case-law but also on the action of the masters of the Treaty and the Community legislator. There is a link between the eventual development of general principles of law and the development of Community law in general. It is evident that the development of Community law may require a development of the general principles, as we know them today. The extension of Community law into new fields of law may give rise not only to a need to develop existing general principles but possibly also to develop new principles. As far as such developments are concerned Members of the Court of Justice are not particularly well placed to forecast the future since they are not well informed of what might be in the course of being decided to that effect.

Let me just point out that certain developments that have already taken place or which are envisaged may trigger such developments. Attention has already been drawn to Title IV of the Amsterdam Treaty on visas, asylum, immigration and other policies related to the free movement of persons. To this one might add two further elements. Even if the Brussels II Convention on recognition and enforcement of judgments in the field of family law deals with recognition and enforcement I would not entirely exclude that the substance of the judgments concerned might necessitate

* Judge at the European Court of Justice.

Ulf Bernitz and Joakim Nergelius (eds.), General Principles of European Community Law, 219–222

the development of new general principles. Secondly, a similar development may occur as a consequence of the meeting of the European Council in Tampere in October this year. The Agenda of that meeting contains items such as criminal and private law. To the extent that may, in due course, result in the creation of a binding instruments of Community law, those new areas may well lead to a development of existing general principles or to the creation of new ones.

In the absence of knowledge about what is going to happen the level of ambition of this presentation is low. It will also be limited to a purely personal view.

Do I believe – and I speak only of my personal impressions – that any tendencies may be deduced from the recent jurisprudence of the Court?

In this respect I would like to start with two words of warning which, hopefully, are unnecessary at a meeting of such distinguished academics. When you read judgments and orders of the Court it may be useful to bear in mind that the task of the Court is to decide cases. For the purposes of our discussions this has two implications. The Court is not involved in an effort to create a general theory on the general principles. So far I have never experienced a discussion on that subject among the Members of the Court and certainly not at the deliberations. You may encounter a discussion on the subject whether a general principle should be introduced. Thus, in Case C-185/95 P *Baustahlgewebe*[1] the applicant submitted that there is a general principle of Community law on promptitude that had been infringed as the Court of First Instance had given its judgment only 22 months after the close of the oral procedure. The delay involved was such that the usefulness of that procedure was negated by the loss of any recollection of it on the part of the Judges. The Court rejected this submission on the ground that the principle of prompt conduct of proceedings, as interpreted by the appellant, does not exist in Community law. It was further stated that neither Article 55 (1) of the Rules of Procedure of the Court of First Instance nor any other provision of those rules or of the EC Statute of the Court provides that judgment must be delivered within a specified period after the oral procedure.[2]

One possible conclusion to be drawn from the case-law of the Court is that it might be daring to extract a general approach to the sources and applications of the general principles. The sources of different principles are different: the protection of human rights and fundamental freedoms has two main sources, namely the Council of Europe Convention and the common heritage of the Member States. The principle of proportionality probably has French administrative law as its main source.

My second word of warning concerns the formulation of judgments. Lawyers frequently work on the assumption that by using different expressions one wishes to express different ideas. In respect of the Court of Justice that is not true all the way. While an effort is made for a coherent use of legal terms this is not necessarily so with other aspects of the Court's language. The fact that the internal working language of the Court is French does affect the style of drafting judgments. In French legal style there are demands not only in respect of precision but also in respect of

1. [1998] ECR I-8417
2. Points 51-52.

style. Thus one avoids repetitions, at least within the same paragraph of a judgment. Occasionally the Court itself falls in a trap and finds that it has slipped into a new doctrine by using a formula slightly different from those used previously. In addition, normally the Court only expresses itself on issues necessary to resolve in each case. This may result in the use of formulations that are not always complete. This may explain why the principle of proportionality is not always expressed in the same manner.

To this may be added that those of you that use other language versions than French may find an explanation to differing wordings that the translator may have slipped. However good they are - and they are good - such mistakes cannot be totally avoided.

It is also obvious that different general principles having been developed with a varying degree of refinement and precision. In some cases the jurisprudence is so rich that it offers an enormous variety of formulations. This may leave the reader with a clear nucleus and a grey zone as to the exact test applied by the Court. This seems to be the case with the principle of proportionality. As Francis Jacobs has recently stated, the Court does not feel constrained to apply the principle in any preordained way.[3]

I shall limit myself to one substantive question that is the protection of *Human Rights and Fundamental Freedoms*.

I believe that you can extract from the case-law that the Court tries to ensure that the protection of those rights and freedoms under Community law at no point is lesser than that under the European Convention for the Protection of Human Rights and Fundamental Freedoms. However, protection under Community law presupposes that the substantive issue in question falls within the scope of Community law.[4] Since 1996 the Court has quoted not only the Convention but also the case-law of the Strasbourg Court.[5] The extent to which the Court seeks to avoid conflicts with the Convention and with the case-law of the Strasbourg Court may be demonstrated by a reference to the Judgment in Case C-249/96 *Grant v. South West Trains Ltd.*[6]

All this does not mean that the protection under Community law could not go beyond that provided for by the Convention. One should not forget that the Convention provides for a minimum standard of protection.

It is probably useful to examine the future development of the protection of Human Rights and Fundamental Freedoms in Community law in the light of these remarks. From time to time one encounters a view according to which the Court in its opinion 2/94 on accession by the Communities to the Convention[7] has taken the position that

---

3. Recent Developments in the Principle of Proportionality in EC Law, Evelyn Ellis (ed), The Principle of Proportionality in the Laws of Europe, Oxford – Portland Oregon 1999, page 3.
4. See, for instance Case C-299/95 Kremzow [1997] ECR I-2629.
5. Joined cases C-74/95 and C-129/95 X [1996] ECR I-6629.
6. [1998] ECR I-636.
7. [1999] ECR I-1759.

an accession is excluded. This view overlooks the fact that the issue before the Court was whether at that time Article 235 would be a sufficient legal basis for an accession. Under those circumstances I do not believe that the Court took a position on the question whether an accession would be possible if the Treaty would be amended in order to enable that.

Nor do I believe that the plans to elaborate a Community or Union Charter on Human Rights would provide an answer to the question. Those plans do, nevertheless, give rise to a number of questions. First, if one would only codify the existing case-law of the Court one would end up with a somewhat strange result. The Court has only answered questions concerning the protection of Human Rights in a limited number of areas. A codification would thus provide a rather insufficient guidance to individuals who might wish to assess the protection under Community law. This would, in particular, be the case in view of the expansion of Community law into new fields that has already taken place or that may be envisaged. A further, hopefully inconceivable, problem would arise if the Charter would not meet the standards of the Convention. If the Charter would be an instrument of a non-binding character it would also be misleading since the protection under the existing case-law is based on binding rules.

Whatever course of action is chosen in respect of the Charter it might be advisable to consider the possibility of an accession by the Community to the Convention. That would also enable the Community institutions to defend themselves before the Strasbourg Court in cases where the compatibility of Community law with the Convention is at stake. That is presently the situation in a case brought against all the Member States and challenging a Judgment of the Court.

The elaboration of a non-binding Charter gives rise to the question whether the Charter would affect the future case-law. I do not think that it is possible at this stage to make any prediction in that respect. The only exception to this seems to be that a non-binding Charter would not likely affect the present role of the Convention as an instrument of fundamental importance for the interpretation and application of Community law.

5.2 General Principles of Community Law in the Future: Some Remarks on their Scope, Applicability and Legitimacy

Joakim Nergelius

The rich and varied contributions of articles to this volume (all originally presented as speeches at the conference, which gives an indication of the rather intense discussions that took place there) raise quite a number of questions related to the role of the General Principles and their future use in EC law, by the Court of Justice (ECJ) as well as the Member States and the other institutions. Being perhaps a bit optimistic but without overestimating the content of this volume too much, I think it could fairly be said that those articles shed substantial light both on the history and concept of the General Principles of EC law as well as on their position in the EC law of today. Starting from the "revelations" made here, or in any case the conclusions that may be drawn from the different articles, it should also be possible to propose or offer some rather qualified perspectives for the future development in this most vital legal area.

Thus, in this final article of the book I intend to discuss at first, once again, the very concept and the various categories of General Principles. After that, I turn to their position and legal status in current EC law, in order to finish with a few words on perspectives for the future. Already from the beginning, I think that the growing importance and dynamic character of this area of EC law should be stressed. The increased use of various General Principles by ECJ as well as by national courts in the Member States show that they have a growing practical importance, while their specific background and their roots in different legal systems guarantee that they will always be of great interest from a purely theoretical point of view, having links to crucial themes both in legal theory, comparative law and legal history. Considering their great importance today and in the future EU, I can only agree with the opinion expressed by the President of ECJ, Judge Rodriguez Iglesias, at a speech in *Folketinget*, the Danish Parliament, on 26 April 1999 (on the occasion of the 150th Anniversary of the Danish Constitution), that no other issue in European law is today in fact more important or better suited for intensified and thorough research than the development of common European legal principles, leading perhaps eventually to some kind of *jus commune europaeum*.[1]

1. This increased interest in the subject has in fact also been visible in the legal doctrine in recent years, as seen *e.g.* in the works of Takis Tridimas, The General Principles of EC law, Oxford 1999, John Usher, General Principles of EC Law (London 1998) and Trevor Hartley, The Foundations of European Community Law, 4th ed., Oxford 1999 chap. 5. So far, however, a vast majority of the work devoted to the subject has focused almost entirely on defining what the principles are and describing the cases in which they have been applied by ECJ. Other issues, like their "travelling back" from ECJ to the national legal systems, are still waiting to be analysed.

Ulf Bernitz and Joakim Nergelius (eds.), General Principles of European Community Law, 223–233

5.2.1 WHICH ARE THE GENERAL PRINCIPLES? CONCEPTIONS AND CATEGORIES

As T. Koopmans puts it in his deep-reaching comparative article on the use of General Principles in European and National Systems of Law, the main problem now facing lawyers somehow active in the area of General Principles is not the dissimilarity of standards to be applied, but rather the conceptual avenues by which similar standards are to be attained. Thus, the question should perhaps be asked right away: What does the expression General Principles of EC law really mean? What's in the idea, the conception?

The long history of the important and influential idea of natural law is of course well known. General Principles of Law is not exactly the same thing, but as Professor Schermers points out in the very beginning of his article on Human Rights as General Principles of Law, neither general principles as such is a new idea in any way. What is striking is rather that their source may vary through time. As Schermers puts it, 200 years ago they were taken from the bible and later from *e.g.* the fatherland or the king. Today, ideas like human rights, democracy or rule of law seem to be in the foreground,[2] which may of course also mean that those important values may be counted as General Principles of Law even in legal systems where they are not codified into positive, binding law. What is important to remember here, however, is that the concept of General Principles of Law was not invented by ECJ and not born through the development of EC law. It existed in public international law long before the birth of European Community, as is shown *e.g.* by the well known reference in Article 38 (1) of the Statute of the Permanent Court of International Justice (now International Court of Justice) to "the general principles of law recognised by civilized nations".

For the purpose of analysing what he calls the *Institutional Principles*, Bruno de Witte defines the General Principles of EC law (which according to him form a different category of principles) as "unwritten principles, recognised by the European Court of Justice, that have a status of higher law by the fact that they may be invoked as a standard for the review of Community acts". Higher law, i.e., at least in regard to the secondary, written EC legislation. But who may invoke or apply them? Historically speaking, this has almost entirely been the task of the ECJ, who "discovered" them and started to make practical use of them. As A.G. Toth shows, they may in fact be resorted to by the ECJ for a number of purposes, *e.g.* to review the legality of the acts of the institutions, to interpret or suppplement provisions of written EC law or to review the compatibility with EC law of the legislation or administrative practice of the Member States.[3] At the same time, however, despite

2. Cfr also the new Art. 7 in the Treaty of European Union (TEU), according to which Member States of the Union may temporarily have their rights as members suspended if they violate any of those principles or idea(l)s.
3. For an overview of early case-law from ECJ (before 1991) in this particular area, see John Temple Lang, The Sphere in which Member States are obliged to comply with the General Principles of Law and Community Fundamental Rights Principles, Legal Issues of European Integration 2/1991 pp. 23-35.

the increased importance that the General Principles tend to have in EC law, we should be aware that the task of ECJ is to decide cases, as Judge Sevón puts it, and that ECJ, with its rather casuistic approach, cannot be described as being involved in an effort to create a general theory on the general principles. This task falls instead on legal science, first and foremost.

Still, no legal scientist could ever go along with this huge and almost scaring mission without relying on the job made in this area and the achievements already reached by ECJ. Among the contributors to this volume, both A.G. Toth and Matthias Herdegen have made brief but still illuminating surveys through some of the early case-law on General Principles and its sources.[4] As is well known, the only article of the Rome Treaty which contains a reference to such a thing as General Principles, Article 288 (former 215) sect. 2, was used as a reference and source of law (or inspiration) for the ECJ when it developed its protection of human rights in the 1970s. Already before that, however, it is interesting to note that the ECJ did not hesitate to fill various gaps in EC law by references to General Principles, which were most often traced from national laws and legal traditions of the Member States.[5] Needless to say, this was easier when the EC consisted of only six Member States than it is today, but it was also seen as necessary in order to avoid the alternative, which was in the early *Algera* case from 1957 described as a pure *dèni de justice*. References were however hardly ever made to the existence of general principles in international law or to such a thing as custom,[6] which illustrates that the General Principles of EC law are to be seen as a genuine, autonomous source of EC law and nothing else. Apart from the laws and common traditions of the Member States, international conventions which all Member States have ratified have also been important sources in the development of those principles, notably of course in the case of human rights and the European Convention of Human Rights (ECHR).

Still, as Herdegen and Sevón both point out, on a more theoretical level it is hard to have a very clear opinion on the methodology used by ECJ when developing those principles (if there is any), due partly to the particular linguistical style used by the court. Without going to deep into this issue, which will be dealt with further in the next section of the article, it may be taken for granted that ECJ, when finding or establishing new general principles, has aimed, generally, not so much at specific legal provisions in national law or ECHR but rather at underlying ideas or principles, as Herdegen expresses it. This has partly to do with the complex issue if a reference to common traditions or laws of the Member States have to include all the Member

4. For another interesting historical view, see T. Koopmans, The Birth of European Law at the CrossRoads of Legal Traditions, American Journal of Comparative Lw 1991 p. 493-507.
5. Perhaps the first time this happened was in the cases 7/56 & 3-7/57, *Algera*, ECR 1957/58 p. 39.
6. Toth explains this fact rather convincingly in this volume by the fact that the practice of the Member States and the EC institutions cannot depart from the rules laid down in the Treaties, which can only be changed by formal Treaty amendments. Thus, custom as an independent source of EC law can in fact never be developed.

States or only a few or a majority of them. Since the first alternative is rarely feasible or realistic, inspiration from "underlying idea(l)s" common to all Member States have probably sometimes seemed like the most likely alternative.

What could be stressed already here, however, is that although the General Principles have been developed and almost "invented" entirely and exclusively by the work of the ECJ, they may of course, once established, be applied also by the Member States and the other EC institutions. Indeed, the fact that they will influence the activities on all those levels is probably one of the most important aspects of their existence. Judge Schäder has explained the relative lack of interest in general principles of law in Swedish law until now with the fact that written sources of law have always been considered as more important, which is of course partly true. However, the increased importance of such principles in recent years[7] is best explained by the profound effect that EC law has already had in Swedish law,[8] combined perhaps with repeated and successful attacks on the legal realism so far prevailing in Nordic legal thinking. Thus, the impact of EC law, including the general principles, in the legal systems of the Member States must never be underestimated.

What are the General Principles of EC law, then? A few words could be said about the different categories of General Principles that may today be said to exist, based partly on some of the contributions to this volume.

As is shown from quite a few articles here (see *e.g.* the contributions from H.G. Schermers and C.S. Kerse), there are today quite a lot of principles to be included among the General Principles of EC law, like propotionality, human rights, legal certainty, legitimate expectations and procedural guarantees like the right of defence and *non bis in idem.* John Temple Lang talks about two different kinds of General Principles, namely principles of fundamental human rights and "what are essentially administrative law principles". Judge Ragnemalm underlines the great importance of transparency and access to documents, while others, like Lawrence Gormley, Graínne de Burca and Bruno de Witte, point to the growing importance of what may be called *institutional principles*, which are of a somewhat different character. As both de Burca and de Witte have pointed out, it seems to be a common feature of the "traditional" General Principles that they are not listed or defined in the Treaties (although the principle of proportionality is now to be found in Article 5 sect. 3 of the Rome Treaty), but have been developed through a case-law where the ECJ has drawn on constitutional and administrative principles common to the Member States. Judge Schäder even makes a distinction between legal systems based on written law, where it is natural that the principles of law are explicitly stated in the legislation, and a

7. Which is shown most clearly by the judgment in the *Lassagård* case, Regeringsrättens Årsbok 1997 ref. 65, where Regeringsrätten, the Supreme Administrative Court or Conseil d'Etat, set aside a Swedish law since it was contrary to General Principles of EC law which had been developed by the ECJ (a particular reference was made here to the case Borelli, C-97/91, ECR 1992 I p. 6313).
8. See *e.g.* Nergelius, The Impact of EC Law in Swedish National Law – A Cultural Revolution, in I. Cameron/A. Simoni (ed.), Dealing with Integration, Vol. 2, Uppsala 1998 pp. 165-82.

system based on case-law, where "the basic principles become the result of all the cases that together form the legal order and the formulation of the general principles becomes the work of judges and scholars". EC law, however, is based both on written law and case-law, which is perhaps the reason why there seems to be such a degree of disagreement even among distinguished scholars as to which kinds of General Principles do in fact exist and how they should be classified. Today, however, I personally think that it is justified to talk of institutional principles like subsidiarity, loyalty and solidarity (cfr Article 10 of the Rome Treaty), institutional balance[9] and the principle of sincere cooperation between the institutions, even if it must then be kept in mind that those principles are, as pointed out in some illuminating articles here, of a somewhat different character than the traditional general principles, not least because they are to such a high degree based on written rules. On the other hand, important, judge-made and to a certain extent "institutional" principles like direct effect and supremacy could hardly be counted as General Principles of EC law, since they rather form some of the very foundations (or pillars or cornerstones) of EU and EC law,[10] without which this whole legal system (and thus the discussion, *e.g.* on the importance and character of the General Principles) would be totally different and in fact hard to imagine.

What is perhaps even more important, though, at least for the time being, is to analyse the legal effects of the use of the General Principles, when they are applied by the ECJ or national courts. What can probably be stated with some kind of certainty, as underlined by Matthias Herdegen, Bruno de Witte and John Temple Lang, is that the General Principles may serve – depending on the circumstances – both as rules of interpretation and as independent and overriding rules of law, which will normally invalidate actions taken in the sphere of EC law which are contrary to the applicable principle(s). Accordingly, H.G. Schermers makes a basic distinction between *regulatory principles* of law, which are used to fill gaps if no other rules exist but are subordinate to written legislation, and *compulsory principles*, which are fundamental principles of a higher level taking priority over written legislation and have to be applied, irrespective of which rules that may come into conflict with them. Remarks like these have a clear connection with questions like the scope and sphere of EC law and the position of the General Principles in the hierarchy of EC law, in relation to primary and secondary EC legislation, issues that will be dealt with in the next section. What could be stated already here, perhaps, is that the courts applying

9. Which has in fact never been referred to by the ECJ as a principle, but simply as an existing fact; this was also my assumption when writing the book Amsterdamfördraget och EU: s institutionella maktbalans (The Amsterdam Treaty and the Institutional Balance of EU) from 1998. Still, the well known cases in this institutional area from the 1980s, 138/79, *Roquette Frères v. Council*, ECR 1980 p. 3333, 294/83, *Les Verts v. Parliament*, ECR 1986 p. 1339 and C-70/88, *Parliament v. Council* (Chernobyl), could be described as expressing some kind of principle, i.e. in terms of democracy, which even overruled some rules of the Treaties.

10. B. de Witte describes them as "meta-norms which help to define the overall nature of the Community legal order", which seems to be an adequate description.

the General Principles may have two options, interpretation and setting aside of conflicting norms, but that the latter may be necessary or compulsory in certain cases, namely when a principle is sufficiently established (and its applicability in the particular case sufficiently clear) in order for it to serve as an an overriding rule of law or "compulsory principle".

One basic difference between the traditional principles and the institutional principles is of course that the latter ones do not serve to protect the position of the individual, but rather to regulate the relations between the EC institutions, as well as sometimes between the EU and the Member States.[11] In order for such a principle to be counted as a "general" principle, it must not, according to de Witte, concern only one specific subject matter or one single institution. It seems clear, however, having regard to recent developments in the jurisprudence of the ECJ,[12] that a principle like proportionality may be invoked both in order to protect individuals and to regulate the relations between the institutions, a development which may have been helped by the mentioning of this principle in Article 5 (3 b) sect. 3 of the Rome Treaty. As for the relations between the EU and the Member States, it seems likely that the principle of subsidiarity, specifically designed to be applied in that kind of situation but so far very seldomly used by the ECJ, is probably better suited for handling various kind of conflicts. Still, the exact scope and applicability of the institutional principles seems to be more unclear than the position of the traditional principles, as de Witte concludes.

This may of course have somehing to do with the fact that they are rather new and that this whole area of law is now rapidly developing, which may also be seen in relation to some other principles. A few words on human rights and access to documents will be given in the next section, but something could already be said here about another new invention of the ECJ from the 1990s, namely State Liability for breach of EC law.[13] Is this to be seen as a General Principle of EC law or not?

In the eyes of A.G. Toth, it seems clear that the ECJ here did develop a new general principle of law, based on the abstract concept of the law or the rule of law which governs the interpretation of the Treaties (cfr Article 220 (164) of the Rome Treaty). It is probably correct, though, as Professor Herdegen has observed, that no such principle could be established through a comparative analysis of the legal systems of the Member States, where the very lack of such rules has in fact been subject to criticism on various occasions. Thus, if the new and crucial EC law concept of state liability should be counted as a General Principle of EC law, which does not seem unreasonable, this shows that there are other methods for the ECJ to establish new principles of this kind than by turning to common legal traditions of the Member States or international conventions. This successful attempt of the ECJ of

11. B. de Witte here talks of horizontal and vertical institutional principles, expressions that are of course relevant in this context.
12. See *e.g.* the case C-84/94, *UK v. Council*, ECR 1996 I p. 5755.
13. See in particular cases C-6/90 and 9/90, *Francovic* ECR 1991 I p. 5357 and C-46/93, 48/93, *Factortame III/Brasserie de Pêcheur*, ECR 1996 I p. 1029.

"weeding out anachronistic features still prevailing in many administrative laws", to use the words of Herdegen, could even be seen as a fine example of what he calls "wertende Rechtsvergleichung", even if the element of establishing or proclaiming (or promoting) a new value here seems to be considerably stronger than the purely comparative one.

5.2.2 Current legal Status of the Principles – Some Observations and Proposals

The question of the current legal status of the General Principles could in fact be divided into a whole group of other issues. One crucial question is of course the position that the principles hold in the hierarchy of norms of EC law. In order to appreciate the impact of the principles for instance in the national laws of the Member States, it also becomes important to analyse the scope and sphere of EC law in general. In this particular context, also the sometimes complicated issue of the relation between EC law and the Eurpean Convention on Human Rights merits attention. This issue also concerns the matter when and how individuals may invoke human rights and other General Principles against the EU institutions and to what extent the institutions are bound by the principles.

As to their position and status in EC law, it must be assumed, as A.G. Toth underlines, that they are superior in relation to secondary EC law. This follows from a huge amount of jurisprudence from the ECJ, concerning classical principles like proportionality and human rights as well as new issues like transparency and access to documents. On the other hand, it seems perhaps a bit far-fetched to imagine, as Toth proposes, that the General Principles should be superior even to the basic Treaties. In fact, some of the very few cases where the ECJ could be said to have used General Principles in a manner which goes beyond and was perhaps even contrary to the wording of the Treaty, happened in the area of institutional law, where the general use of those principles have otherwise been, as discussed above, rather limited. I am referring here of course to the *Les Verts* and *Chernobyl* cases,[14] where the ECJ upheld or discovered some prerogatives of the European Parliament that did not in fact exist in the Treaty.[15] Controversial as those cases may be, they preceded a subsequent Treaty change with only a few years and may thus not have been quite as revolutionary as they are sometimes described as having been. It may in fact also be argued that those two judgments were not *contrary* to explicit provisions in the Treaty and that the court merely used principles of democracy and institutional balance to fill a gap in the Treaty, which has later been filled by the Member States. Anyhow, it seems difficult to find cases that would support the idea hat the General Principles should be superior to primary EC law. A hierarchy of norms based on primary law at the top,

14. 294/83, ECR 1986 p. 1339 and C-70/88, ECR 1989 I p. 2041 respectively.
15. For some rather harsh criticism against this line of reasoning, see Trevor Hartley, The European Court, Judicial Objectivity and the Constitution of the European Union, Law Quarterly Review 1996 p. 95-109.

General Principles in the middle and secondary law (cfr Article 249) at the "bottom" seems to be more realistic, albeit perhaps more traditional and from that point of view more dull.

Even Toth, who seems inclined to bestow upon the General Principles a superiority over any other EC rule, admits that there are limits to the power of the ECJ to invoke the principles. One of those limits follow of course from the relatively new Article 5 (3 b) of the EC Treaty, which says that the Community shall act within the limits of the powers conferred upon it by the Treaty (the so-called principle of attributed powers). Thus, the General Principles can only be resorted to within the limits determined by the objectives adressed by the Treaty. The scope and sphere of EC law is nowadays, since the entry into force of the Maastricht Treaty, simply more limited than before. This limited scope and applicability of EC law has also been shown in some recent human rights cases, notably perhaps the Irish Abortion case, where a group of Irish students who informed about medical clinics in the UK could not invoke EC law when they were prosecuted, since they had no economic relation with the clinics and the case did thus not amount to an exercise of the rules on free movement of services.[16] In other words, EC law offers a protection against violations of human rights committed by Member States only in spheres of law which form part of EC law, as underlined here by Judge Sevón.[17] The same is probably true for violations of other General Principles, where Temple Lang identifies the sphere of EC law (not yet clearly defined by the ECJ) as the situations when a national authority is implementing or applying EC law, when it is acting on behalf of the Community and when it is regulating or restricting any right given or protected by EC law.[18] Within this sphere, however, the principle of supremacy applies and the national courts must give priority to EC law over conflicting national rules, as Temple Lang stresses; in cases of doubt, a preliminary ruling should be requested from the ECJ.[19]

Concerning the level of protection when the General Principles are in fact applicable, however, the standards laid down by the ECJ – which are to be followed of course by national courts – must certainly be, as Judge Ragnemalm puts it, European, i.e. common to the Member States and to the EU as a whole. Thus, they must also be followed by the EU institutions. Still, some problems occur here, which have once again been seen perhaps most clearly in the field of human rights. The question is, as regards the reference to the common constitutional traditions of the Member States, if, in order for ECJ to protect a particular right, it is necessary for that right to be enshrined in the Constitutions of all the Member States or if it is sufficient that it is perhaps guranteed by some of them (or by a majority). As Toth stresses, the ECJ has never answered that question in clear words, but in most of the important human

16. C-159/90, *SPUC v. Grogan*, ECR 1991 I p. 4685.
17. Here it could also be noted, as underlined by Toth, that Article 6 (2) of TEU, which proclaims that the Union shall respect fundamental rights, is judicially unenforceable against the Member States.
18. See also Temple Lang, The Sphere... p. 33.
19. See also The Sphere... p. 34.

rights cases[20] it seems that ECJ has referred to the constitutional traditions "common to the Member States" or, when this was the case, the constitutional rules and practices of the nine Member States. This is perhaps in contrast, then, with the approach adopted when other General Principles have been recognised as parts of EC law: the principle of proportionality, *e.g.*, was essentially imported into EC law from French and German Administrative Law in 1957 and, to take a fresh example, the principle of transparency and access to documents, which was acknowledged by the ECJ and the Court of First Instance before it found its way into the EC Treaty by the Amsterdam modifications,[21] was in fact only acknowledged by a few Member States (mainly Netherlands and the Nordic countries) and even fiercely opposed to by many other Member States. Here it is in fact difficult to talk of such a thing as a common principle, which does however not exclude the possibility of such a principle later being common for the Member States, once adopted by the ECJ. General Principles may obviously be developed in different ways. In the first case, concerning proportionality and many other principles, which are only clearly to be found in some Member States but not exactly contrary to traditions of others, it may be the case, as Herdegen has it, that even if a highest common denominator could in fact be discerned, this would probably be on such a level of abstraction that it would not provide a rule which would be useful in individual cases. What the comparative analysis can do, then, is not to solve individual cases but to provide "a normative framework within which a concrete rule may be developed". We will return to this point in the last section of the paper.

Indeed, the importance of the protection of the individual against the EU institutions and the fact that the General Principles do also bind the latter could be stressed here. As seen from the many recent cases referred to by Judge Ragnemalm, the ECJ seems to be driven by an ambition to "lead by example", as he describes the situation. It is perfectly clear, I think, that what he calls the "occasionally quite cumbersome structure" of the EC legal order cannot be used as an argument against applying what could be described as common national standards when protecting fundamental rights at the EU level. As Ragnemalm says, arguments of the kind that this would jeopardize the efficiency of the institutions miss the main point here, namely that such standards are in fact not national but European and therefore binding also for the institutions of the EU.

In this context, a few words could also be said about the position in EC law of human rights in particular and the relation between EC law and ECHR. This seems to be one of the most complicated issues in this area from a legal point of view, with a tremendous capacity for gaining continued attention and being analysed from different perspectives, as seen in the last years after the opinion from ECJ on the possible accession of EU to the convention (which was not recommended)[22] and after

20. See *e.g.* 44/79, *Hauer*, ECR 1979 p. 3727.
21. See notably cases C-58/94 *Netherlands v. Council*, ECR 1996 I p. 2169 and T-194/94, *Carvel and Guardian Newspapers v. Council*, ECR 1995 II p. 2765.
22. Opinion 2/94, ECR 1996 I p. 1759.

the important Matthews judgment from the Strasbourg court in February 1999.[23] Not least the relationship between the two courts give rise to a number of questions, as illustrated here by the sharp analysis provided by Schermers, among others. What must be assumed for the foreseeable future, I think, is that no incorporation of ECHR into EC law will take place (as indicated here also by the rather hostile view towards incorporation expressed by Judge Sevón). Whether the attempts to create a new convention or charter on human rights for EU will lead anywhere remains to be seen. For the time being, therefore, we will have to live with Article 6 sect 2 of TEU, which may not be legally invoked against the Member States and which "only" grant ECHR and human rights the position of a General Principle of EC law, as Schermers point out. As shown in this volume and as the jurisprudence of the ECJ reveals, however, this needs not amount to too little, even if a stronger protection could of course always be desired. As long as this is the situation, though, it must be assumed that the Strasbourg court has the last word on the interpretation of ECHR; here, the situation could in fact be much more unclear and blurred should the convention be a full and integrated part of EC law.

5.2.3 A Quick View to the Future

Traditionally, the way in which the General Principles have been created and developed into a part of EC law, with further effects in the national legal systems, has given rise to expressions like "re-transplantation" (de Búrca), since they have in most cases originated somehow from the national legal systems and then been "re-accomodated" by those systems once again, having been "shaped by ECJ and moulded to fit the EC's different legal and constitutional framework". On a purely methodological level, also an expression like cross-fertilisation (Temple Lang) may be used, the latter then referring to importation of Community rules into national law and further importation of national rules into EC law. However, for the future the question if such a phenomenon like true General Principles not only of EC law but of European Law in general, i.e. nothing less than a *ius commune europaeum*, could be developed (and in that case how this should come about) is perhaps more crucial.

Needless to say, this task could not only be fulfilled by the ECJ, but would also need to involve activities of the national courts and the European Court of Human Rights. Only then could such a development ever take place and be endowed with some degree of legitimacy, from the legal actors as well as from the public (as underlined here by Herdegen). This seems to me to be a more important condition than what is recommended here by Toth in order to achieve the same goal, namely a codification of General Principles (here human rights) by turning them from unwritten principles of law into written and binding legal norms.

It might be stressed that the role of comparative law in this process (as well as in the development that has hitherto taken place) shall not be underestimated. This

23. *Denise Matthews v. UK*, 18 February 1999, case No. 24833/94 (not yet published or reported).

could even be seen as one of the main areas where comparative law does have a true practical use, even if such a comparative approach may only very rarely result in the finding of directly applicable solutions in individual cases. As Koopmans has stressed in an earlier article,[24] courts may use comparative law in at least two different ways, namely to find a solution to the problem they are faced with or to justify a solution arrived at on different grounds (*e.g.* after an interpretation of national law). Only the first of those methods does of course amount to any comparation in the true sense of the word, but I think Koopmans is right in claiming that the legal climate generally speaking has changed in the last ten or fifteen years and that the interest in comparative law seems to be growing in many courts in different parts of the world. Koopmans points to the Netherlands but some recent examples could even be given from Swedish law or from the fact that members of the US Supreme Court have begun to take an interest in the constitutional debate in other legal systems, *e.g.* in EU or Germany.[25]

As far as the ECJ is concerned, the impact of comparative law (in the true sense) has undoubtedly been considerable.[26] In fact, the importance that is given to comparative law was one of the striking elements of the work of the ECJ that surprised me when I worked in the research and documentation department there in 1997-98. Still, in order to achieve the true *ius commune europaeum*, which is perhaps only a futile illusion but could on the other hand be a most useful tool for further legal integration in a unified and otherwise harmonised Europe, a bolder attempt might be required. Thus, not only the creation and development of the General Principles but also their impact in EC law and the various legal systems of the Member States must be analysed, all with a view, *de lege ferenda*, of turning them into some kind of ground for this future "common law of Europe".[27] Then, whether this is a good idea or not is of course another question. The only thing that can be said on that topic here, is that the whole idea seems considerably more realistic to me than would have been the case only some five years ago.

---

24. Comparative Law and the Courts, International and Comparative Law Quarterly 1996 p. 545-56.
25. In the summer of 1998, four members of the US Supreme Court visited the courts in Luxemburg and Strasbourg as well as the Bundesverfassungsgericht in Germany and Conseil Constitutionnel in France. Justice Breyer gave a vivid report on the journey at a round table meeting of the International Association of Constitutional Law in New York in November 1998.
26. See Koopmans, op. cit. p. 546 ss for further examples.
27. This is in fact the idea of an ambitious research project on the General Principles of Community Law undertaken at the University of Lund by LL.M. Xavier Groussot, contributor to this volume.

About the authors

Joxerramon Bengoetxea is Professor of Legal Theory at the University of San Sebastian, Spain. He worked as a référendaire at the European Court of Justice from 1993–98 and is currently a minister in the Basque regional government. His works include his dissertation The Legal Reasoning of the European Court of Justice from 1993.

Ulf Bernitz is Professor of EC Law and European Integration at the University of Stockholm and has published a huge amount of work in this area, as well as in civil law. He is the chairman of the Swedish Network for Research in European Law and was President of FIDE from 1996–98.

Grainne de Burca is Professor of EC law at the European University Institute in Florence. Together with P.P. Craig she has published a well-known textbook on EC law and she has also written a number of articles on EC law in recent years, notably on theoretical issues like legitimacy.

Laurence W. Gormley is Professor of European law at the University of Groningen (Jean Monet Centre of Excellence) and has published a huge amount of well-known works, notably in the area of free movement of goods but also institutional issues.

Xavier Groussot is a doctorate student at the University of Lund. He is Maîtrise de Droit public, Université Jean Moulin, Lyon; Master of Public International Law, Raoul Wallenberg Institute, Lund; Master of European Affairs, Lund.

Matthias Herdegen is Professor of EC law and Public Law at the University of Bonn and has published many articles and books, notably in the field of human rights and constitutional law.

C.S. Kerse is a legal adviser for the Select Committee on the European Communities in the House of Lords. He has also worked as a solicitor and as a law professor and published many articles on General Principles of EC law.

T. Koopmans was a judge in the European Court of Justice from 1979–90. Before and after that he has been a Professor of Constitutional Law at the University of Utrecht. He has also been visiting professor in Cambridge. His extensive work in this area include some pathfinding articles on the relationship between General Principles and Comparative Law.

Ulf Bernitz and Joakim Nergelius (eds.), General Principles of European Community Law, 235–237

Joakim Nergelius is Associate Professor of Constitutional Law at the University of Lund. He has published a number of books and articles on various issues in Constitutional Law and EC law, notably in the institutional field, in recent years and also worked at the Division of Research and Documentation at the European Court of Justice in 1997–98.

Hans Ragnemalm is a judge at the European Court of Justice since 1995. Before that, he has been a Professor of Public Law at the University of Stockholm, Parliamentary Ombudsman and judge at the Swedish Supreme Administrative Court (Regeringsrätten). He has published many academic works, notably in the field of administrative law.

Hjalte Rasmussen is Professor of European Law at the University of Copenhagen. Among his works in the field of EC law, his dissertation On Law and Policy in the European Court of Justice from 1986 is probably the best known.

Henry G. Schermers is a distinguished scholar with a long academic career and a huge production, mainly in the fields of human rights and international law, where he has held a chair for many years in Leiden. He has also been a member of the European Commission on Human Rights for a long time.

Göran Schäder is a judge at Regeringsrätten, the Swedish Supreme Administrative Court. Before that, he was director of legal affairs at the Ministry of Justice. He is the co-writer of one of the most used Swedish textbooks on EC institutional law.

Leif Sevón is a judge at the European Court of Justice since 1995. Before that, he has among other things been a judge at the EFTA Court and a director in the Ministry of Justice. In 1999, he was awarded the title of honorary doctor at the University of Stockholm.

John Temple Lang is Director at the Directorate General Competition of the European Commission and Professor of Law at Trinity College, Dublin. He has published a huge number of works in EC law, notably on institutional principles and competition law, and in 2000 also at the University of Helsinki.

A.G. Toth is Professor of EC law at the University of Strathclyde, Glasgow. He has written extensively on General Principles in recent years, both on human rights and *e.g.* the principle of subsidiarity.

Ola Wiklund is Associate Professor of EC law at the University of Stockholm. His publications include a doctoral dissertation on the judicial discretion of the European Court of Justice from 1997. He also worked in the same court, at the Division of Research and Documentation, 1995–96.

Bruno de Witte has very recently been appointed Professor of EC law at the European University Institute in Florence. Before that, he held a chair in the same field in Maastricht for many years. De Witte is today a leading scholar in EC law, notably in the fields of human rights and institutional law.

Table of Cases

Ulf Bernitz and Joakim Nergelius (eds.), General Principles of European Community Law, 239–244

www.ingramcontent.com/pod-product-compliance
Lightning Source LLC
LaVergne TN
LVHW020642300926
849161LV00004B/771
* 9 7 8 9 0 4 1 1 1 4 0 2 0 *